Pro-ecological Restructuring of Companies: Case Studies

Edited by Dr Aleksandra Gąsior

Department of Microeconomics
Institute of Economics
Faculty of Economics and Management
University of Szczecin

]u[

ubiquity press
London

Published by
Ubiquity Press Ltd.
6 Osborn Street, Unit 2N
London E1 6TD
www.ubiquitypress.com

Text © the authors 2019

First published 2019

Cover designed by Amber MacKay
Front cover art by stux | Back cover art by DavidZydd
Cover art licensed under CC0 Public Domain and sourced from Pixabay.com

Print and digital versions typeset by Siliconchips Services Ltd.

ISBN (Paperback): 978-1-911529-48-4
ISBN (PDF): 978-1-911529-49-1
ISBN (EPUB): 978-1-911529-50-7
ISBN (Mobi): 978-1-911529-51-4

DOI: https://doi.org/10.5334/bbk

The full text of this book has been peer-reviewed to ensure high academic
standards. For full review policies, see http://www.ubiquitypress.com/

Suggested citation:
Gąsior, A. (ed.) 2019. *Pro-ecological Restructuring of Companies:
Case Studies*. London: Ubiquity Press. DOI: https://doi.org/10.5334/bbk.
License: CC-BY 4.0

To read the free, open access version of this
book online, visit https://doi.org/10.5334/bbk
or scan this QR code with your mobile device:

Contents

Acknowledgements

On behalf of myself and the authors, I would like to say a massive thanks to the staff at Ubiquity Press for making this book better! I particularly thank our editor Imogen Clarke for forbearance, kind support and a great deal of unwavering patience during the publishing process, and our copy editor Rebecca Mosher for extremely meticulous linguistic correction, which definitely contributed to improving the entire presentation of the book.

Special thanks to reviewers Alexandrina Pauceanu and Gernot Mühge for carrying out a detailed review of the book.

In addition, I would like to thank the European Commision that financed the book in the form of the project PRORES (269251), part of the 7th Framework Program, PEOPLE, Marie Sklodowska Curie Action.

Last but not least important for me personally, I'd like to express my sincere gratitude to Professor Tomasz Bernat, who provided support, advice and kind words in the process of publishing this book.

Dr Aleksandra Gąsior, Editor

Introduction

Business-driven pro-environmental measures were the inspiration behind collating practical examples from both within and outside the EU into one book. Another impulse to conduct a case-study type analysis was research carried out within the 7th Framework Program of the EU on "Proecological restructuring for jobs". Three countries participated in the research: Poland as the leader, Lithuania and Ukraine. It consisted of surveying the research target group – i.e. large companies that either already restructured themselves or were planning to do so. In the book, readers will find a three-way approach to restructuring processes. In the first part, the cases look at how political and legal factors are embedded in a company's strategy and how they influence the company's behaviour. The next part analyses direct companies' activities on matching restructuring with ecology. The final part gives the approach to ecoinnovations in the companies.

The main objective of this book is to present a practical approach to pro-environmental challenges faced by companies in the process of restructuring. To meet this aim, the basic research method used was a qualitative one in the form of case studies with interviews with business owners. Moreover, for the case studies the following research methods were used: literature review and mass media reviews, in-depth interviews with company staff or experts, direct observations and face-to-face discussion, analyses of source documents from companies, state administration or statistical offices, and finally, surveys or questionnaires.

This book incorporates material and experience from Ukraine, Romania, Germany and Poland. Yet another positive feature is that the authors are from an interdisciplinary scientific milieu, related to both engineering and the economy. This allowed us to collate a set of case studies from different countries, different economic sectors, and large and small businesses, with diverse approaches to research. Through this, three main areas have been defined in which individual cases, characteristic of those areas, were presented.

The first chapter, relating to a turbulent environment, puts special emphasis on aspects of politics and law, the international market, technology and environmentalism. Interviews and direct observation material allowed the authors to present both positive and negative experiences of companies in the process of restructuring with a focus on pro-environmental measures taken. Here, readers will find good practices developed to solve problems readers may frequently encounter in turbulent environments. An exceptional follow-up of the first chapter is the subject of subsequent case studies from the second chapter, referring to pro-environmental activities recognized as a determinant of effective restructuring of an enterprise. Here, both practitioners and academics can find topics related to reduction of the ecologically harmful activity of a company in Ukraine. The next topic is related to environmental management and its functioning both in Poland and Ukraine. Special attention is drawn to the presentation of the achievements of Polish enterprises in the scope of environmental investments in new technologies. The book is enriched here with a practical example of investing in renewable energy in Germany. The last chapter is about the essence of world economy objectives, namely eco-innovation. The case studies presented here relate to companies and the environmental benefits of their products. Pollution and legal changes affecting eco-innovation are discussed here as well, along with the final benefits of the users and the issue of energy consumption. This chapter relates very precisely to environmental aspects through the company using or manufacturing pro-environmental products. The three areas presented in the book and mentioned above, are, according to the researchers, extremely important for an enterprise to operate on the market while maintaining symbiosis with the environment. On the other hand, restructuring seems to be one of the better moments for an enterprise to take on pro-environmental actions. Having read the book, the readers will able to validate this assumption themselves.

The intention of the book is not to develop the theoretical concepts of the restructuring processes. The main idea is to present real examples of these companies' activities to see how they work and what problems can appear and have to be solved. In this light, the book offers all readers a practical perspective from the different companies, markets and countries.

The book is intended for a wide variety of audiences, and the authors trust that the experiences and good practices of others will prove valuable both for future businessmen (i.e. students), but also for academics and representatives of local government, central environmental agencies, owners and managers of enterprises to be restructured.

Aleksandra Gąsior

SECTION I

Turbulent Environment

Introduction

Rodica Milena Zaharia

PhD, Bucharest University of Economic Studies,
Department of International Business and Economics, CCREI

The landscape of business all around the world may today be characterized by one word: *turbulent*. Turbulent, because there are many uncertainties and threats related to political, legal, economic, social and ecological factors. Among these factors, ecological factors act silently and businesses tend to ignore them. Often, businesses invoke economic or social pressure when they postpone measures meant to protect the environment or to change their operations to be more pro-ecological. However, in the last decades, more and more businesses started to consider ecological factors in the core of their activity. Ignoring ecological factors from the business strategy means transforming *turbulence* from an acute to a chronic state.

This section provides a series of business case studies from Romania, Poland and Ukraine. The case studies present situations that show what the attitude towards pro-ecological behaviour is and what the barriers for encouraging or discouraging pro-ecological conduct are.

The first case study presents a situation where political factors have intervened in changing the law following pressure from different interest groups. There are situations in which laws related to environmental protection are considered too strict or impossible to apply because they induce economic burden. The case study describes the pressures exercised by large retailers from Romania

---

How to cite this book chapter:
Zaharia, R. M. 2019. Turbulent Environment: Introduction. In: Gąsior, A. (ed.)
   Pro-ecological Restructuring of Companies: Case Studies, Pp. 3–4. London: Ubiquity
   Press. DOI: https://doi.org/10.5334/bbk.a. License: CC-BY 4.0

because of a tax on recycling waste, and it demonstrated that companies have rather a reactive than a proactive attitude towards pro-ecological action when environmental protection is seen mostly as a cost, not a competitive advantage.

The second case study presented in this section shows a different situation: how a Ukrainian company strengthened its competitive position on the international egg market by adapting to the consumers' needs and by integrating international ecological standards into its production process. In this case, the company understood the importance of the ecological dimension and how this is a competitive advantage.

The third case study aims to evaluate a small Polish company's (including both the employees and management) awareness of the impact of technology on the pro-ecological decisions taken in the restructured enterprise. Using a survey and in-depth interviews, the study concluded that ecological awareness is demonstrated through management decisions and actions. However, most employees need further information about the pro-ecological measures, which could be provided through individual talks, an informational campaign about pro-ecological steps, or through the very simple method of using posters concerning the basic economic operations of the company.

Political and Legal Factors' Influence in Motivating Pro-ecological Behaviour of the Firm: The Case of the Queen Monaco Company (Romania)

Laura Wahed* and Rodica Milena Zaharia*

*PhD, Bucharest University of Economic Studies,
Department of International Business and Economics, CCREI

Introduction

The importance of political and legal factors in orienting firms towards a pro-ecological behaviour is crucial. It is a truism that in countries that promote the pro-ecological legislation and where the application of the law is consistent, the companies are encouraged to promote actions that imply a pro-ecological vision towards their businesses. Also, when political and legal factors are in consonance, companies transform their behaviour from a reactive one (to adapt to the law) to a proactive one (to anticipate the environmental legislation trends and to find out how upcoming legislation can affect the business).

The legal context represents the central system that shapes competition, orients the companies' actions towards employers, regulates the relationships between companies and public authorities or determines the balance of power between the customers and the company. The political factors are those that implement the legal system and may disrupt or accelerate the implementation

How to cite this book chapter:
Wahed, L. and Zaharia, R. M. 2019. Political and Legal Factors' Influence in Motivating Pro-ecological Behaviour of the Firm: The Case of the Queen Monaco Company (Romania). In: Gąsior, A. (ed.) *Pro-ecological Restructuring of Companies: Case Studies*, Pp. 5–14. London: Ubiquity Press. DOI: https://doi.org/10.5334/bbk.b. License: CC-BY 4.0

of the legal framework. Political factors may also change the legal context and control how laws and regulations are respected. Mostly in the area of environmental protection, the legal and political factors are essential.

Political and legal factors are, probably, among the least predictable factors that influence businesses. Pressure groups tend to change government policies, and these policies may diverge in different directions, according to the power of the interest group. In some cases, consumers are the winners; in others, businesses manage to enact their visions. Political and legal factors also influence the quality of the competition. Some firms survive and grow by offering bribes to government officials. The success and growth of these companies are not based on their competitiveness, and the consumers are prevented from having fair access to the most competitive products. Sometimes, the safety of the consumers is affected, when the legal and political factors do not follow the principles of correctness, law enforcement, equal opportunities and fair competition.

Objectives and Methodology

The case study analysed in this section shows how political and legal factors are embedded in a company's strategy and how they influence the company's behaviour. It explains a reactive behaviour, as a consequence of unpredictability of legal framework and political actions. The research method used here is the case study, a qualitative method that underlines the importance of the context when a specific situation is analysed. Case study research allows the exploration and understanding of complex issues, mostly when a holistic, in-depth investigation is required (Zainal 2007). Yin (1984:23) defines the case study research method "as an empirical inquiry that investigates a contemporary phenomenon within its real-life context; when the boundaries between phenomenon and context are not clearly evident; and in which multiple sources of evidence are used."

The appropriateness of a case study methodology for this situation is determined by the importance of the context over the pro-ecological behaviour of the company. Environment is a very delicate subject. Many times, issues related to environmental protection are placed in antagonist positions with issues related to economic development. This view expresses mostly the priorities of developing and less developed countries, according to which feeding and sheltering people is more urgent than protecting the environment. Even at the level of the EU there are differences between Northern Europe, much more concerned with environmental protection, and countries from the South or former socialist states where environmental protection, both at the level of framing legislation and implementation of the law, are weaker. The environmental policy in the EU "rests on the principles of precaution, prevention and rectifying pollution at source, and on the 'polluter pays' principle" (European Parliament

2016). In the absence of a strong institutional frame, and a clear legislation related to environmental protection, the reactive behaviour of the companies towards a pro-ecological attitude is encouraged. Also, the fact that a common legislation regarding the environment in the EU does not exist, that there are double standards related to environmental protection, induces some difficulties in implementing strong environmental policies across Europe and explains differences among countries in the performances related to environment quality and consumer protection.

Romanian Context: How Legal, Institutional and Political Factors Influence the Behaviour of Companies in the Area of Environmental Protection

Romania, as a member of the EU since 2007, constantly improved its legislation in the area of environmental protection. The current regulations are based on several legal principles, as in the case of other EU member states, such as: (i) compliance with the environmental acquis communitaire; (ii) integration of environmental concerns into sectoral policies; (iii) monitoring and reduction of climate change risks; (iv) application of the "polluter pays" principle; (v) preservation of biodiversity and specific ecosystems; (vi) sustainable use of natural resources; (vii) disclosure of environmental information and public participation in decision-making; and (viii) international cooperation for environmental protection (UNECE 2012).

There are three main authorities having competencies in the environmental protection field, each covering a specific activity area (KPM 2016, p.127):

The Ministry of Environment, Water and Forest (MEWF) is the central environmental authority, having environmental legal framework, policy-making and strategy development. The MEWF also acts as liaison with the European Commission for fulfilling Romania's reporting obligations under various EU directives.

The National Environmental Protection Agency (NEPA) is the central implementation authority and ensures the necessary training process for all parties involved in environmental matters. It is mainly in charge of the coordination of various permitting procedures through its regional and local agencies (43: one for each county, one for Bucharest, and a special authority for the Danube Delta).

The National Environmental Guard (NEG) is the main enforcement authority, having competences mainly in respect of verifying compliance with applicable environmental regulations and norms by companies. The NEG is represented by a Local Environmental Guard (LEG) in each county and in Bucharest. For noncompliance, LEGs impose penalties, according to the amount of environmental damage or risk caused by the non-compliance.

However, the National Environmental Protection Agency (NEPA) and the National Environmental Guard (NEG) do not have a joint database that would facilitate information-sharing on both the technical characteristics of regulated entities and their most recent compliance behaviour and enforcement actions taken against them (UNECE 2012).

Despite many improvements in enforcing a strong legislation and imposing strong norms towards environmental protection, environmental problems persist in Romania. A variety of illegal forestry and resource activities persist, stemming from corruption and weak oversight on behalf of the government. In spite of the actions taken by the Ministry of Environment, Waters and Forestry, the country faces significant challenges in managing its relations with large multinational corporations that seek to operate under the weakly regulated environmental regime. Increased taxation on landfill waste and penalties imposed by the National Environment Guard has marginally contributed to improving the environmental situation, but also yields corruption concerns (Sustainable Governance Indicators 2016).

There are many areas of environmental protection where Romania has a critical position. One of them is the recycling process. Romania is among the last EU countries in terms of recycling waste. Romania should reach 50% of waste recycling in 2020, otherwise, according to the treaties Romania has signed, the infringement procedure will be applied and penalties of 200,000 euro per day will be paid. Also, the legislation in the area of waste recycling was updated with the European directive only at the last moment. The new Emergency Government Ordinance 68/2016 transposes into the national legislation the provisions of Directive 2008/98/EC of the European Parliament and Council dated November 19th, 2008, regarding the waste and repeals certain directives. Among many provisions of the new legal act, the EGO 68/2016 imposes on waste producers and holders the obligation to separately collect all waste categories in the event that such is technically, economically appropriate and environmentally safe. At the same time, the obligation for such materials not to be mixed with other waste or materials with different features is expressly stipulated (Pachiu & Associates 2016). Also, for keeping track of waste management, the EGO 68/2016 mentions that producers of non-hazardous waste, units and undertakings conducting waste treatment activities, hazardous waste producers, economic operators authorized for collecting and carrying hazardous waste or acting as waste sellers or brokers have the obligation to ensure chronologic record of waste management for each type of waste, as well as of the amount, nature and origin of waste and, as applicable, of the destination, frequency of collection, means of transportation and treatment, capitalization or removal of waste according to the provisions of the 2014/955/EU Commission Decision and make it available to the competent control authorities, upon the request of these entities (Pachiu & Associates 2016).

The Ministry of Environment, Water and Forest discovered that many companies actively recycling waste broke the law and reported higher values of recycled wasted than they had done in reality. DIICOT descended on 59 companies and individuals suspected to have produced a difference of 54 million euro (Zaharia 2016). The authorities imposed fines and asked for real reports until the end of January 2016. According to law no. 24/ 2015, any company that delivers market-packaged goods has to recover packaging waste resulting from consumption. The law applies to any EU country, not only in Romania. To comply with this responsibility, businesses can organize themselves in associative structures called *responsibility transfer organizations* or may recover waste placed on the market through its own resources. If operators do not fulfil the assumed targets, they are legally required to contribute to the Environment Fund with 2 lei per kilogram of non-recycled packaging (packing tax).

Large protests were organized at the beginning of 2016 against this penalty and many companies, producers and retailers associations asked for fiscal amnesty for 2015 and for the reduction of the tax for the future. They threat the authorities with street protests, claiming that this tax will lead to insolvency for many producers and large unemployment in the food industry (Zaharia 2016). They also claimed that the ministry was not able to establish a functional system of recycling waste packages and these penalties should punish the government for incompetency, not the producers and retailers. After many discussions between the Ministry and the representatives of larger retailers and producers, the "packing tax" a new law was proposed in the parliament, to reduce this tax from 2 lei per kilogram to 0.30 lei per kilogram (Breniuc 2016). Despite the opposition coming from environmental NGOs, even against the opposition expressed by the Ministry of Environment, Water and Forest, the politicians gave in to the pressures of the different business interests groups and moved the law forward for approval. By the beginning of November 2016, the law had passed the Senate. There will be further discussion in the Chamber of Deputies, which is the last approval forum.

This demonstrates how politicians may change the law at the pressure of different interest groups. When the politicians can be forced to postpone the enforcement of the law, this raises suspicions about incompetency or corruption, creates unfair competition, does not motivate companies to be proactive towards environmental protection and does not educate consumers in demanding pro-ecological behaviour. Also, these changes do not induce predictability from the point of legislative stability. This lack of predictability could stand as an explanation for the reluctance of some Romanian economic agents to show proactive behaviour towards environmental protection.

Within this context, most companies have a reactive attitude towards environmental protection. The case study analysed here demonstrates reactive behaviour towards the legislation, inducing the idea that companies use precaution in investing in a pro-ecological action. This precaution may be explained by the fact that the only pressures the companies face derive from the legislation. Company's competitiveness is not positively influenced by the pro-ecological attitude, investments in protecting the environment are not rewarded by society and investments in pro-ecological activity are not justified by a predictable evolution of the legislation. The politicians may change the legislation to a less protective law for the environment or may postpone the enforcement of the law, if the pressure from producers and retailers is big enough. Under these circumstances, companies do the minimum in this area, preferring to rest on complying with the law and adopting those measures that are most economically beneficial.

Company Performance and History of Activities

Set up in 1996, Queen Monaco is an important company in the fast-moving consumable goods (FMCG) market in Romania, having more than 140 employees in several business locations and an annual turnover that increased over time to an estimated €20 million in 2016, according to the data provided by the management of the company. During the past 20 years, the company evolved and developed gradually from a small local business to a holding that today entails several companies specializing in different business activities such as retail, distribution, logistics, and import-export and business consultancy.

Currently, Queen Monaco has a diversified portfolio of business partners, including multinational companies, such as Lavazza Coffee, Kimbo Coffee, XL Energy Drinks, Philip Morris, La Festa, Imperial Tobacco or Maspex. In addition, Queen Monaco developed business partnerships with the most important Key Accounts on the Romanian market, its most significant partners being Carrefour, Hypermarche Romania (Cora), Auchan, Kaufland, Metro and Selgros, besides the other 6000 traditional retail customers that enrich the customer portfolio.

Protecting the Environment: The Role of Political and Legal Factors in the Environmental Policy of the Company

As with many other companies, Queen Monaco has a reactive attitude towards environmental protection. From this perspective, the management of the company complies with the regulations and procedures imposed by the governmental institutions, and limits the integration of the pro-ecological principles to the adaptation to the national legislation. However, as some of its commercial partners adopted pro-environmental behaviour, the company has also undertaken some strategies to respond in a positive manner to the environmental pressures and to improve the environmental outcome.

Ecological issues have become an important issue in Romania, and Romania has implemented new laws and regulations that try to reduce the negative impact of business activities on the environment. For example, the new Fiscal

Code has introduced an additional ECO tax for plastic bags in order to discourage the use of the polluting materials. With operations in the import-export of food products and their distribution on the Romanian retail market, Queen Monaco was directly influenced by this regulation and it had to enforce it by replacing the plastic bags with eco-friendly paper bags. However, not following the legislation would have worse consequences on the company, mainly the penalties, bad publicity and retaliation from (few) business partners who would consider that being associated with somebody who is not concerned about the environment is not good for their image. Besides this regulation, the Marketing Department has shown a constant preoccupation in recent years for the quality of packaging of imported products, requesting the suppliers use non-polluting materials (or the less-polluting ones), with a minimum impact on the environment. Moreover, in agreement with the Romanian law no. 249/2015, which refers to the management of packaging and the waste derived from packaging, the company drew up a contract with a *responsibility transfer organization,* which takes the responsibility for recycling the packaging delivered by the company. As a consequence of this legislation, the amount of materials recycled by the company has considerably increased in the last year. This reactive, and not proactive, attitude the company adopted towards the legislation responsible for environmental protection is also explained by the costs generated by complying the law. For example, in 2015, as compared to 2014, the tax paid by the company for waste and packaging recycling more than doubled for the same quantity of waste.

As regards the operations of storage of food products, the company complies with the national legislation, which imposes very high standards related to the prevention of food contamination and, therefore, to the avoidance of ecological risks. For this purpose, Queen Monaco made investments in purchasing new environmentally-friendly technologies as well as in training the employees in adopting pro-ecological behaviour in food storage areas. The HACCP (Hazard Analysis Critical Control Point) system was implemented, achieving accreditation ISO 9001- quality management system, the procedures aiming at protecting the environment. The HACCP principles were adopted by the *Codex Alimentarius Commission* established by Food and Agriculture Organization (FAO) and World Health Organization (WHO) to protect consumer health. From this perspective, the company identifies, evaluates and controls the potential risks that might occur in the process of food product storage and distribution. Moreover, a specialized manager is currently in charge of these environmental procedures, being bound to implement and control all the measures and to encourage the pro-ecological behaviour among the employees. This program also has resource efficiency purposes, that is, the person delegated to perform this process has elaborated an Environmental Management Program (EMP), which includes specific **procedures** in order to reduce the business impact on the environment:

- To minimize the use of natural resources, such as fuel, by grouping the merchandise and transporting it towards the customers, avoiding several transports (the company owns 60 vehicles, from small cars to trucks; therefore, the fuel use is significant on a daily basis, especially for the distribution operations).
- To avoid material waste (for example, the pallets received with the imported goods are reused on the internal market, and the cardboard boxes or the plastic thin sheets are reused to package other goods).
- To manage the waste (in the warehouses, as well as in the offices, the waste resulting from commercial activity is carefully collected in separate units, being subsequently delivered to the waste collector for recycling).
- To minimize energy consumption (an intelligent lighting system was introduced, eliminating traditional bulbs).
- To reduce paper use by printing only the important documents, to electronically archive the fiscal documents and to issue electronic bills.
- To encourage employees to actively engage in environmental protection.

The legislative changes and standardized procedures related to the environmental issues imposed measures that created short-term high costs for the company (acquiring innovative technologies, training employees etc.), but in the long run the effects are beneficial, being reflected in cost production and storage cuts as well as in the contribution to a healthier environment.

The company accomplishes the standards imposed by the consumer protection legislation in Romania, that is, it stores and distributes the products in optimal conditions. For this purpose, the warehouse manager is in charge of achieving the standards of storage and transportation with special vehicles (designed for food transportation and authorized for this purpose only) in compliance with the legislation in force as well as the producers' recommendations imprinted on the package or the quality certificates. Moreover, the warehouse manager is responsible with controlling the warehouse temperature and humidity, which should be between minimum 5°C and maximum 25°C and the relative humidity RH between a minimum of 25% and a maximum of 75%, keeping a daily register of all these data.

Another measure that considers consumer protection relates to the employees who handle the merchandise. They have medical tests regularly in order to protect the consumers and to secure a healthy work environment and are continuously trained to improve their performance in adopting pro-environmental behaviour. In addition, each batch of products is tested by authorized laboratories in order to assure the quality standards of the goods.

The warehouses comply with the European standards of hygiene (being periodically controlled by the Sanitary Veterinary and Food Safety Department), having a specially painted floor for keeping a clean environment and doors equipped with filters against dust and insects. Moreover, the company is checked monthly by the same institution that evaluates the sanitary standards of food product storage. Regularly, a pest control company is in charge of the warehouse inspection in order to control the pest issues and to maintain a clean environment for consumer protection.

Conclusions

Political and legal factors are essential in shaping the business environment and in determining the behaviour companies have towards the environment. This case study demonstrates how legal and political factors influence the restructuring policy of a company.

Romania has made much progress in protecting the environment. From a legal point of view, Romania adopted a legislation that is in consensus with the European laws and regulation towards environmental protection. Also, Romania established institutional framework responsible for the laws' enforcement, control and fines for those which do not comply with the law. Not too much has been done in the prevention area, which explains why companies are reactive rather than proactive. Also, politicians proved to be quite sensitive towards the business pressure and interests and didn't promote a strong commitment towards environmental protection.

The case study analysed here demonstrates that companies have a reactive rather than a proactive attitude towards pro-ecological action when environmental protection is seen mostly as a cost, not a competitive advantage. This is possible when legal and political factors are unpredictable.

References

Breniuc, I 2016 Legea privind reducerea taxei pe ambalaje a trecut de Senat. Available at http://www.green-report.ro/reducerea-taxei-pe-ambalaje-senat: [Last accessed 15 June 2017].

European Parliament 2016 Environment policy: general principles and basic framework. Available at http://www.europarl.europa.eu/atyourservice/en/displayFtu.html?ftuId=FTU_5.4.1.html: [Last accessed 15 June 2017].

KPMG 2016 Investment in Romania 2016. Available at https://assets.kpmg.com/content/dam/kpmg/pdf/2016/04/ro-investment-in-romania-2016.pdf: [Last accessed 18 June 2017].

Pachiu & Associates 2016 Legal Update ENVIRONMENT. Available at http://www.pachiu.com/wp-content/uploads/2016/10/Legal-Update_Environment_EN.pdf: [Last accessed 20 June 2017].

Stan, L & Zaharia, R 2016 Romania. European Journal of Political Research Political Data Yearbook 2015, Vol. 55, No. 1, pp. 224-230. DOI: https://doi.org/10.1111/2047-8852.12152

Sustainable Governance Indicators 2016 Romania. Available at http://www.
sgi-network.org/2016/Romania/Environmental_Policies: [Last accessed 20
June 2017].

UNECE 2012 Environmental Performance Reviews. Romania. Available at
http://www.unece.org/fileadmin/DAM/env/epr/epr_studies/Romania_
II.pdf: [Last accessed 10 July 2017].

Yin, R K 1984 *Case Study Research: Design and Methods.* Beverly Hills, Calif:
Sage Publications.

Zaharia, C 2016 Taxa pe ambalaj scoate oamenii în stradă. Industria alimentară
va picheta sediul Ministerului Mediului. Available at http://www.green-
report.ro/taxa-pe-ambalaj-scoate-oamenii-in-strada-industria-alimentara-
va-picheta-sediul-ministerului-mediului/: [Last accessed 20 June 2017].

Zainal, Z 2007 Case study as a research method. *Jurnal Kemanusiaan bil.9.*
Available at http://eprints.utm.my/8221/3/ZaidahZainal2007_CaseStudy
asaResearchMethod.pdf: [Last accessed 20 June 2017].

The Role of International Factors and International Market in a Turbulent Company Environment

Tetiana Mostenska*, Oksana Piankova† and
Oleksandra Ralko‡

*PhD, Professor, National University of Life and
Environmental Sciences of Ukraine
†PhD, Associate Professor, Kyiv National Trade and Economics University
‡PhD, Associate Professor, National University of Life and
Environmental Sciences of Ukraine

Introduction

Carrying out a study of pro-ecological restructuring at Ukrainian enterprises, the authors came to the conclusion that these processes are in the development stage by both qualitative and quantitative criteria. At the level of top management, pro-ecological changes are not a priority. In Ukraine, historically (due to the fact that Ukraine was part of the USSR) entrepreneurs' attitudes show some disregard to the value of resources, both natural and labour, and therefore the main incentives for changes at the macro and micro levels are precisely external factors. Thus, various laws and development programs are being adopted at the state level, sustainable development strategies are being developed, but they are mostly declarative in nature. The main motivation for changes at the state level at the moment are commitments to the IMF, EBRD, the EU and deterioration of relations with Russia. The last one is mainly displayed in energy-intensive industries and is associated with an increase in prices for gas and other fuel resources. At the enterprise level, any changes that can be attributed

How to cite this book chapter:
Mostenska, T., Piankova, O. and Ralko, O. 2019. The Role of International Factors and International Market in a Turbulent Company Environment. In: Gąsior, A. (ed.) *Pro-ecological Restructuring of Companies: Case Studies*, Pp. 15–44. London: Ubiquity Press. DOI: https://doi.org/10.5334/bbk.c. License: CC-BY 4.0

to pro-ecological mainly occur due to economic feasibility. Fuel costs have been raised for the enterprises, and so to reduce the cost of production in view of the low purchasing capacity of the population, they implement energy-saving technologies. Another motive for carrying out pro-ecological processes is the enterprise's entrance to foreign markets. All other factors – environmental, social and cultural – have no impact on pro-ecological restructuring. At a business forum that was held in Kiev in November 2017 that was devoted to issues of inclusive and sustainable development, business representatives voiced a simple idea that can be reduced to the following: as long as fines for harm to the environment are minimal, no one will introduce technology that will reduce this harm. The issues of the same corporate social responsibility are mainly dealt with by companies whose products causes the most harm to the population, namely the tobacco and alcohol industry.

In general, if we consider the degree of development of corporate social responsibility towards issues of ecology and energy conservation, it is very low. If we consider the prevalence of pro-ecological restructuring processes in all sectors of Ukraine, it should be noted that in the past few years, due to strained relations with Russia, the rise in fuel costs and gas supply disruptions, most of the enterprises were forced to introduce energy-saving technologies.

The sectoral structure of Ukraine over the last 10 years has been characterized by the high proportion of agro-industrial products. So both in the structure of the domestic market and in Ukraine's exports, agricultural and food production occupies about 35%. It is the export orientation of these sectors that determined the most dynamic pro-ecological processes in enterprises that were forced to adapt to the demands of foreign markets. Therefore, the authors selected the agricultural and food industries as a vivid example of pro-ecological restructuring. From the agricultural and food industries, we selected the market for eggs and egg products as the most developed and export-oriented.

In conditions of worsening of food security problems and environmental challenges in food production, the issues of ensuring humanity in quality and inexpensive food are particularly relevant. Eggs and egg products belong, in particular, to the category of quality and inexpensive food products.

The international market of eggs belongs to growing markets, due to the fact that eggs are one of the cheapest products. "Eggs are a superfood that can help alleviate malnourishment and protein poverty" (Davies 2018). The volume of production and consumption of raw eggs in most countries covers the domestic market, due to shorter product shelf life. At the same time, export of dry egg products has grown. However, the egg market is very vulnerable due to the significant influence of external environmental factors.

Except public consumption of eggs (eggs are the cheapest source of animal protein), the largest consumers of egg products are enterprises of the confectionery and oil fat industry, as for them eggs are raw materials. Egg product consumers are also bakeries, the meat processing industries and HoReCa (hotels, bars, cafés and restaurants).

Growth in the food industry will stimulate additional demand for both dry and liquid egg products. Given the annual increase in the production of eggs and egg products, and expansion of markets of their use, both markets will certainly grow. Egg product manufacturers will strengthen their market positions by improving production technology, increasing production volume, expanding the range of egg products, finding new ways of marketing, increasing exports and so on. With the growth of the production the issues of ecologization of eggs and egg products has become particularly relevant.

AVANGARDCO IPL is one of the largest agro-industrial companies in Ukraine, specializing in the production of eggs and egg products. To maintain and extend its positions both in domestic and foreign markets, the company implements measures to reduce production costs and enhance product quality control.

The Objective and Methodology

People around the globe need a safe, plentiful and inexpensive food supply, to provide a balanced diet, essential for sustained human health. Producers of eggs and egg products help to solve the food problem by providing population with animal proteins. On the efficiency of eggs and egg products producers influence the following international environment factors: currency fluctuations, supply and demand, prices etc.

The purpose of writing the case study is to determine the international factors and the requirements of the international market that affect the activities of the vertically integrated company AVANGARDCO IPL, as well as determining the impact of production ecologization on the effectiveness of the company.

Reorientation of different enterprises on low-waste cycles is based on implementing innovative cleaning and abatement equipment, ecologization of technological processes. Environmentally safe production should become the leading branch, expand the scope of employment and bring considerable profit. Environmental regulations must not conflict with economic interests when the deterioration of the environment is less profitable than the solution to environmental problems.

The subject of the research is methodological and practical approaches to determining the impact of external environmental factors on company activity and the ability to adapt the company's strategy to external exciters by enhancing flexibility and making effective management decisions.

The object of the research is process of influence of international factors on the internal environment of AVANGARDCO IPL with the aim of developing mechanisms to neutralize the negative effects of changes in the external environment and increased production volumes. Such an approach allows us to define the priority areas for decision-making in the field of environmental control processes of the company.

The state of international and national markets of eggs and egg products is analyzed using statistical materials from the World Egg Organization (www.internationalegg.com), the Ministry of agrarian policy and food of Ukraine (www.minagro.gov.ua) and State Statistics Service of Ukraine (www.ukrstat.gov.ua). Analysis and characterization of AVANGARDCO IPL was conducted on the basis of the official website of the company (www.avangardco.ua/en/). Analysis and characterization of the biggest competitor of AVANGARDCO IPL – the company Ovostar – was conducted on the basis of the official website of the company (www.ovostar.ua/en/).

Short History and Performance of the Company

The Ukrainian company AVANGARDCO IPL ranks second among the world leaders in egg producers by the number of laying hens in production – 27 million hens – and ranks first as producer of eggs and dry egg products in Ukraine and first in Eurasia.

AVANGARDCO IPL's major activities include:

- Breeding of industrial laying hens, production and sales of shell eggs.
- Production and sales of dry egg products.
- Incubation and sales of one-day-old laying hens, breeding and sales of young laying hens and sales of poultry for slaughter.
- Production and sales of feed.
- Other activities include sales of goods and services, poultry meat and by-products, organic fertilizer etc.

AVANGARDCO IPL consists of 19 laying farms, 10 rearing farms, six feed mills, three hatcheries, two poultry complexes, Avis and Chornobaivske, and the egg processing plant Imperovo Foods. Production facilities in 14 regions of Ukraine allow the company to meet the demand of Ukrainian consumers in an efficient and timely manner.

The main stages of the company development are summarized in Table 1.

In 2015, Avangardco IPL added seven new countries to its already impressive portfolio of 42 country markets by starting to export its shell eggs to Qatar and Israel and its egg products to the UK, Bangladesh, Iran, Latvia and Italy. However, the deterioration in the market, accompanied by reduction in the consumption of eggs was the reason that the volume of shell eggs in 2015 decreased by 46%, while their sales fell by 35%, accompanied by a decrease in company revenue by 43%. Main company performances are in Table 2. Gross profit from production of shell eggs decreased by 84% to 14,636 thousand USD. In 2015 there was also a decrease of gross profit margin to 9%.

Production of dry eggs also decreased. If in 2014 83% of dry eggs were marketed outside Ukraine, then in 2015 the share of exports dropped to 78%

Table 1: Main stages of the AVANGARDCO IPL development.

Year	Event
2003	Purchase of the Avangardco poultry farm located in West Ukraine not far from Ivano-Frankivsk
2003–2009	The company purchased additional 18 laying farms, three hatcheries, three rearing farms and four feed mills.
2009	The company commissioned a modern egg processing plant.
2010	Avangardco IPL made itself known on the international financial markets by successfully completing an IPO on the London Stock Exchange and attracting 208 million USD in investment. An additional 200 million USD was raised through a Eurobond placement.
2011–2013	The company modernized poultry complexes, laying capacity increased to 30.1 million hens, while annual production capacity reached 8.6 billion eggs.
2014	Imperovo Foods received official authorization to export dry egg products to the European Union. The company's eggs and dry egg products became Kosher certified.
2015	The company added seven new country markets to its export destinations for a total of 42. The share of the EU in egg powder exports rose to 40%.
2015	The company successfully restructured a 200 million USD Eurobond that represents a lion's share of the company debt portfolio.

Source: AVANGARDCO IPL. Available at: http://www.avangardco.ua/en/.

Table 2: Company effectiveness in shell and dry egg production.

Performances	Production of shell eggs, billion eggs			Production of dry eggs, tons		
	2014	2015	%	2014	2015	%
Production	6,306	3,434	−46	21,323	9,057	−58
Sales	4,288	2,798	−35	185,592	11,445	−38
Revenue, thousand USD	275,585	155,789	−43	116,993	64,735	−45
Exports, % of sales	21	24	−	84	89	−
Revenue, % of total sales	66	68	−	28	28	−
Gross profit, thousand USD	89,698	14,636	−84	40,365	11,805	−71
Gross profit margin, %	33	9	−	35	18	

Source: Avangardco, 2015. Available at: http://avangardco.ua/fileadmin/files/INVESTOR_RELATIONS/Avangardco_IPL_Annual_Report_2015_final.pdf.

Table 3: Shell egg sales by channel, % of volume.

Channels	Years	
	2014	**2015**
Retail chains	35	44
Wholesalers	52	41
Exports	13	15

Source: Avangardco, 2015. Available at: http://avangardco.ua/fileadmin/files/INVESTOR_
RELATIONS/Avangardco_IPL_Annual_Report_2015_final.pdf.

(by 5%). While revenue of total sales remained unchanged (28%), gross profit decreased by 71%, which was the reason for the reduction of the gross profit margin to 18% in 2015. The company uses one- and two-tier distribution channels: retail chains and wholesalers (Table 3).

In the studied period, there was a change in the structure of the distribution channels of AVANGARDCO. Thus, shell egg sales by retailers increased by 9% while sales through wholesale traders were reduced by 11%. In addition, during the year, exports grew by 2%.

Role of international factors and international market in a turbulent company environment

In order to determine the impact of international factors and changes at international markets on AVANGARDCO activity, let's analyze international and Ukrainian markets of eggs and egg products.

The world market of eggs and egg products, key regional markets – importers

The traditional world leader in production of eggs, since 1990, has been China; after the collapse of the Soviet Union the United States occupied the second place and India and Japan are competing for the third place. In 2000 Ukraine did not belong to the 15 world leader countries in the production of eggs, but in 2010–2013 Ukraine has ranked ninth (Table 4). There is a correlation between large amounts of egg production and the population of the country: eight world leaders are the countries with the biggest population.

In 2015 the geographical structure of production remains unchanged. The leading position in terms of egg production was occupied by China, its share exceeded the nearest competitor – the United States – by four times, and India was in the third place.

Table 4: World leaders in egg production.

Place	1990	2000	2010	2013
1	China	China	China	China
2	Soviet Union	The United States	The United States	The United States
3	The United States	Japan	India	India
4	Japan	India	Japan	Mexico
5	Brazil	Russia	Mexico	Japan
6	India	Mexico	Russia	Russia
7	Mexico	Brazil	Indonesia	Brazil
8	Germany	France	France	Indonesia
9	France	Germany	Ukraine	Ukraine
10	Spain	Turkey	Turkey	Turkey
11	Italy	Italy	Spain	Germany
12	Netherlands	Netherlands	Iran	France
13	Great Britain	Spain	Italy	Iran
14	Thailand	Indonesia	Germany	Spain
15	Poland	Iran	Netherlands	Italy

Source: summarized by authors on materials of the journal "Poultry and poultry products".

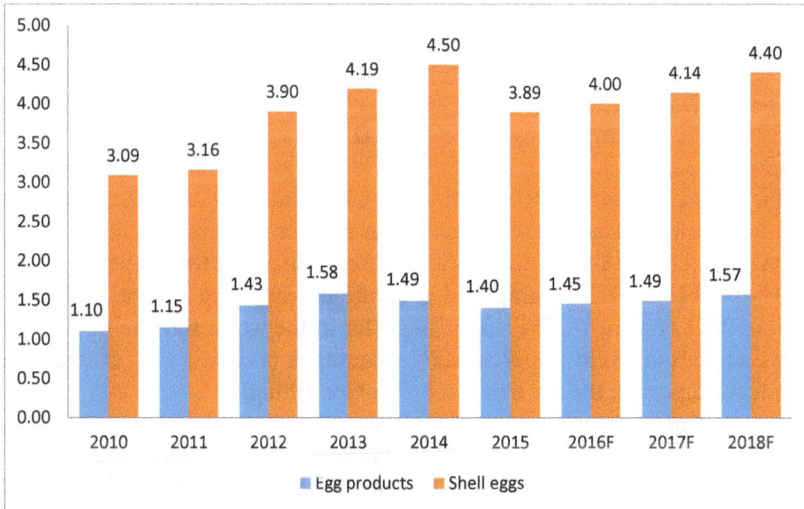

Fig. 1: World import of eggs and egg products, billion USD.

Source: Pro-Consulting. Egg market review. International Trade Centre. Available at: https://pro-consulting.ua/base/analiz-rynka-ukrainy.

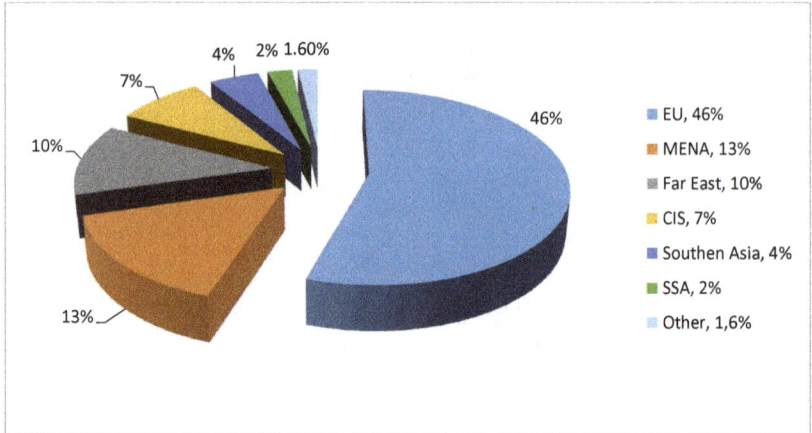

Fig. 2: Breakdown of world imports of eggs and egg products in 2015.

Source: Pro-Consulting. Egg market review. International Trade Centre. Available at: https://pro-consulting.ua/base/analiz-rynka-ukrainy.

Asian countries demonstrated the highest growth rates, the impetus related to the growth in demand for animal proteins by increasing population and the inability to meet the demand through domestic production.

However, despite globalization, egg production is traditionally national; 97% of eggs are consumed within the country of original production, and only 3% of the products are offered on the world market (International Egg Commission, 2017).

World imports of eggs and egg products (Figure 1) are characterized by stable growth during 2010–2014, as confirmed by the positive dynamics of consumption. The main reasons for the decline of egg imports (by 0.61 billion USD) and egg products (by 0.09 billion USD) in the world are simultaneous reduction in demand in EU, MENA and CIS markets in 2015. According to the International Trade Centre forecast, in 2016 imports will resume gradual growth, and in 2018 the volume of purchases in financial terms will reach the level of 2014. In 2015 geographical structure of world imports was similar to that of 2011 (Figure 2). The largest importer in the world was the EU, with a share of 46% of world imports; MENA countries occupied 13% of total egg products imported; the Far East, 10% (Pro-Consulting).

Detailed information on the regions is given in Table 5.

The EU market is characterized by significant domestic production in the amount of 7.4 million tons of eggs; annual per capita consumption is 221 eggs (Table 5). The fall in imports (by 16%) was due to increased supply of domestic producers who have met the requirements of the European Council Directive 1999/74/EC. In 2015, the foreign trade balance of eggs in the EU was 1040 thousand tons. Significant import is caused by the need for egg products (55% of world imports).

Table 5: Key features of regional markets of eggs and egg products.

Region	Eggs						Egg products			
	production	consumption	% of world imports	export	import	key importers	% of world imports	export	import	key importers
UA	7.4	221	43	2035	995	Germany – 41%, Netherlands – 18%, Italy – 6%	55	986	779	Germany – 19%, UK – 18%, France – 10%
MENA	3.7	104	15	88	337	Iraq – 64%, UAE – 7%, Syria – 7%;	7	–	102	Qatar – 23%, UAE – 17%, Saudi Arabia – 14%
CIS	4.8	230	10	138	119	Russia – 69%, Turkmenistan – 6%, Tajikistan – 6%.	Self-sufficiency in region			
Sub-Saharan Africa	2.1	35	3	18	72	Angola – 33%, Mozambique – 9%, Liberia – 8%.				
South East Asia	Self-sufficiency in region						5	92	72	Thailand, 30%, Indonesia, 24%, Vietnam, 17%

Source: International Egg Commission. Available at: https://www.internationalegg.com/.

The main importers of eggs were: Germany – 41%, Netherlands – 18%, Italy – 6%; egg products: Germany – 19%, United Kingdom – 18%, France – 10%.

In 2015, MENA countries were produced 3.7 million tons of eggs, and the eggs trade balance was negative (–249 thousand tons). The region is a net importer by egg products, since there is no domestic production. MENA countries bought 15% of the world imports of eggs and 7% of egg products respectively. The market is growing and attractive; the level of its consumption is two times less in comparison with Europe – only 104 eggs per capita. The main regional importers of eggs were: Iraq – 64%, UAE – 7%, Syria – 7%; egg products: Qatar – 23%, UAE – 17%, Saudi Arabia – 14%.

CIS countries are able to meet their own needs within the Eurasian Union. The main regional importers of eggs were: Russia – 69%, Turkmenistan – 6%, Tajikistan – 6%.

The countries of Sub-Saharan Africa have remained import-dependent (consumption is 35 eggs per capita), among the main regional importers of eggs were: Angola – 33%, Mozambique – 9%, Liberia – 8%.

The Far East region had negative balance of 251 million USD and 18% of world imports. The main regional importers of eggs were: Japan – 77%, Taiwan – 9%, South Korea – 8%.

The egg and egg product market of Ukraine

Egg production in Ukraine had a weak upward trend till 2013. The period of 2014 is characterized by a decline in production by 27.5 thousand pieces or 0.1%. The beginning of the antiterrorist operation and occupation of Crimea caused the loss of production capacity for the production of eggs in eastern Ukraine and the Crimean Autonomous Republic, which led to a significant decline in production. In comparison with indicators of 2014, production cuts were 14.3% (2804.4 thousand pieces); however, compared with the index of production in 2005, production of eggs increased by 28.6%.

In the near future in Ukraine, there will be a tendency towards declining egg production. The trend may change if the export of eggs will show growth. Decommissioning of the operating capacity of enterprises producing eggs has caused changes in the producers' structure. Thus, in 2014 agricultural enterprises produced 64.0% of the eggs; in 2015 the share of industrial production dropped to 58.2%. Reduction in industrial egg production was 2804.4 million pieces or by 14, 3% (table 6), while households were reduced their production only by 30.4 million pieces (0.4%).

However, over the studied period industrial egg production has increased by 3.3 times, while households increased production only by 1.2 times.

There is a concentration of production in the industry. Distributions of companies that produce eggs by capacity and production volumes in 2015 are presented in Table 7.

Table 6: Structure of production of eggs by types of agricultural holdings.

Production of eggs	2000	2005	2010	2011	2012	2013	2014	2015
Total								
million pieces	8808.6	13045.9	17052.3	18689.8	19110.5	19614.8	19587.3	16782.9
Agricultural enterprises								
million pieces	2977.3	6458.1	10249.6	11738.2	11977.4	12234.2	12536.2	9762.2
percentage of total production	33.8	49.5	60.1	62.8	62.7	62.4	64.0	58.2
Households								
million pieces	5831.3	6587.8	6802.7	6951.6	7133.1	7380.6	7051.1	7020.7
percentage of total production	66.2	50.5	39.9	37.2	37.3	37.6	36.0	41.8

Source: Agriculture of Ukraine 2015. Statistical Yearbook. Available at: http://www.ukrstat.gov.ua.

Table 7: Groupings of agricultural enterprises by production of eggs in 2015.

	Number of enterprises		Production of eggs	
	units	percentage to total enterprises	million	percentage of total production
Enterprises producing of eggs – total of which, thousand pieces	392	100.0	9762.2	100.0
no more than 10.0	116	29.6	0.3	0.0
10.1–50.0	56	14.3	1.4	0.0
50.1–100.0	24	6.1	1.6	0.0
100.1– 500.0	50	12.8	12.6	0.1
500.1–1000.0	7	1.8	5.1	0.1
1000.1–5000.0	24	6.1	58.5	0.6
5000.1–10000.0	26	6.6	187.9	1.9
10000.1–50000.0	41	10.5	932.6	9.6
more than 50000.0	48	12.2	8562.2	87.7

Source: Agriculture of Ukraine 2015. Statistical Yearbook. Available at: http://www.ukrstat.gov.ua.

Thus, 48 enterprises, which produced more than 50 thousand eggs, had a 12.2% share of all enterprises producing eggs. They produced 87.7% of the total egg production in Ukraine, while 253 other enterprises (64.5% of total enterprises) produced only 0.2% of all eggs that were produced in Ukraine.

An important indicator for the market characteristics is the level of self-sufficiency of the country by certain products. Self-sufficiency by eggs in Ukraine was 113.9% in 2015.

The balance of egg production and consumption is shown in Table 8. Throughout the study period, egg production has exceeded consumption. However, if in 1995 the difference was 6.4%, then in 2015, it was 28.4%. Thus, the increase in the volume of egg production is oriented to external markets.

Consumption of eggs per capita in Ukraine from 2000 to 2014 has risen from 166 to 310 eggs or by 86.7%. The increase of prices for eggs and reduction of purchasing power in 2015 led to a significant reduction in the consumption of eggs per capita to 280 eggs.

The reduction of capacity and the decrease of purchasing power led to the reduction of capacity in the domestic market in Ukraine. If from 2000 to 2011, consumption of eggs in Ukraine has grown, in 2011–2013 it remained almost unchanged, then in 2014–2015 consumption of eggs in Ukraine declined: in 2014 by 42 thousand tons, compared with 2013 (5.2%); in 2015 the tendency was stronger and led to decrease of 77 thousand tons.

Since 2007, foreign trade of eggs in Ukraine has been positive. The largest share in exports egg production had was in 2015 – 18.1%. In 2014, 147

Table 8: Balance of egg production and consumption (including egg products), thousand tons.

Indicators	1995	2000	2005	2006	2007	2008	2009	2010	2011	2012	2013	2014	2015
Output	544	508	753	822	812	863	919	985	1079	1104	1133	1131	969
Change of stocks at end of year	−11	2	13	35	10	20	12	9	14	7	0	0	−4
Import	5	2	5	3	3	7	7	7	3	4	5	7	11
Total of resources	560	508	745	790	805	850	914	983	1068	1101	1138	1138	984
Export	4	0	1	1	16	23	58	75	83	82	105	147	126
Expenditures of fodder and hatching	47	36	91	100	100	115	120	125	145	172	180	163	136
Loses and wastes	0	1	6	12	11	15	14	16	22	37	40	37	21
Consumption	509	471	647	677	678	697	722	767	818	810	813	771	694
Excess (+) lack (−) of consumption over production	35	37	106	145	134	166	197	218	261	294	320	360	275
Consumption to production, %	93.6	92.7	85.9	82.7	83.5	80.7	78.6	77.9	75.8	73.4	71.8	68.2	71.6
Share of export volume of production, %	0.7	0	0.1	0.1	2.0	2.7	3.0	7.6	7.7	7.4	9.3	13.0	18.1

Source: Agriculture of Ukraine 2015. Statistical Yearbook. Available at: http://www.ukrstat.gov.ua.

thousand tons of eggs was exported from Ukraine, in 2015, it was 126 thousand tons (Figure 3).

Dynamics of prices on eggs is presented below (Figure 4).

Over the study period prices increased by 3.5 times. The biggest price increase is typical for 2014 – by 2.4 times compared with 2013 and for 2015 – by 1.7 times comparing with 2014. Such increases in 2014 and 2015 can be attributed to the rising cost of production, caused by the rising cost of energy resources.

The reduction of the domestic market was accompanied by a decrease in egg exports from Ukraine. In 2015 the pace of the decline in exports was 14.3%, compared with 2014 (Figure 5).

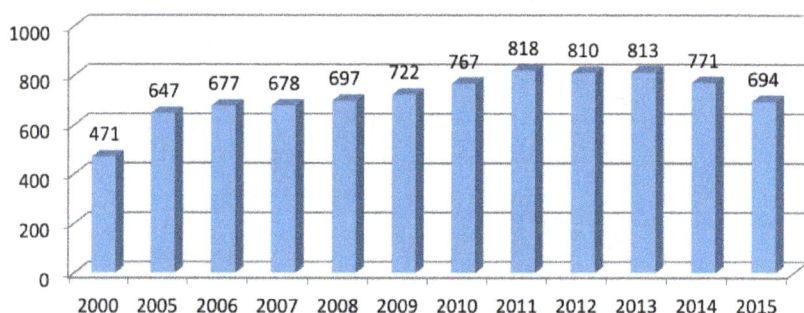

Fig. 3: Dynamics of eggs consumption in Ukraine, thousand tons.

Source: The Ministry of agrarian policy and food of Ukraine. Available at: www.minagro.gov.ua. Agriculture of Ukraine 2015. Statistical Yearbook. Available at: http://www.ukrstat.gov.ua.

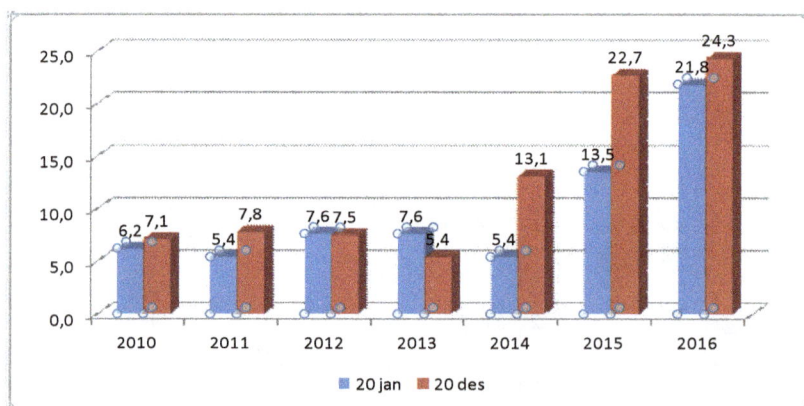

Fig. 4: Dynamics of prices on chicken eggs, UAH for 10 pieces.

Source: Agriculture of Ukraine 2015. Statistical Yearbook. Available at: http://www.ukrstat.gov.ua.

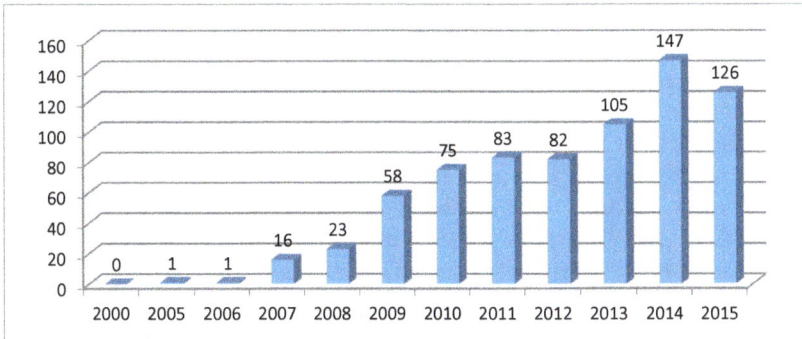

Fig. 5: Dynamics of eggs export, thousand tons.

Source: Agriculture of Ukraine 2015. Statistical Yearbook. Available at: http://www.ukrstat.gov.ua.

So, in 2015 consumption of eggs decreased by 77 thousand tons and exports decreased by 21 thousand tons.

Major competitors in the egg and egg product market of Ukraine

The egg and egg product market is sufficiently formed; powerful new players do not appear in it, and among those that are active players, there is fierce competition.

The main producers of egg products in Ukraine are AVANGARDCO (whose main specialization is the production and export of dry egg products) and Ovostar (whose main specialization is the production of a complete range of liquid and dried egg products; the export is an additional sales channel, strategically oriented to the domestic market). Due to increasing demand for higher quality and safety of food, the demand for liquid egg products is growing every year.

"Ovostar Union N.V. is a holding entity incorporated under the laws of the Netherlands consolidating companies with production assets located in Ukraine. Ovostar shares have been quoted on the Warsaw Stock Exchange since June 2011. Ovostar's mission is to produce ecologically clean and healthy food for Ukrainians. Also as Ovostar grows and gradually increases the volume of eggs produced, Ovostar develops the export markets and supplies shell eggs and egg products of consistently high quality to different international clients. Within the egg segment, Ovostar constantly focuses on meeting the demand of Ukrainian middle-class consumers" (Ovostar(a)).

With a shell egg portfolio of over 20 sub-brands, the company supplies branded eggs to the largest retail chains in Ukraine. Additionally, as a result of gradually increasing egg production, Ovostar is developing a presence on export markets. Within the egg products segment, Ovostar offers the full range of egg products in both liquid and dry forms. By adjusting the products to the clients' needs (while maintaining the superior quality) Ovostar achieves the loyalty of largest food-processing companies in Ukraine and outside.

Ovostar production sites "employ the most up-to-date poultry and processing equipment and progressive technological concepts in order to ensure the efficiency of production processes and superior quality of final products" (Ovostar(b)). Having initially adopted a large-scale production approach, Ovostar's vertically integrated business model spans the full production cycle, from parent flock to egg processing. In addition to core business, Ovostar maintains their own fodder production, processing of rapeseeds and grain storage in order to ensure the high quality of the poultry fodder provided to Ovostar's poultry flock. Ovostar products are compliant with international quality standards ISO 9001:2008 and ISO 22000:2005, FSSC 22000 as well as applicable national Ukrainian standards and sanitary norms. Ovostar also possess the Halal Certificate to export internationally.

The share of Ovostar Union in production of liquid egg products in Ukraine is 94% (2014: 90%); the share of Ovostar Union in production of dry egg products in Ukraine is 13% (2014: 6%); the share of Ovostar Union in industrial egg production of Ukraine is 12% (2014: 8%).

The volume of eggs sold in 2015 grew by 18% to 862 million eggs, resulting in USD 53.2 million of total revenue (2014: USD 48.6 million). Ukraine is Ovostar's major market and Ovostar's supply of eggs on the local market remained the same year to year: 634 million eggs or 73% of Ovostar's sales volume (2014: 644 million eggs or 88%). The growth the volume of shell eggs for sale was mainly directed for export. In 2015, the volume of eggs exported increased 2.6 times, from 89 to 229 million eggs. The export price during the first three quarters of 2015 was higher than the local price in USD terms. Ovostar's average selling price of shell eggs over the year increased by 68% to 1.374 UAH/egg compared to 0.819 UAH/egg in 2014.

"In 2015 Ovostar processed 347 million eggs (2014: 319 million eggs) producing 6787 tons of liquid and 1924 tons of dry egg products. The production plan of egg products was adjusted to a stronger focus on export-oriented dry egg products. In 2015 this segment generated USD 18.2 million of total revenue" (Ovostar(b)).

"The revenue from export sales over 2015 increased by 85% to USD 21.6 million and was received mostly in USD. The Middle East is Ovostar's key export market as the region is rather close in distance via sea transportation and can offer an attractive price for eggs and egg products. As the deep and comprehensive EU-Ukraine free trade agreement was enforced, Ovostar started to export the egg products to the EU in June 2015" (Ovostar, 2015).

Under the influence of changes in foreign and domestic markets and the actions of their major competitor, the company AVANGARDCO began restructuring their businesses.

Enterprise's risks and directions of structural changes of AVANGARDCO IPL under the influence of international factors and international market

The development of enterprises is only possible if they are ready to adapt to new consumer demands, including issues related to ecological compatibility of the production and product quality. The basic risks of AVANGARDCO have been investigated in order to identify "bottlenecks" and the prospects for overcoming them for consumers. Information about such risks and ways for overcoming them is on the company's official website and product packaging, as an element of the safety strategy of the company (www.ovostar.ua/en/).

"The risk of getting a foodborne illness from eggs is very low. In addition to food, bacteria also need moisture, a favorable temperature and time in order to multiply and increase the risk of illness. In the rare event that an egg contains bacteria, consumer can reduce the risk by proper chilling and eliminate it by proper cooking.

Over recent years, the bacterium *Salmonella enteritidis (Se)* has been found inside a small number of eggs. Scientists estimate that, on average across the U.S., only 1 of every 20,000 eggs might contain the bacteria. So, the likelihood that an egg might contain Se is extremely small – 0.005% (five one-thousandths of one percent). At this rate, if you're an average consumer, you might encounter a contaminated egg once every 84 years.

Other types of microorganisms could be deposited along with dirt on the outside of an egg. So, eggshells have to be washed and sanitized to remove possible hazards.

But, like all natural organic matter, eggs can eventually spoil through the action of spoilage organisms. Although they're unpleasant, spoilage organisms don't cause foodborne illness. The bacteria Streptococcus, Staphylococcus, Micrococcus and Bacillus may be found on egg shell surfaces because all these species can tolerate dry conditions. As the egg ages, though, these bacteria decline and are replaced by spoilage bacteria, such as coliform and Flavobacterium, but the most common are several types of Pseudomonas. Pseudomonascan grow at temperatures just above refrigeration and below room temperatures and, if they're present in large numbers, may give eggs a sour or fruity odor and a blue-green coloring.

Although it is more likely for bacteria to cause spoilage during storage, mold growth can occur under very humid storage conditions or if eggs are washed in dirty water. Molds such as Penicillium, Alternaria and Rhizopus may be visible as spots on the shell and can penetrate the shell to reach the egg" (Gun, Salo, 2008; Eggs & Food Safety).

As part of measures to minimize the loss risk of the safety of eggs and egg products through contamination or epidemics among livestock, a biological safety system has become particularly relevant, namely:

- Location of production at a distance of more than 0.3–1.2 km from the residential places;
- Location of poultry plants in different regions of the country to the fastest localization of possible outbreaks of infectious diseases;
- Poultry management in closed-type industrial premises;
- Prevention of contact with wild birds;
- Usage of disinfectant barrier;
- Prevention of contact between birds of different ages through the separate retention of young birds;
- Minimize contact of employees with poultry population;
- Prohibition of poultry management in the household for employees;
- Strict control of food reserve through checking the raw materials and released products of the combine fodder factories of the company;
- Growth of their own breeding generation;
- Scheduled vaccination against Newcastle disease, Marek's disease, bronchitis and other diseases;
- Creation of own specialized laboratories in the company;
- Staff training and testing on biosafety.

The company has implemented the integrated quality management system in order to effectively manage production in the context of sustainable development. Focusing on the requests of priority export markets, the producer is guided in its activity by standards established by the International Organization for Standardization (ISO), Good Manufacturing Practice (GMP) and Good Agricultural Practices (GLOBALGAP (EUREPGAP)) on crop and livestock, namely: adherence to the international standard "Quality Management System" (ISO 9001: 2008); international standard "Food safety management systems – Requirements for any organization in the food chain" (ISO 22000: 2005); International Code of practice general principles of food hygiene (CAC / RCP 1-1969); FSSC 22000.

In the context of the quality standards the three-level security control system is applied:

- Introduced plan of HACCP;
- Developed quality auditing system by internal auditors;
- External independent bodies on certification that are involved in control.

"AVANGARDCO IPL is a socially and environmentally responsible business. The company pays special attention to the relationships with its clients, contractors, suppliers, investors and other target audiences" (Annual Report, 2015a).

Building partnerships allows for faster adjustment to the changing market environment, implementation of state-of-the-art technologies and joint creation of added value. AVANGARDCO's advantage lies in vertical integration, which makes it possible to effectively control every step of the production process. The company's key production facilities include hatcheries, rearing farms and laying farms. Thanks to strict control at every stage of the production process, as well as the availability of warehouses for long-term storage, the company can adjust production volumes to match demand and minimize the consequences of price fluctuation. The egg processing plant Imperovo Foods allows the company to produce high-quality egg products. The company owns six compound feed mills, which allows it to meet up to 64% of the demand for poultry feed – a key component of production costs. The company is under the process of constructing biogas plants, which will help it to resolve the environmental issue of chicken manure disposal while producing electricity and heat as well as bio fertilizers. Company products such as shell eggs and egg products are widely sold domestically, as well as exported to 42 countries.

"The investment community, creditors, government agencies, suppliers, equipment producers and NGOs also play an important role in AVANGARD-CO's eco-system" (Avangardco, 2014). The desire for further development stimulates enterprise to reconsider its strategic objectives.

AVANGARDCO's mission is to promote public health by giving consumers access to affordable, healthy and safe animal proteins globally.

"AVANGARDCO IPL's focus areas are:

• Improving product quality;
• Doing business in line with global best practices;
• Combining socially and environmentally responsible business practices" (Avangardco, 2014).

Based on the research findings, some priority directions for the company development were defined, among them:

• Maintenance of the leader position in the production and supply at the domestic egg market;
• Regional expansion of the exports of eggs and dried egg products;
• Step up in exports of dried egg products for priority external markets.

Implementation of planned measures requires:

• Quality assurance through improving the ecological compatibility of the production by deepening upstream integration;
• Future steps to address biological safety issues;
• Restructuring of the product portfolio of dried egg products in accordance with the changing demand of importer;
• Obtaining of permission documentation for exports to priority markets.

According to the growing requests of foreign markets and worsening of internal problems caused by the loss of production capacity through the annexation of the Crimea and military operations in 2015, AVANGARDCO developed and implemented a new sustainable development strategy.

The strategy envisages changes in the structure of their product portfolio, which will be formed according to customer demands. This is necessary because of the imbalance in the structure of the commodity groups of dried egg products.

World imports of dried egg products include: yolk powder – 42%; albumen – 39%; dried egg yolk – 19%. Demand for different groups are formed according to the purpose of further usage, and as it is known, egg products are the subject of industrial producers' attention.

Seeking to meet the growing demand of importers of albumen led to significant stock forming of dried yolk powder. At the same time, consumption of yolk in the domestic market did not compensate for the commodity surplus of this product. So, AVANGARDCO moved towards the formation of a product portfolio strictly according to the order of products in accordance with the specifications of the customer with the aim of avoiding overproduction of some product groups and maintaining profitability.

Adherence to high quality standards is ensured by deepening upstream integration based on environmental orientation. The company underwent certification. The plant is fully equipped with production lines SANOVO (Denmark) and is certified according to the standards FSSC 22000, ISO 22000: 2005 and ISO 9001: 2008. In 2014 "Imperovo Foods" received official permission for exports of egg products to the European Union, as well as a certificate on kosher products (Avangardco, 2015).

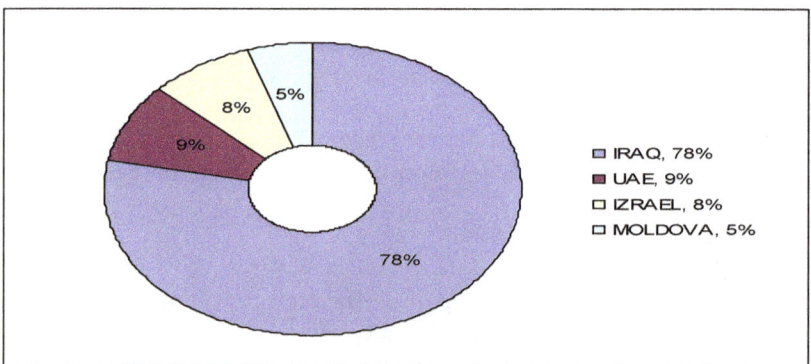

Fig. 6: AVANGARDCO top egg export markets, 2015, % of revenue.

Source: Avangardco, 2015. http://avangardco.ua/fileadmin/files/INVESTOR_RELATIONS/ Avangardco_IPL_Annual_Report_2015_final.pdf.

In order to diversify the regional structure of exports, AVANGARDCO has found some prospects in boosting the egg and egg product supply from Ukrainian to foreign markets, as well as researching the special demands of priority markets.

The most attractive export markets are the European Union and countries of MENA, the market of Judaic countries. In order to ensure compliance with the requirements of foreign markets on ecological compatibility of the production and quality of egg product, the company got the status of authorized exporter to the EU, and was certified halal and kosher.

The most rapidly growing market importer was the MENA region till 2015. It consists of countries of North Africa, the Middle East, the Gulf States and Turkey. Among key characteristics of the market, there are rapid population growth, increasing middle class; pent-up demand as a result of low self-sufficiency that is connected with difficulties in setting up of local production due to adverse climatic conditions. Among the threats, there are economic instability caused by military actions (Syria, Iraq). Today the MENA region has dependence on imports of eggs; it is a net importer in the segment of egg products (Figure 6).

There is further re-orientation of the market towards increasing egg product purchases and the gradual withdrawal of import eggs.

Because the popular majority of MENA countries are Muslims, permission for export of products must be confirmed by certified halal. The certificate confirms that the eggs obtained from hens that were fed without meat and bone meal. Compliance with the halal food standards applies strict control over

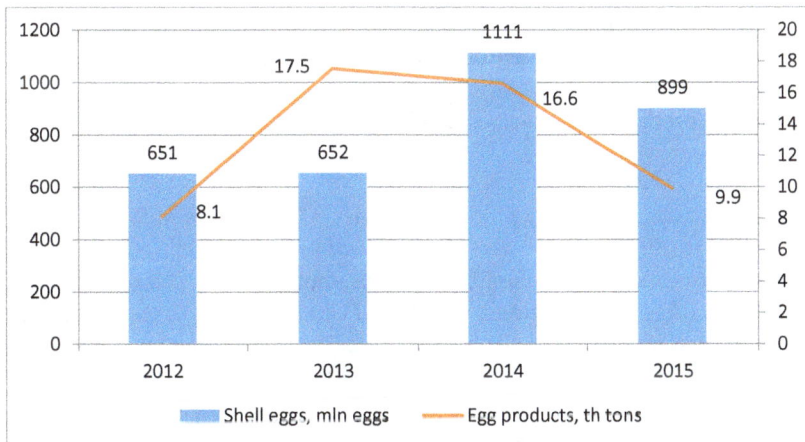

Fig. 7: Export of shell eggs and egg products from Ukraine.

Source: Avangardco, 2015. http://avangardco.ua/fileadmin/files/INVESTOR_RELATIONS/
Avangardco_IPL_Annual_Report_2015_final.pdf.

chickens' nutrition. The company has confirmed the quality of halal production by the halal certification, and they received automatic access to the markets of all Muslim countries in the world. However, a significant symptom of missing the most profitable market is the import reduction of the region by 18%, in particular by 33% in Iraq in 2015. It is because of further escalation of military conflicts.

Also, in order to expand export deliveries to the markets of kosher product's consumers AVANGARDCO has been certified as kosher, which is evidence of "purity" of the product, abidance by the terms of feeding and keeping chickens.

The growing interest of Avangardco in the market of the EU is explained:

- Geographical availability;
- Need for re-orientation of egg product deliveries because of sanctions to the Russian Federation (before -2% of exports), decrease in demand of MENA countries (18%);
- Significant profitability (less costs than those of European producers through upstream integration, the devaluation of the hryvnia);
- Significant difference in price of export and realization in the Ukrainian market.

Avangardco IPL successfully completed environmental restructuring in accordance with the requirements of European legislation in 2012. In 2014 the company received the status of an authorized exporter, "Imperovo Foods Ltd" (Ukraine Eggs and egg products Approval number 09-15-36 EGG 25/07/2014).

Features of the EU market for exports:

- of eggs – the narrowness of the quota for duty-free supply and the complexity of its receipt. At delivery over the quota, a company is unable to compete with the local producers.
- of egg products – pent-up demand, price competitiveness even without duty exemption.

The priority country for egg product deliveries is Denmark, which bought 38% of exports in 2015.

A step up in exports to the EU will be promoted because according to the Association Agreement between the EU and Ukraine, a duty-free quota for the supply of egg products and albumen was received in the amount of 1500 tons per year in conversion to eggs in their eggshells, followed by a gradual increase in quotas over five years up to 3000 tons per year (in conversion to eggs in egg-shells) and 3000 tons per year in net weight.

Thus, the domestic producer AVANGARDCO is a powerful exporter whose products are represented in the markets of 42 countries and the company consistently provides eggs and egg products at the national market.

Table 9: Regional structure of the eggs and egg products' exports by Avangardco, 2014–2015.

Commodity	2014	2015
Eggs	Iraq – 69.1% Liberia – 25.6% Moldova – 4.8% Turkey – 0.3% UAE – 0.2%	Iraq – 78%, UAE – 9%, Israel – 8%, Moldova – 5%
Egg products	Jordan – 24% Taiwan – 19% UAE – 18% Indonesia – 14% Turkey – 7% Other – 18%	Denmark – 38% Taiwan – 17% Indonesia – 14% Thailand – 8% Pakistan – 7% Other – 16%

Source: Avangardco, 2015. http://avangardco.ua/fileadmin/files/INVESTOR_RELATIONS/ Avangardco_IPL_Annual_Report_2015_final.pdf.

In 2015 Ukrainian exports of eggs fell by 19% (in physical terms) [According to "Agriculture of Ukraine 2015. Statistical Yearbook." Available at: http:// www.ukrstat.gov.ua], AVANGARDCO retained the share of exports, at 48% (Table 9).

Among the importers of eggs that successfully work with AVANGARDCO there are: Iraq – 78%, UAE – 9%, Israel – 8%, Moldova – 5%; importers of egg products: Denmark – 38%, Taiwan – 17%, Indonesia – 14%, Thailand – 8%, Pakistan – 7%.

The MENA region has remained the most profitable for the company because it consumes more than 90% of Ukrainian egg exports.

Conclusions

The international market of eggs belongs to growing markets, due to the fact that eggs are one of the cheapest products.

The egg market is very vulnerable due to the significant influence of external environmental factors.

The traditional world leader in production of eggs, since 1990, has been China; the United States occupied the second place and India and Japan are competing for the third place. In 2010–2013 Ukraine has ranked ninth in the production of eggs. Egg production is traditionally national; 97% of eggs are consumed within the country of original production, and only 3% of the products are offered on the world market.

The EU market is characterized by significant domestic production in the amount of 7.4 million tons of eggs; annual per capita consumption is 221 eggs. In 2015, the foreign trade balance of eggs in the EU was 1040 thousand tons. Significant import is caused by the need for egg products (55% of world imports).

Egg production in Ukraine had a weak upward trend till 2013. The period of 2014 is characterized by a decline in production by 27.5 thousand pieces or 0.1%. The beginning of the antiterrorist operation and occupation of Crimea led to a significant decline in production. In comparison with indicators of 2014, production cuts were 14.3% (2804.4 thousand pieces); however, compared with the index of production in 2005, production of eggs increased by 28.6%.

In the near future in Ukraine, there will be a tendency towards declining egg production. The trend may change if the export of eggs will show growth.

Agricultural enterprises produced 64.0% of the eggs in 2014. In 2015, the share of industrial production dropped to 58.2%. Reduction in industrial egg production was 2804.4 million pieces or by 14.3%, while households were reduced their production only by 30.4 million pieces (0.4%).

48 enterprises, which produced more than 50 thousand eggs, had a 12.2% share of all enterprises producing eggs. They produced 87.7% of the total egg production in Ukraine, while 253 other enterprises (64.5% of total enterprises) produced only 0.2% of all eggs that were produced in Ukraine.

Consumption of eggs per capita in Ukraine from 2000 to 2014 has risen from 166 to 310 eggs or by 86.7%. The increase of prices for eggs and reduction of purchasing power in 2015 led to a significant reduction in the consumption of eggs per capita to 280 eggs.

Over the study period prices of eggs increased by 3.5 times. The biggest price increase is typical for 2014 – by 2.4 times compared with 2013 and for 2015 – by 1.7 times comparing with 2014. Such increases in 2014 and 2015 can be attributed to the rising cost of production, caused by the rising cost of energy resources.

The main producers of egg products in Ukraine are AVANGARDCO (whose main specialization is the production and export of dry egg products) and Ovostar (whose main specialization is the production of a complete range of liquid and dried egg products; the export is an additional sales channel, strategically oriented to the domestic market). Due to increasing demand for higher quality and safety of food, the demand for liquid egg products is growing every year.

The company that aims to be the leader in the Ukrainian egg and egg product market and strengthen its competitive position in foreign markets has to adapt to changing conditions, in both national and global markets.

A complex set of external and internal factors has influenced AVANGARD-CO's activity in the Ukrainian market; moreover, negative domestic economy factors led them to strengthen their positions in international markets, namely:

- political and legal factors, among which are: military actions and the annexation of Crimea (loss of capacity); lack of legislative stability and a high degree of government influence on the economy, particularly changes in currency legislation in terms of exchange controls for foreign economic activity of enterprises (adjustment of period inflow of foreign currency, part of the obligatory sale of foreign exchange earnings, complications of purchase foreign currency for import transactions), revision of tax laws (VAT refunds, functioning of special regimes).
- economic factors, among which are: decrease in demand in the Ukrainian market; devaluation processes because the currency is a favourable factor for the development of an exporter, less than inflation, adjusting domestic demand; lack of access to credit resources; an oligopoly in the egg market and a duopoly in the egg product market.

Analyzing the factors of international environment, it is appropriate to note that the greatest impact on the aspiration to implement the new strategy for AVANGARDCO to enhance their competitive position as a producer and exporter were made: the fall in food prices in the world and the reduction in world imports of eggs and dry egg products.

An integral part of the strategic reorientation implementation, aimed to expand presence at foreign markets, was the environmental component (biosafety, improving the conditions of keeping chickens). The bases for its implementation were the following factors of international environment included increasing requirements for quality and environmental friendliness of products in the EU (mandatory for obtaining status of Permanent Exporter) and the MENA countries' market requirements regarding product conformity to the Muslim religion (obtaining Halal Certificate) and the Jewish faith (Kosher Certificate).

Among the favourable international factors in the EU market (ranged from most to least influential) were:

- Signing of an agreement with EU;
- Open borders of the European market by providing quotas for a duty-free supply of eggs and egg products;
- Stability law (legal security of supplier through compliance with the contract);
- Significant difference in price between the EU and Ukraine;
- High demand; and
- Progressive population that reflected an interest in ecological/organic/environmental-friendly food, the aspiration to a healthy lifestyle.

Among the favorable international factors at market of MENA countries are:

- Growing population;
- Increasing middle class;
- Lack of domestic production of eggs and egg products; and
- Transparency of requirements for quality and safety products.

However, despite the substantial decline in imports of egg products, especially by Iraq, it is worth noting that among threats to further cooperation, the following factors (ranged from most to least influential) are included:

- Threat of deepening military conflict;
- International activities of terrorist organizations;
- Decrease in demand for products through mass migration from some countries;
- Reduction in prices for egg products; and eggs;
- Risks in foreign trade agreements implementation due to the instability of the political situation.

The level of influence of each determinant on company activity under its restructuring processes is demonstrated in Table 10.

Table 10: Levels of influence of determinants on the company's activity under its restructuring processes.

	Determinant	Points
Economic factors		
1	Interest rates	9
2	Inflation rate	8
3	The national currency exchange rate	9
4	The unemployment rate	2
5	The degree of savings and debt society	3
6	Salaries	3
7	The availability of credits for businesses and households	8
8	Competition in core market	9
9	Consumer confidence	6
10	Access to capital	10
11	Level of taxes change	10
Political and legal factors		
12	Stability of legislation in the country	10
13	The degree of intervention of the government in the economy	10

14	The national political situation	10
15	International trade regulations and legislative restrictions	10
16	Consumer protection law	5
17	Labour Law	4
Political and legal aspects of the international market		
18	Preventing of monopolistic tendencies and unfair competition	2
19	Increasing of entry barriers for particular activities	2
20	Ensuring the safety of the products	10
21	Protecting the interests of weaker market participants	3
22	Protection of the environment.	7
23	The global political situation	10
Socio-cultural factors in both national and international sense, and the relationships between them		
24	The civilizational progress (lifestyle and its changes, the knowledge of the living standards in other countries)	7
25	Society mobility	6
26	The level of education	1
27	Local community initiatives	1
28	The awareness of civil and consumer rights	2
29	Religion	10
The technological factors		
30	State or company expenditures for Research and Development	8
31	The speed of up-to-date technology transfer	7
32	The level of transport development	9
33	The frequency of the new products' appearance	10
34	New tendencies of changes in realisation of business challenges, mobile technologies	9
35	The level of technological modernity industry	8
36	New inventions and development of science	8
37	Opportunities and the knowledge transfer and technology costs	7
38	The life cycle of products and the speed of technological changes	6
International factors		
39	The economic situation on the world	8
40	The opening of the borders	10
41	The stability of political, economic and tax systems in the countries that are the area of the industry interest	10

Continued.

42	The international agreements and regulations	10
43	The probability of an international armed conflict	10
44	International activity of terrorist organizations	10
Ecological aspects		
45	The deliberate use of air conditioners (switch off during airing rooms, no use after working hours)	1
46	Heating of water and space by using solar energy	4
47	Switched off lights when they are not needed	8
48	Unused administrative units are disconnect from the electricity network	6
49	Permanent monitoring of water consumption (e.g. control of leaking taps)	8
50	Trainings of personnel in effective waste management	10
51	Signed contracts with suppliers to reduce the amount of unnecessary packaging	4
52	Ecological innovations	10
53	Encouraging environmental awareness of employees and business' stakeholders	10

Source: results of investigation „Management of enterprises in terms of ensuring food security" that were held by the authors in National University of Food Technologies in terms of Scientific and Research Work financed by Ukrainian Goverment (project ID: 0112U004638). Answers provided on a scale from 1 (factor almost wasn't influenced on proecological restructuring) to 10 (factor was high influenced on proecological restructuring).

Expert assessment led to the following conclusions. The role of environmental factors (economic, political and legal, socio-cultural, technological) remains the leading one. The determinants received the highest assessment of experts such as: access to capital; level of taxes change; stability of legislation in the country; the degree of intervention of the government in the economy; the national political situation; international trade regulations and legislative restrictions; ensuring the safety of the products; the global political situation; the frequency of the new products' appearance. These determinants form the highest level of efficiency in carrying out pro-ecological restructuring – 10 points.

The lowest score (1-2 points) received environmental factors such as: the unemployment rate; preventing of monopolistic tendencies and unfair competition; Increasing of entry barriers for particular activities; the level of education; local community initiatives; the awareness of civil and consumer rights; the deliberate use of air conditioners. These determinants have little effect on the company's activity under its restructuring processes.

The study of the level of influence of individual determinants on the company's activities in the process of environmental restructuring revealed the following trends:

- the highest score among the environmental determinants were: training of personnel in the effective waste management (10 points); ecological innovations implemented by companies (10 points); encouraging environmental awareness of employees and business stakeholders (10 points);
- switched off lights when they are not needed (8 points); continuous monitoring of water consumption (e.g. control of leaking taps) (8 points); unused administrative unit are disconnect from the electricity network (6 points).

Significantly modest assessments have been made regarding unnecessary packaging (4 points) associated with the specifics of the analyzed product and the lack of reuse of packaging in the supply of eggs and egg products, especially on external markets. The question of use in the practical activity of Ukrainian producers of solar energy products (4 points) becomes of particular urgency; however, it is appropriate to emphasize the prospects rather than the possibilities of realization today.

Effective pro-ecological restructuring of Ukrainian enterprises is possible through providing the combined components, such as:

- an intellectual component through acquiring environmental knowledge;
- a value component through the formation of ecological consciousness;
- a legal component due to the increase of legal awareness about normative acts on ecology of Ukraine and counterpart countries; including the introduction of amendments to the legislation, namely the definition of investment priorities, along with economic and social effects, environmental impact on investment activities;
- a security component through the formation and implementation of environmental safety requirements at the micro-macro level;
- a practical component as an activity through acquiring theoretical knowledge and implementing practical skills in environmental restructuring.

Enterprises will be interested in implementing the strategy of pro-ecological restructuring only if the state establishes strict requirements for the environmental component of the production and sale of products.

At the same time, enterprises should concentrate their efforts to train personnel on effective waste management issues; implementation of environmental innovations that are implemented by companies; environmental awareness of employees and stakeholders; implementation of practices of saving material resources (electricity, water, materials). The implementation of the strategy of proecological restructuring as a component of the corporate strategy will lead to the sustainable development of enterprises and the economy of the country.

References

Agriculture of Ukraine (2015). Statistical Yearbook. Available at: http://www.ukrstat.gov.ua

AVANGARDCO IPL. Available at: http://www.avangardco.ua/en/

Avangardco (2014), Annual Report (2014). Available at: http://avangardco.ua/fileadmin/user_upload/AVGR_Annual_report_2014.pdf

Avangardco (2015), Annual Report 2015. Available at: http://avangardco.ua/fileadmin/files/INVESTOR_RELATIONS/Avangardco_IPL_Annual_Report_2015_final.pdf

Davies, J. (2018), Eggs' role in ending protein poverty Available at: https://www.poultryworld.net/Eggs/Articles/2018/5/Eggs-role-in-ending-protein-poverty-283827E/

Eggs & Food Safety. Available at: https://www.incredibleegg.org/egg-nutrition/egg-safety/

Gun Wirtanen, Satu Salo, (2008). Risk Assessment of Microbial Problems and Preventive Actions in Food Industry. 2-nd Open Seminar arranged by SAFOODNET – Food Safety and Hygiene Networking within New Member States and Associated Candidate Countries. Istanbul, Turkey, 22–23 Oct. 2007 Available at: https://www.vtt.fi/inf/pdf/symposiums/2008/S251.pdf

International Egg Commission. Available at: https://www.internationalegg.com/

International Egg Commission (2017), Annual Report (2017). Available at: https://www.internationalegg.com/new-report-on-the-dynamics-and-patterns-of-the-egg-industry-in-apec-member-countries/

Ovostar. Available at: http://www.ovostar.ua/en/

Ovostar (2015), Annual Report 2015. (Available at: http://www.ovostar.ua/data/file/financial_reports/ovostar_union_nv_annual_report_2015.pdf

Ovostar(a). Available at: www.ovostar.ua/ru/ipo/general_information/

Ovostar(b). Available at: https://mfa.gov.ua/.../sites/.../WEB_Katalog_Ovostar_2015.p.

Pro-Consulting. Egg market review. International Trade Centre. Available at: https://pro-consulting.ua/base/analiz-rynka-ukrainy

State Statistics Service of Ukraine. Available at: http://www.ukrstat.gov.ua

The Ministry of agrarian policy and food of Ukraine. Available at: www.minagro.gov.ua

World Egg Organization. Available at: http://www.internationalegg.com

World leaders in egg production. *Poultry and Poultry products* (2013) Vol.2

Ecological Awareness at the Age of Developed Technology in the Example of the Restructuring of a Medium-sized Enterprise "X"

Aleksandra Gąsior

Dr, Department of Microeconomics, Institute of Economics,
Faculty of Economic and Management, University of Szczecin

Introduction

Scientific and media reports on the constantly deteriorating state of natural human surroundings force contemporary society to search for more effective ways of caring for the environment that are currently available. Living in harmony with nature requires taking action in at least three areas (Majchrowska 2013):

1. Natural and technological sphere.
2. Political and social activities, legal and economic activities.
3. Popularization activities concerning individual and social awareness (Frątczak 1995).

The enterprise environment – both micro and macroeconomic – tries to respect the above-stipulated areas through active measures, aiming to achieve harmony. One might presume that human beings are fully aware of how big a role nature plays in the proper functioning of the life of man and nature, as well as in economic life. Unfortunately, constant reports from the economic world, which is controlled by humans, cast a doubt on that presumption.

How to cite this book chapter:
Gąsior, A. 2019. Ecological Awareness at the Age of Developed Technology in the
Example of the Restructuring of a Medium-sized Enterprise "X". In: Gąsior, A.
(ed.) *Pro-ecological Restructuring of Companies: Case Studies*, Pp. 45–57. London:
Ubiquity Press. DOI: https://doi.org/10.5334/bbk.d. License: CC-BY 4.0

This chapter will discuss the problems faced by restructured enterprises in terms of ecological aspects and the pro-ecological measures they undertake for the improvement or prevention of any deterioration of an enterprise's nearest natural surroundings.

An attempt was made in the paper to analyse the activities of a purposefully chosen medium-sized enterprise, "X"[1], which within the scope of conducting permanent restructuring, focusing on its fixed assets, impacts the natural environment. The fundamental question that at this point needs to be posed is whether the employees, together with the management personnel, are aware of these activities. The following deliberations should answer that question.

Methodology

At present, the performance of restructuring activities is of permanent nature, as R. Borowiecki (2010) and R. Borowiecki and A. Jaki (2015) rightly observed. It is worth noting that permanent restructuring, constituting a thorough change, is an answer to the turbulent environment, which is increasingly less predictable, while every enterprise, be it small or large, must still be able to function in it.

However, it is hard not to notice that it is easier to pinpoint the exact dates set for the fulfilment of restructuring processes in large enterprises (which results from their structure and greater formality of works called for in that kind of enterprise, but also from their obligations to a large stakeholders' group), than in medium-sized enterprises. Significant differences occur in the approach to ecological aspects: large enterprises implement programmes especially dedicated to ecological issues, and they establish departments responsible for environmental protection. Medium-sized enterprises, even though they undertake activities for environmental protection, do not articulate it in their strategy or operations policy, but oftentimes they do it involuntarily. It is not due to their unwillingness or inaction, but rather because they lack the need to incorporate it in the strategy of enterprise operations, which is reflected in the case of an example company, "X", presented below. The described differences inspired the author to deliberations concerning the restructuring of fixed assets and the use of modern technology in the company's economic activity. Therefore, the fundamental objective of the paper is to evaluate the awareness, of both the employees and the management of company "X", of the impact of technology on the pro-ecological decisions taken in the restructured enterprise.

It corresponds to the above-listed areas: natural and technological activities as well as popularization activities in respect of individual and social awareness.

An attempt at answering the following, more detailed questions will be helpful in achieving the main objective of the paper, namely:

1. Do the employees as well as the management demonstrate ecological awareness?
2. Does the technology employed in the production process performed by company "X" have a positive impact on the natural environment?
3. Can the entire process of operations be considered as pro-ecological activity or only its individual stages?
4. Do the employees perceive the conducted restructuring process as pro-ecological activity in the company?

The results of a survey conducted on large enterprises in 2014, which will serve for the comparison of results of a survey conducted at company "X" in 2016, will be helpful in an attempt to answer the questions posed above.

It needs to be emphasised that the survey of 2014 concerned the evaluation of pro-ecological restructuring for employment. A research sample included large enterprises (defined as those employing more than 249 people), which underwent or were in the course of undergoing restructuring. Out of 1677 enterprises that constituted a research group, complete surveys were obtained in the research period from 120 companies. Mostly companies from the following four sectors took part in the survey: mining industry; industrial processing; generation and supply of electrical energy, gas, water; sewage and waste management as well as operations related to reclamation. The reason for the selection of companies from those sectors was a significant (undesirable) impact that business activities conducted by the enterprises from those sectors have on the natural environment.

It is believed that a comparison of the research results ought to be interesting because of the possibility of comparing the obtained average values from the replies of large enterprises with the results of a medium-sized enterprise, "X". The choice of the entity was intentional, on account of it being part of the "industrial processing" sector as well as the activities undertaken by the entity.

The results of observations and in-depth interviews will be used for the purpose of deepening the comparative analysis, aiming at answering the questions posed.

Short History and Activities of Enterprise "X"

Enterprise "X" is a medium-sized company operating in the industrial processing sector for over fourteen years and with a fully Polish capital. The organisational and legal form of the entity is a limited liability company. Enterprise "X" is a manufacturing company, whose core business activity is manufacture of workwear according to the Polish Business Activity Classification. Additionally, company "X" provides laundry and repair services, and rents utility rooms and production machines. During the research period, over 90 people were employed by the company. The idea for this type of operation was taken from western countries, where people started paying attention much earlier than in Poland to the quality of the clothes in which a labourer works, to the method of its cleaning and most importantly to transferring a part of the company's activity outside by way of commissioning the service (clothes outsourcing).

In order to ensure a better evaluation of the employees and management of enterprise "X", it is worth focusing on the scope of enterprise "X"'s activities (manufacture of workwear). First of all, a diagram of the process of the service rendered by the company will be presented, which was devised on the basis of the observations conducted in the company (Diagram 1).

It must be emphasised that the process of manufacture of workwear by company "X" requires suitably, individually selected fabrics, specialised for each customer, preceded by consultancy, in order to ensure the right choice of a proper cut and garments. Apart from a personalised cut, the clothes also feature a label identifying the customer's employee.

The provision of clothes rental and servicing requires the following activities, ensuring high quality and the improvement of the competitive position that company "X" holds in the market:

1) *Water cleaning.* Proper washing technologies ensure the cleanliness and aesthetics of the final effect of the service. It is important to maintain suitable properties of the washed assortment in terms of colour, fabric resistance or their technical parameters, to which the company pays special focus and which it guarantees. For the purpose of the service the company uses agents that are safe to humans, clothes and the environment, which is guaranteed by a permit held by the enterprise from the National Institute of Hygiene in Warsaw and the opinion of the Children's Memorial Health Centre Institute in Warsaw. The process is under constant supervision and control by qualified technologists. Water cleaning is completed

---

Contract signing → consultancy regarding individual customer needs→ manufacture of clothes → delivery of lockers for storage of clean clothes and lockers for dirty clothes → constant care over contract fulfilment and systematic exchange of dirty clothes to clean clothes after its washing, maintenance and repair → generation of documentation evidencing the acceptance-delivery process → systematic reporting of servicing → settlement of the service rendered according to the terms agreed upon in the contract

---

Diagram 1: The process of clothes: production, rental and servicing at enterprise "X".

Source: Own work on the basis of active observation.

with a Tunel Finisher machine, which smoothes out, extracts dust from and disinfects washed garments. For the customers from pharmaceutical companies, on account of their requirements, apart from washing and drying, the company also offers the service of airtight packaging.

2) Footwear disinfection. Footwear is disinfected with the use of a bactericidal device.

Additional activities of the basic process (of clothes rental and servicing) include:

1. Storage of customer's unused clothes.
2. Handling of claim notices.

Apart from the composite services of clothes rental and servicing, another asset of company "X" concerns the sales offer of industrial safety articles.

It worth emphasising that company "X" is one of very few companies with Polish capital, and although it is categorised as a medium-sized enterprise, it is one of the major companies in its sector.

Research Results

Before the deliberations on the survey results and on company "X" operations are presented, it must be stressed that multiple definitions can be found in the literature (Borowiecki and Jaki 2015; Borowiecki and Wysłocka 2012; Myers 1977; Karpiński 1986; Sadzikowski 1989; Falińska in Rudek 1992, Jsiński 1992; Kowalczuk-Jakubowska and Malewicz 1992; Szulc in Kukliński 1993; Chomątowski 1994; Pełka 1994;Czapiewski and Kreft in Borowiecki 1994; Jagoda and Lichtarski 1994; Kamela-Sowińska and Mirecki 1995; Stabryła 1995; Sapijaszka 1996; Nalepka 1997; Wanielista and Miłkowska 1998; Durlik 1998; Nalepka 1998; Malara 1998; Gabrusewicz 1999; Nogalski and Waśniewski 1999; Belka and Pietrewicz in Mączyńska 2001; Malara 2001; Romanowska 2004; Stabryła 2005; Lachiewicz and Zakrzewska-Bielawska 2005) for restructuring in Poland from the onset of transformations through the present day. Nevertheless, for the purpose of the research, the definition of S. C. Myers (1977) was adopted, which continues to reflect well what the process of restructuring is for an enterprise. In turn, the definition of ecological awareness was taken from J. Penc (2003), which was supplemented with the approach of, inter alia, K. Niziołek (2004), J. Frątczak (1995) or A. Papuziński (2006).

During passive observations, the knowledge of processes performed in the enterprise was deepened, particularly regarding the processes related to the functioning of labourers' work positions. In order to reply to the questions posed in this paper, active observation and interviews were employed. Three conversations were conducted with the company's management representatives and with employees, which gives a total of over 47 interviews of a non-categorised, open and individual nature.

Before evaluating the ecological awareness of the employees and management of company "X", first of all, the survey results will be presented concerning the decision taken by the examined enterprise regarding restructuring in a turbulent environment for technological reasons. This will enable a preliminary assessment as to which of the determinants played the most significant role in making that decision.

As previously mentioned, results of the survey conducted in company "X" will be compared with the survey results for all of Poland that was conducted in 2014.[2] (Chart 1).

The following determinants characterising technological aspects were chosen for the survey: state/enterprise expenditure on research and development; the speed of modern technologies transfer; level of transport development; frequency of new products appearing; new trends of changes in tackling business challenges, mobile technologies; degree of industry technical modernity; new inventions and scientific development; possibilities and cost of knowledge and technology transfer; life cycle of goods and the speed of technological changes.

After calculating a weighted average for large enterprises, the results of which are presented in Chart 1, it occurred that the most significant factor for them was the degree of transport development when deciding on the conduct of enterprise restructuring. In the case of the analysed enterprise "X", the major factor that helped make the decision to restructure entailed the speed of modern technologies transfer. In the comparison of the obtained results, in the case of large enterprises the speed of modern technologies transfer ranked only in fourth place, with a weighted average of 8.78, to which an interviewed representative of company "X" assigned a weight of 6 and it was the highest weight for the factors in the area of technology. From the evaluation of enterprise "X", it follows that the technological aspect of a turbulent environment was not too significant in the making of the decision to restructure. Contrary to large enterprises, the above-mentioned factors were not attributed with equally high significance, quite the reverse; they are typically smaller by more than a half. In the case of a medium-sized enterprise it may mean difficulties with investing in technology or in relatively high-quality equipment, so that it does not constitute the main driving force of restructuring.

In search for an answer to the basic question posed in the paper concerning the ecological awareness of both the employees and management of enterprise "X", which undergoes permanent restructuring with a particular focus on fixed assets, the answers will be formulated on the grounds of the conducted observations and in-depth interviews.

In the interviews conducted with the company's co-owner, the following areas shaping the ecological awareness of the analysed company were identified:

1) The knowledge of the processes taking place in the enterprise as well as their impact on the environment.

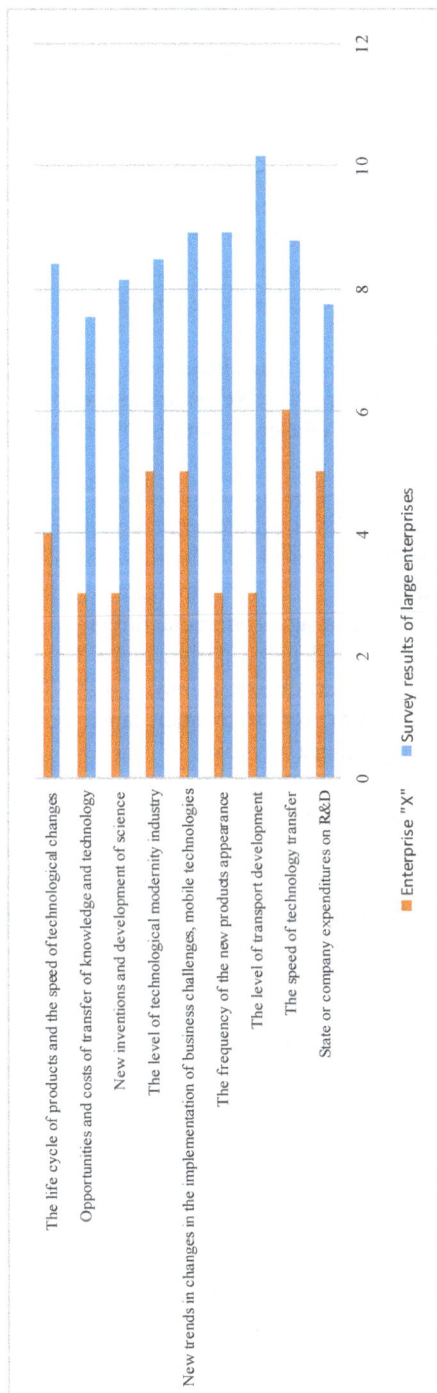

Chart 1: Weighted average of the significance of technological factors affecting the decision on restructuring used in the survey study.

Source: Own work on the basis of survey studies for all of Poland conducted in 2014 and a purposefully selected enterprise "X" – survey of 2017.

2) Permanent restructuring, which is conducted for, inter alia, pro-ecological purposes reducing the negative effects of the conducted operations.
3) Planning of changes in the enterprise activities, contributing to environmental protection.

Regarding 1: The service provided by the analysed company "X" entails the performance of the first stage of clothes water cleaning. It requires the use of proper machines with suitably selected chemical agents. The company management and employees care about minimising threats to both employees and the environment, so that the quality of the service rendered is maintained or even raised.

The basic operation depending on the management's knowledge involves frequent investments in washer-extractors. Newer and newer models improve the results in the sphere of washing efficiency, but also in terms of energy-saving and water-saving results.

The employees exercise special care and minute exactitude when dosing suitable chemical mixtures for clothes washing, which oftentimes, depending on the customer, requires proper treatment in order to maintain the parameters of the fabrics used in work clothes. In turn, the management keeps an eye on all the recommendations of chemical agents manufacturers provided on a regular basis being correctly implemented, particularly when a decreased dose is recommended with the same effect as the one achieved with a larger portion of a mixture. It forces the company to exercise constant care in terms of modernisation of the systems securing against any toxic substances penetrating into the environment.

Regarding 2: Pro-ecological activities undertaken by company "X" also involve the next stage of the main process, namely drying and ironing of washed clothes, for which a highly specialised device, a Tunel Finisher, is used. The purchase of the machine contributed to the restructuring of the entire drying and ironing process. Until 2014 the service was performed on a mass scale with the use of dryers – to dry clothes, and with human labour – to iron them. However, in order to reduce the costs related to the process, currently Tunel Finisher – a high-tech machine of improved efficiency and capacity – is used. Clothes are automatically put into the machine. They are treated with hot water, compressed steam, which on the one hand irons garments, while on the other dries them. Human labour has been limited only to putting given items of clothing into the machine on the one side and collecting them on the other side upon the conclusion of the entire process. To compare, a clothes dryer can dry (depending on the fabric thickness) up to 100 items of clothing in an hour. Such clothes still need ironing. A worker using a hand-held iron is able to iron 20–30 items of clothing in an hour. In turn, the above-mentioned machine can dry and iron 1600 garments in an hour with the involvement of only two workers. The use of Tunel Finisher has resulted in reorganisation of employment and of drying and ironing processes.

Regarding 3: Another pro-environmental measure the company intends to implement is a water reclamation system. It involves reclaiming water from a washer-extractor from the third programmed rinsing cycle and using that water for the first rinsing cycle in the subsequent washing load. What is more, during operation the Tunel Finisher generates serious noise. Therefore, the company is currently restructuring the organisation of the work in the hall where Tunel Finisher operates, with the aim of minimising the effects of the above-mentioned noise.

Conclusions

The region in which the company has its seat boasts many special bird protection areas or special habitat protection areas. There are over 90 nature reservations found in the area. The local community greatly appreciates having access to such attractive nature gifts as forests full of mushrooms, berries and game or rivers, in which community members unwaveringly enjoy angling. Unfortunately, the image does not translate to the immediate environment of the examined company X. The nearest surroundings of the company feature buildings and yards, which the company uses for the benefit of its employees, e.g. by creating a car park. Unfortunately, the entire area is covered in concrete and it does not correlate to what can be seen in more distant surroundings, i.e. forests, garden allotments and fields. Despite the unfavourable conditions, the owner is making efforts to add greenery around the company seat. Thus, it seems that the natural environment surrounding the company seat inspires to act for its benefit, which can be seen in the change of landscaping around the premises of company "X". Still, the company's interior is equally important. For that reason, the presented results of the conducted survey, the observations made and the conclusions drawn from interviews enable a subjective evaluation of the basic problem posed in the paper concerning the awareness of the employees and management of company "X" of the impact of the technologies on pro-ecological decisions taken in the restructured enterprise.

In order to fulfil the main goal, detailed questions had to be answered. The first one concerned a determination: Do employees as well as the management demonstrate ecological awareness? Both the employees and the company's management show ecological awareness, but the focus of their awareness has to be differentiated. From the interviews with the employees, it arises that they are not indifferent to ecological aspects in their closest surroundings, namely in their households. Regrettably, they are completely indifferent to what goes on at their work place. They shift the entire responsibility for the matter to the management, while adhering only and exclusively to the guidelines given to them.

Another issue regarded the use of technology in the provision of services by company "X" and its positive impact on the natural environment. Although the management and the majority of employees are convinced that the technology implemented in the company's operations, and particularly the speed of modern technology transfer, enables them to reduce the harmful impact on the environment, still only few employees, after a moment of consideration, pessimistically declared that no technology, even the most modern one, serves the environment in any positive way. Nevertheless, they all agree that in such a technologically advanced world, only pro-ecological measures are acceptable, ones that aim to support and protect, not harm the environment.

The next question concerned the functioning of the entire process, whether all of it can be perceived as pro-ecological, or only its individual stages, and the answer can be found above. The basis of the service provided by company "X" – clothes rental and servicing – features aspects that stand in conflict with not harming the environment, since the service entailing washing demands the use of proper chemical agents that need to be neutralised in order to prevent their harmful effects. It means that the enterprise needs other high-technology machines and devices, i.e. it expects that companies specialising in such machinery will manufacture a product satisfying its demand. It is common knowledge that such production requires proper materials and energy. Thereby, discrepancy occurs in the network of needs, which at the same time harm the environment. It means that in the entire process of rental and servicing there are processes of more pro-ecological nature – washing, drying and ironing, and less pro-ecological ones, such as administrative issues that require better coordination (document circulation, their double printing etc.), and the ensuing expansion of activities, which, if being pro-ecological, will contribute to environment protection.

The last issue referred to the question: Do employees perceive the conducted restructuring process as pro-ecological activity in the company? Unfortunately, this area has been neglected by the management, which during restructuring focused most on the information of what the restructuring will entail, what its effects are going to be for the present personnel. The information concerning pro-ecological aspects was missing.

Summing up, if it is assumed that ecological awareness means knowledge and the way of thinking, which is constantly deepened and updated, in order to undertake activities for the protection of nature and the environment, one needs to conclude that:

a) The management is highly knowledgeable about the impact of technology when making decisions on pro-ecological measures for the protection of the environment, as well as about the minimisation of damage resulting from the activities performed in the course of the enterprise restructuring. The respondents demonstrate an ethical attitude through their approach and convictions in relation to the principles of environment protection.

b) Even though employees largely operate on a pro-ecological basis – in line with the guidelines and the rules represented by the management – they do not entirely realise that they do so. It results from their lack of interest in such aspects of their work place.

In conclusion, the ecological awareness at the times of developed technology in restructuring of a medium-sized enterprise "X" is demonstrated through management decisions and actions. On the other hand, most employees need further information about the pro-ecological measures, which could be provided through individual talks, an informational campaign about pro-ecological steps, or through an equally effective, yet simple method of using posters concerning the basic economic operations of company "X".

Notes

1   The owners did not consent to the publication of the company's business name.
2   The results of large enterprises were more extensively presented in the following articles: Gąsior A 2015, Salaries as a Determinant of Restructuring Large Companies in Poland. *Transformations in Business & Economics*, 14(3C): 36C, p. 372–389. Gąsior A 2016, Poziom rozwoju transportu jako determinanta procesu restrukturyzacji dużych przedsiębiorstw, [in:] Polityka ekonomiczna, ed. Sokołowski J, Węgrzyn G, Research Papers of Wrocław University of Economics, Wrocław, nr 450, p. 150–160. Gąsior A 2017, Restrukturyzacja a poprawa aspektów ekologicznych w dużych przedsiębiorstwach [in:] Zarządzanie restrukturyzacją: procesy i struktury w obliczu zmian, ed. Jaki A, Rojek T, Fundacja Uniwersytetu Ekonomicznego w Krakowie, Kraków, p.173–182.

References

Belka, M and Pietrewicz, L 2001 Kluczowe czynniki sukcesu restrukturyzacji dużych przedsiębiorstw w Polsce. In: Mączyńska, E (ed.). *Restrukturyzacja przedsiębiorstw w procesie transformacji gospodarki polskiej*, Warszawa, DiG.

Borowiecki, R 2010 Permanentna restrukturyzacja jako czynnik rozwoju i sukcesu przedsiębiorstw w dobie globalizacji rynku, *Zeszyty Naukowe Uniwersytetu Ekonomicznego w Krakowie*, No. 836.

Borowiecki, R and Jaki, A 2015 Restrukturyzacja – od transformacji do globalizacji, *Przegląd Organizacji*, No. 9.

Borowiecki, R and Wysłocka, E (eds.) 2012 *Analiza ekonomiczna i ocena ekspercka w procesie restrukturyzacji przedsiębiorstw*, Warszawa, Difin.

Chomątowski, S 1994 Kierunki i metody oceny oraz realizacji restrukturyzacji przedsiębiorstw, *Przegląd Organizacji*, No.12.

Czapiewski, M and Kreft, Z 1994 Koncepcja restrukturyzacji Portu Handlowego Gdynia S.A. In: Borowiecki, R. *Restrukturyzacja przedsiębiorstw w procesie transformacji rynkowej*, Kraków, AE-TNOiK.

Durlik, I 1998 *Restrukturyzacja procesów gospodarczych, Reengineering, Teoria i praktyka*, Warszawa, Placet.

Falińska, J 1992 Sposób wprowadzania zmian restrukturyzacyjnych w przedsiębiorstwie. In: Rudek, J. *Przekształcenia własnościowe i strukturalne w gospodarce polskiej*, Wrocław, Wyd. Politechniki Wrocławskiej.

Frątczak, J 1995 *Świadomość ekologiczna dzieci, młodzieży i dorosłych w aspekcie edukacji szkolnej i nieszkolnej*, Bydgoszcz, Wyd. WSP.

Gabrusewicz, W 1999 Restrukturyzacja przedsiębiorstw i metody oceny jej efektów, *Przegląd Organizacji*, No. 3.

Gąsior, A 2015 Salaries as a Determinant of Restructuring Large Companies in Poland. *Transformations in Business & Economics*, Vol. 14, No. 3C (36C), p. 372-389.

Gąsior, A 2016 Poziom rozwoju transportu jako determinanta procesu restrukturyzacji dużych przedsiębiorstw. In: Sokołowski, J and Węgrzyn, G (eds.). Polityka ekonomiczna, *Research Papers of Wrocław University of Economics*, Wrocław, No. 450, p. 150-160.

Gąsior, A 2017, Restrukturyzacja a poprawa aspektów ekologicznych w dużych przedsiębiorstwach. In: Jaki, A and Rojek, T (eds.). *Zarządzanie restrukturyzacją: procesy i struktury w obliczu zmian*, Kraków, Fundacja Uniwersytetu Ekonomicznego w Krakowie, p.173-182.

Jagoda, H and Lichtarski, J 1994 Problemy i wytyczne restrukturyzacji naprawczej przedsiębiorstw. In: Borowiecki, R (ed.). *Restrukturyzacja przedsiębiorstw w procesie transformacji systemowej*, Kraków, AE-TNOiK.

Jasiński, Z 1992 Restrukturyzacja systemu zarządzania przedsiębiorstwem, *Ekonomika i organizacja przedsiębiorstwa*, No. 8.

Kamela-Sowińska, A and Mirecki, AB (eds.) 1995 *Restrukturyzacja jako proces podnoszenia efektywności przedsiębiorstwa*, Bydgoszcz, OPO.

Karpiński, A 1986 *Restrukturyzacja gospodarki w Polsce i na świecie*, Warszawa, PWE.

Kowalczuk-Jakubowska, D and Malewicz, A 1992 *Restrukturyzacja jako technika ratowania i rozwoju przedsiębiorstwa*, Warszawa, Instytut Organizacji i Zarządzania w Przemyśle, "Orgmasz".

Lachiewicz, S and Zakrzewska-Bielawska, A 2005 *Restrukturyzacja organizacji i zasobów kadrowych przedsiębiorstwa*, Kraków, Oficyna Ekonomiczna.

Romanowska, M 2004 *Leksykon zarządzania*, Warszawa, Difin.

Majchrowska, A 2013 Świadomość ekologiczna i postawy wobec środowiska naturalnego wśród mieszkańców Lubelszczyzny. Kapitał Intelektualny Lubelszczyzny 2010–2013 Available at http://www.kil.lubelskie.pl/wp-content/uploads/2013/08/%C5%9Awiadomo%C5%9B%C4%87-ekologiczna-i-postawy-wobec-%C5%9Brodowiska-naturalnego.pdf [Last accessed 15 September 2016].

Malara, Z 1998 *Metodyka dokonywania zmian restrukturyzacyjnych w obszarze organizacji i zarządzania przedsiębiorstw*, Wrocław, Politechnika Wrocławska.

Malara, Z 2001 *Restrukturyzacja organizacyjna przedsiębiorstwa*, Prace Naukowe Instytutu Organizacji i Zarządzania Politechniki Wrocławskiej. Monografie, No. 32, Wrocław, Oficyna Wydawnicza Politechniki Wrocławskiej.

Myers, SC 1977 Determinants of Corporate Borrowing. *Journal of Financial Economics*, Vol. 5.

Nalepka, A 1997 Istota, zakres i metodyka restrukturyzacji przedsiębiorstwa. In: Borowiecki, R (ed.). *Restrukturyzacja a konkurencyjność przedsiębiorstw*, Kraków, Wyd. AE w Krakowie.

Nalepka, A 1998 *Zarys problematyki restrukturyzacji przedsiębiorstw*, Kraków, Antykwa.

Niziołek, K 2004 Kompleksowe zarządzanie jakością środowiska (TQEM) – koncepcja zarządzania przedsiębiorstwem w XXI wieku. In: Lewandowski, J (ed.). *Zarządzanie organizacjami gospodarczymi w zmieniającymi się otoczeniu*, Łódź, Wyd. Politechniki Łódzkiej.

Nogalski, B and Waśniewski, J 1999 Restrukturyzacja jako wyznacznik rozwoju przedsiębiorstwa budowlanego, Zeszyty Naukowe Uniwersytetu Gdańskiego, *Organizacja i Zarządzanie*, No. 13, Sopot.

Papuziński, A 2006 Świadomość ekologiczna w świetle teorii i praktyki. (Zarys politycznego modelu świadomości ekologicznej), *Problemy Ekorozwoju*, Vol. 1, No. 1, p. 33-40.

Pełka, B 1994 *Restrukturyzacja przedsiębiorstwa przemysłowego*, Insytut Organizacji i Zarządzania w Przemyśle, Warszawa, Orgmasz.

Penc, J 2003 *Zarządzanie w warunkach globalizacji*, Warszawa, Difin.

Sadzikowski W 1989 Finansowanie procesu restrukturyzacji przemysłu w Polsce, *Finanse*, No. 1.

Sapijaszka, Z 1996 *Restrukturyzacja przedsiębiorstwa. Szanse i ograniczenia*, Warszawa, Wydawnictwo Naukowe PWN.

Stabryła, A 1995 *Zarządzanie rozwojem firmy*, Kraków, Księgarnia Akademicka.

Stabryła, A 2005 *Zarządzanie strategiczne w teorii i praktyce firmy*, Warszawa, Wyd. Naukowe PWN.

Szulc R, 1993 Restrukturyzacja gospodarcza, pojęcie i doświadczenia międzynarodowe. In: Kukliński, A (ed.). *Studia regionalne i lokalne*, Warszawa, Wyd. Uniwersytetu Warszawskiego.

Wanielista, K and Miłkowska, I (eds.) 1998 *Słownik menedżera*, Wrocław, Fraktal.

SECTION 2

Pro-ecological Performance of the Enterprises

Introduction

Tomasz Bernat

Dr hab., University of Szczecin, Faculty of Economics and Management, Department of Microeconomics

The following section is a continuation of the solutions from section 1, which presented the turbulent environment companies are set in. Unlike that part, the case studies presented here describe measures taken by business entities as part of the restructuring processes. These activities are closely linked with pro-environmental decisions.

The first part of the section is an extended case study on the pro-environmental activity of a large company, ThyssenGas. The analysis posed a question of whether the activity of this German gas supplier was related to ecological processes. A high-technology solution was identified here, one which enables mixing natural gas supplied to the end users with biogas from local suppliers. This example shows how even a large entity can restructure its operation to make it as green as possible.

The next section describes the situation in Ukraine through the example of the "LLC Leader" pig farm and its problems with the disposal of bio-waste such as faeces. With large livestock production, dealing with bio-waste constitutes a significant problem. The disposal method proposed in this chapter is the production of biogas. This is shown through the example of the farm as an environmentally friendly way to recycle biological waste.

How to cite this book chapter:
Bernat, T. 2019. Pro-ecological Performance of the Enterprises: Introduction. In: Gąsior, A. (ed.) *Pro-ecological Restructuring of Companies: Case Studies*, Pp. 61–62. London: Ubiquity Press. DOI: https://doi.org/10.5334/bbk.e. License: CC-BY 4.0

The third part describes the activities of HS Company, an industrial processing company that manufactures components of machinery and equipment. The company decided to take a strategic reorientation with participation of its core stakeholders, namely employees. The adopted strategy, related to financial and organisational problems, resulted in new solutions not only in the organization of the processes but also as regards the staff.

In the fourth subsection, an example of a Ukrainian producer of alcoholic beverages, "Obolon", is presented. The main area of interest of the company is the production of beer for domestic and international markets. The purpose of the analysis of this entity is to indicate the influence of environmental factors on its activity as well as a broader discussion of actions taken by the company, especially with regard to CSR. In this case, the analysis is focused on measures taken to reduce the environmental burden caused by the company's activities.

The next part is going to present an interesting example from one of the world leaders in business consulting, the Pricewaterhouse Coopers (PwC). The case study is concentrated on their strategy of corporate responsibility developed on a global company level and implemented in a national branch, namely in Romania. The focus of the paper is to investigate the measures taken to implement the strategy on a local scale.

The last part describes pro-environmental investments in new technologies. With the example of Poland and selected actions of the European Commission, ecological measures taken by business entities are presented. Two projects have been analysed: GreenEvo and ETV, as flagship examples of pro-environmental investments in new technologies. The subject is further illustrated by means of analysis of statistical data as regards the chapter's subject.

Business activity can and should be conducted in such a way so as to make it the least harmful to the environment. The six case studies presented in this section confirm the assumption that any business can be restructured to become more environmentally friendly.

Investment in Conventional or Renewable Energy Sources: Thyssengas – A Green Energy Provider?

Tomasz Bernat

Dr hab., University of Szczecin, Faculty of Economics and Management, Department of Microeconomics

Introduction

Pro-environmental business activity takes different forms. One of them is a complex approach to technological progress aimed at increased involvement in environmental protection. As an example of such an attitude this paper presents Thyssengas, the leading natural gas supplier in Germany. The technological solutions described below combine conventional energy sources with the renewable ones. This shows that even in large-scale business activity economic entities can use pro-environmental methods by changing their basic technology.

The Objectives and the Methodology

Companies operating in market economies often make efforts intending to show their best side to stakeholders. One such endeavor is involvement in promoting environmentally friendly solutions. In the majority of cases such initiatives are undertaken by large and very large businesses as they can allocate adequate financial resources and assign staff to dedicated organizational units. Such activity is closely related to public relations because its main objective is to give the company a positive image. Moreover, businesses initiate real actions

---

How to cite this book chapter:
Bernat, T. 2019. Investment in Conventional or Renewable Energy Sources: Thyssengas – A Green Energy Provider? In: Gąsior, A. (ed.) *Pro-ecological Restructuring of Companies: Case Studies*, Pp. 63–73. London: Ubiquity Press. DOI: https://doi.org/10.5334/bbk.f. License: CC-BY 4.0

associated with organizational, technological, structural or financial changes. Such activities can be referred to as operational restructuring that is aimed at implementing pro-environmental or CSR-related solutions.

The above concept is exemplified by the activities initiated by the object of the present analysis, namely Thyssengas GmbH. It is one of the leading economic entities in Germany. Its main field of operation is transporting natural gas to individual and industrial customers. Here, several elementary questions arise regarding whether businesses in this particular sector are able to introduce environmentally friendly solutions on a large scale. If they are able to do so, how is this performed and what are the benefits for the company, its customers, the economy in general and for the society? Such posed questions allow for the hypothesis that a natural gas supplier is able to implement cutting-edge pro-environmental technology on a large scale.

In order to verify the above hypothesis, we need to examine the company history together with the changes to its profile, technological advancement and the environmental impact on its operation. The major research method is the analysis of source documents and literature. Then, based on these findings, the company operation will be evaluated in the context of the technological changes. Finally, the conclusions of the analysis will be presented.

Company Performance and History of Activities

Thyssengas GmbH is an independent network operator and one of the leading German natural gas transport network companies. It was founded in 1921 and operates Germany's first long- distance gas pipeline (from Duisburg-Hamburg to Wuppertal-Barmen), which was built in 1910. Today, Thyssengas is an independent "carrier" for national and international natural gas trading companies. Its transport system extends from wide areas of North-Rhine Westphalia to Lower Saxony. Natural gas is transported safely and *in an environmentally friendly way* from the state borders to the centres of consumption and to the natural gas storage facilities. Thyssengas independently transports up to 10 billion cubic metres of natural gas via 4200 kilometres of underground transmission pipelines.

The company has a long-standing history, employs thousands people, and realizes its allowed revenues largely under the regulation of the German Federal Network Agency (Bundesnetzagentur). All functions of traditional gas transport are supplemented by adding new service offerings. Tasks range from transport capacity booking to constant analysis of natural gas fed in by natural gas traders, which is necessary for consumer protection.

With its current and potential new partners, Thyssengas takes an active part in shaping the future by developing and expanding the NCG market area in the long run in order to make it one of the most liquid gas markets in Europe. In 2016 Thyssengas was acquired by the consortium DIF Infrastructure IV and

EDF Invest, as equal shareholders. The agreement of the Thyssengas acquisition takes under consideration that a German gas transportation network belongs to the company.

Regarding the situation in Germany, the demand for energy and competition continue to grow. Thus, active participation in the gas transport market and permanent improvement of natural gas logistics are at company's centre of attention. This is the reason that Thyssengas has joined NetConnect Germany (NCG), the largest market area in Germany, which links the former H- and L-gas market areas of six transport network operators with connection points to more than 500 distribution networks.

Investments in Renewable Energy – Europe and Germany

The importance of renewable energy sources has been increasing in every country all over the world (Schweitzer and Persson 2014). This can be seen in particular in highly developed countries. Germany is a leader in implementing such solutions (Biogazownie na Świecie 2017). Politicians develop a vast range of economic or social policies supporting and encouraging both individuals and organizations to initiate environmentally friendly activities (Bartosik 2007). Funds spent on renewable energy sources are growing year by year, reaching record levels. According to Raport (Raport 2016), global expenditure on investments rose by 5% in 2015, attaining USD 285.9 billion worldwide. Global expenditure on those investments from 2004 to 2015 is shown in Figure 1.

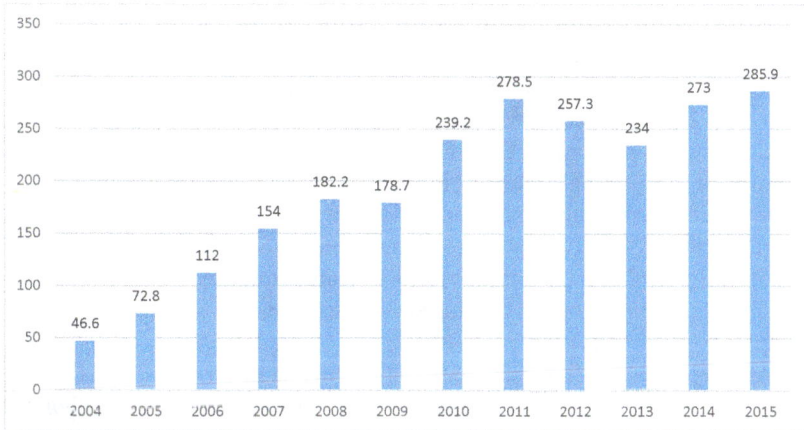

Fig. 1: Global expenditure on new investments in renewable energy in 2004–2015 in billions of US dollars.

Source: UNEP, Bloomberg New Energy Finance.

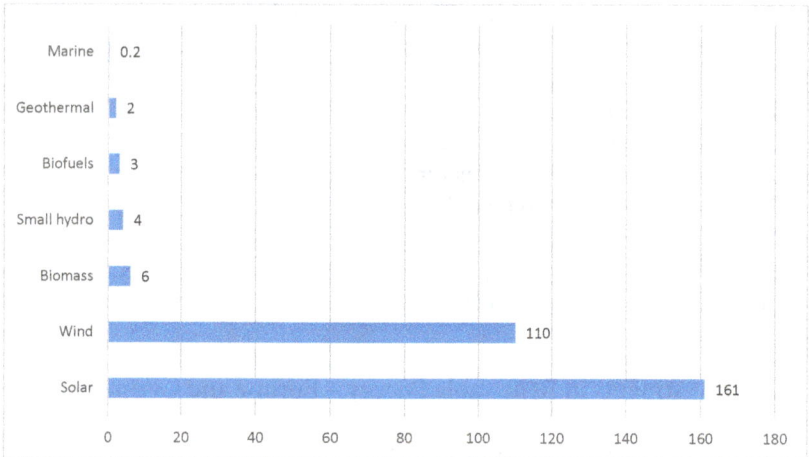

Fig. 2: Global investment in renewable energy by sectors in 2015 and in billions of USD.

Source: UNEP, Bloomberg New Energy Finance.

When looking at the chart, it should be noted that over the observed period the expenditure rose more than six times, from 46.6 to 285.9 billion US dollars. Additionally, when analyzing the data in developed and developing countries, a steadily accelerating upward trend can be seen in the latter. In the record year of 2015, the investments in green energy in the developing countries were higher than in the developed ones (156 and 130 billion US dollars respectively).

To assess the growth of green energy market, we should look at its individual sectors. The two leading ones that attracted the most investment in 2015 were solar technology (photovoltaics) and wind farms (see Figure 2).

Figure 2 shows the distribution of new investments in renewable energy. As seen from the diagram, there were two dominating sectors, namely solar and wind energy technologies. The remaining sectors did not attract significant investment. Interestingly enough, in comparison to 2015, the major increase in investments was seen in solar energy technologies, while the other sectors, excluding wind power, experienced declines. In conclusion, in 2015 the major sector that pulled this part of the world economy upwards was solar technology, primarily due to the fact that it provides solutions that generate cheap electric power (DOE 2011).

Another interesting fact concerns the countries that invest the most in renewable energy. In 2015, the biggest spenders were China (more than 102.9 billion US dollars) and the USA (USD 44.1 billion). In Europe it was the United Kingdom that spent the most (USD 22.2 billion), followed by Germany (USD 8.5 billion).

Germany is the sixth global leader in investments in renewable energy. It started the energy revolution by investing enormous amounts of money for that purpose. Over the past decade "green" politicians, supported by ecologically aware voters, decided to move on to a green energy transition, called *Energiewende* in German. They offered substantial subsidies for those who decided to invest in green energy sources, which considerably increased public involvement in solar and wind technologies (formerly regarded as a niche market), thus contributing to their lower manufacturing costs. As a consequence, they gained a competitive edge in relation to fossil fuels (Ball 2017). The major elements of that revolution were both an increased involvement in the production and use of solar and wind energy, as well as the change in approach of companies selling such conventional fuels as natural gas. A good example of this is Thyssengas, a German trader and distributor of natural gas.

Thyssengas – On the Path to Change

Rapidly changing global energy markets are facing challenges that force them to change (Valladares and Jensen 2011). The challenges result from growing consumers' awareness, new and innovative technological solutions as well as from the increasingly better quality of products and services (Schweitzer and Formanski 2017). However, the major challenges are environment-oriented requirements that companies must comply with. This also refers to energy traders, such as Thyssengas. As mentioned above, Thyssengas is a leader in the German gas distribution market. It annually transports over 10 billion cubic meters via 4200 kilometers of its own pipelines.

Despite the gas supply, the main responsibility of the company is to ensure that the gas is transported safely, both in terms of the risk of system failure and its consequences, and that its supply to the customers is uninterrupted. What is nevertheless important for the company itself and for German society is such business operation that does not pose a threat to the natural environment. The pipeline failure or possible consequences of gas leak or explosion cause not only material damage for the company and the society, but also result in substantial environmental costs. Therefore, the company has to guarantee proper functioning of its systems in every aspect. At the same time, whenever it is technically possible, the company should participate in efforts to maximize the use of renewable energy sources. Such operational restructuring means that the offer should be supplemented with a whole range of biogases that can be produced as fuels coming from renewable energy sources. The answer to the question of how these goals are being met is to be found further in this work.

Safety of natural gas transmission

Safe transmission of natural gas is one of the essential objectives of every economic entity dealing with such services (Wit 2006), such as Thyssengas.

One of the mottoes incorporated in the company mission is: Energy reaches its goal safely and pollution-free. To this end Tyssengas joined NetConnect Germany (NCG) with the intention of proactively shaping its future and optimizing the logistics of natural gas transmission in response to the consumers' expectations. Today, the company's plans include even closer cooperation with natural gas suppliers and new consumers for the benefit of further growth of the NCG market in Germany and building such a market in Europe. Such market consolidation creates the opportunity to expand the offer for customers, add new options and promote competitiveness in the area.

It is important to mention other members of NetConnect Germany: Bayernets GmbH, Eni Gas Transport Deutschland S.p.A., Open Grid Europe, GRTgaz Deutschland GmbH and GVS Netz GmbH. These business partners ensure both safe transmission of natural gas and a broad range of services encompassing trading with gas and supplying it to consumers (Wit and Andersen 2012). These services include: accounting grid management, the provision and operation of a virtual trading point, the online provision of data relating to settlement and balancing energy, and balancing energy management.

Such a solution permits the otherwise difficult combination of services: the comprehensive availability of an energy source and transport channels that are extremely reliable and pollute neither rivers nor roads. Safety and environmental protection procedures are incorporated in all Thyssengas organizational procedures. Every activity addresses security and environmental challenges. In this sense, the creation of the European natural gas grid is an investment in a cutting-edge, effective and safe system of gas transmission that has not been possible before on such scale. One of its basic elements is building new pipelines that will make it possible to include diverse energy sources, both renewable and non-renewable, in the system. This solution secures a reliable and uninterrupted gas supply.

Pipelines built by Thyssengas comply with the highest international and German legal requirements that meet the consumers' increasing expectations regarding the transmission safety and the network accessibility. For instance, new natural gas plants and pipeline systems, such as five new facilities located in North-Rhine Westphalia and connecting the German system with the Dutch grid, or a new facility in Saxony-Anhalt that offers the opportunity to better adjust to the local customers' needs are all built in accordance with the latest trends in technology in terms of security, functionality or strength of the safety equipment. All these initiatives are always inspected by independent security consultants.

How is the operational activity of the company monitored? All the pipelines are regularly inspected and analyzed for safety by a helicopter. The main purpose of these inspections is to assess if new construction projects in the proximity of a pipeline are not a threat to their safety. When problems are detected, measures are taken in order to neutralize the risk.

One serious risk to pipeline safety is uncontrolled gas leaks. In such a case, preventive steps include specialist checks for leakage and emergency shut-off systems. To this end, ultramodern methods such as *intelligent pigs* are used to react instantly to the detected leakage and to initiate maintenance and repair works. What poses an additional problem is the very nature of the material of which pipelines are made. Metal, being a basic component of pipes, is subject to corrosion. Therefore, a special electric anticorrosion system is installed (Spiegelhauer, Persson and Kildsig 2017).

In general, the safety of the network is monitored from a central control desk in Dortmund that focuses mainly on the pipeline pressure and quality. The around-the-clock service is ready to react immediately to emergency situations and to start repair works.

Furthermore, it is worth mentioning the measures regarding direct protection of the natural environment. Thyssengas incorporated the need for environmental protection in all its operational plans. New building works needed to expand transmission grids are designed along with protective measures. When a new pipeline is laid, its natural environment is restored to a state that is not worse than before the works. What is more, decisions are made to leave it in an even better condition. Once the investment has been completed, the pipeline can only be traced by special signposts.

Combining renewable and non-renewable energy sources

One of the elementary opportunities offered by modern technology is the combination of conventional and renewable energy sources. In reference to Thyssengas this means the possibility of mixing natural gas with biogas. It is known that the use of biogas helps to prevent climate change. It can be utilized in almost every aspect of business activity.

Special generators are used to feed biogas in the natural gas grid, thus creating a more environmentally friendly product. Such technology is both economically sound and effective. For instance, this product can be used to generate electricity or heat new facilities. This creates new opportunities to improve the cost-effectiveness of biogas generators.

Thyssengas has developed technology for feeding biogas into natural gas pipelines and supplying the mixture to consumers. The simplified process is shown in a Diagram 1 below.

Diagram 1 shows the technology used to transmit natural gas mixed with biogas to consumers. Apart from natural sources of biogas produced from agricultural waste, the technology obtains electricity from renewable energy sources (Kostowski and Górny 2010). The technology allows the use of biogas as fuel for gas cogeneration systems in the scattered power industry (combined production of electric power and heat) and allows for heating inside areas by means of gas-fired boilers or heating food on gas cookers. The importance

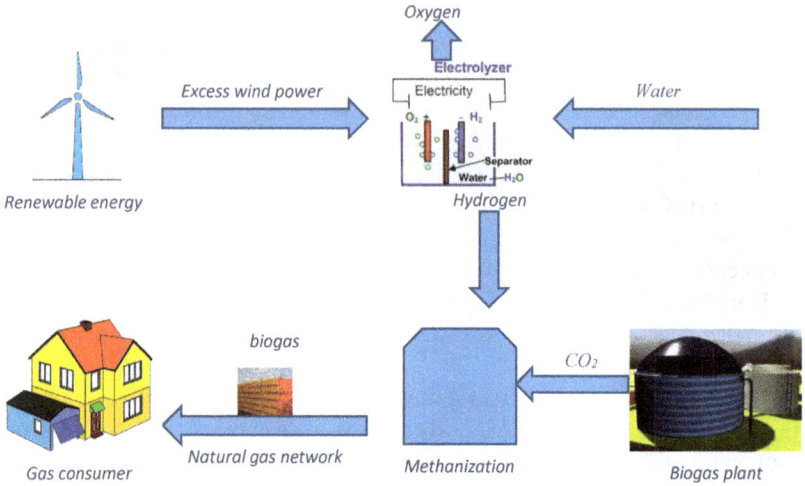

Diagram 1: Thyssengas technology to produce, mix and supply biogas to consumers.

Source: http://www.thyssengas.com/en/biogas/.

of these methods is growing because due to gradual depletion of natural gas deposits, it will become necessary to mix it with biogas. However, there are several serious problems that either have been already solved by modern technology or will be addressed in the near future.

The elementary issue is the process of biogas refining followed by its conversion in order to meet specified calorific and technological parameters according to the quality standards of mains gas. The conversion process is usually based on CO_2 water absorption (see Diagram 1), but other methods are applied as well. Another problem arises when it comes to feeding biogas into natural gas grids, as it must be scrubbed of harmful components (such as sulphur compounds, carbon monoxide, water vapor or oxygen). There is also a question of whether biogas should be upgraded, which means scrubbing it of carbon dioxide and nitrogen, thus obtaining higher or lower calorific value in comparison to mains gas. The next important issue is the location of the existing biogas plants, which should be situated near transmission and distribution grids.

According to Jonasson et al. (2003), Skorek and Kalina (2005), Dupoint and Acrosi (2006), Rasi et al. (2007), Barczyński (2009), and Kostowski and Górny (2010), it is possible to mix biogas with natural gas while keeping certain standard parameters. Basing on findings concerning the high-methane gas (E), the infusion of 5–10% of low-methane biogas allows for maintaining appropriate fuel quality. In practice, this proportion has been tested in solutions developed by Thyssengas. However, the company itself points to the following several technical complications:

- a problem with achieving adequate calorific value of biogas that would correspond to the natural gas quality. It is a condition of generating a high quality end product.
- a problem with high sensitivity of the technological system to the fluctuations in the quality of natural gas and biogas. These factors both affect the efficiency of the machinery and pollute the natural environment.
- a problem with the end quality of the product as stipulated by the calibration law. Consumers should always receive the product of the same quality, which is difficult to obtain when two gases are mixed.

Thyssengas – A Greening Company

The activity of the leading gas supplier on the German market demonstrates the opportunities provided by renewable sources of energy. The elementary questions to be answered in this part of the paper have been as follows:

- Is it possible for a business entity operating in this particular economy sector to implement ecological solutions on a large scale?
- How does it happen and what are the benefits for the company, its customers, the economy and society?

The following research hypothesis was made: *A company dealing with natural gas supply is able to implement a cutting-edge biogas technology on a large scale.*

The study results provide answers to the questions above as well as positive verification of the hypothesis. The example of Thyssengas GmbH proves that even a massive scale of operation does not constitute a barrier to implementing technological and practical solutions related to the use of renewable energy sources. Despite diverse technological or legal problems, the technology of mixing natural gas with biogas allows for greening the end product and its extensive economic use.

What benefits are gained? First of all, any business in the natural gas transmission sector is able to incorporate the latest solutions into its operation. This will be advantageous not only for the company itself (e.g. company promotion, good PR, competitive edge and research into the technology of the future), but for society in general (green solutions, reductions of environment pollution, reliable product suppliers). Additionally, the fact that the companies from this sector have created a Union-wide network allows for the assumption that the range of their impact can be wider than just one country.

In conclusion, the hypothesis that a company dealing with natural gas supply is able to implement a cutting-edge biogas technology on a large scale has been verified. This conclusion has been supported by the results of the analysis of Thyssengas GmbH operation. The impact of the solutions implemented by the company has been highly rated.

The technologies that have been used by the natural gas and biogas providers allow us to draw several conclusions. The gas market is constantly evolving, which is due to both natural and political or social factors. The use of modern technology ensures the greening of businesses and transforming a conventional product into an innovative solution that meets the society needs on an increasingly high level. Therefore, we can expect more revolutionary technological solutions employing renewable energy in our everyday lives.

References

Ball, J 2017 *Germany's High-Priced Energy Revolution*, Fortune 2017. Available at http://fortune.com/2017/03/14/germany-renewable-clean-energy-solar/ [Last accessed 15 Nov 2017].

Barczyński, A 2009 *Wprowadzanie biogazu do systemu dystrybucyjnego - szanse i możliwości*. Materiały konferencji „Rynek Gazu".

Bartosik, M 2007 Globalny kryzys energetyczny - mit czy rzeczywistość? Wybrane możliwości działań antykryzysowych w elektrotechnice. "X Międzynarodowa Konferencja „Nowoczesne urządzenia zasilające w energetyce" Zakopane.

Biogazownie na Świecie 2017 Available at http://ioze.pl/energetyka-biogazowa/biogazownie-na-swiecie [Last accessed 17 Nov 2017].

Borbely, A-M and Kreider, J F 2000 Distributed Generation The Power Paradigm for the New Millennium. Boca Raton, Florida: CRC Press.

Dupont, L and Accorsi, A 2006 *Explosion characteristics of synthesised biogas at various temperatures*. Journal of Hazardous Materials, BI 36.

Gorzelik, J 2010 *Nowe przepisy dotyczące biogazu i biogazowni w kontekście zmian w prawie energetycznym*. Available at http://www.cire.pl/item,50712,14,0,0,0,0,0,nowe-przepisy-dotyczace-biogazu-i-biogazowni-w-kontekscie-zmian-w-prawie-energetycznym.html [Last accessed 17 Nov 2017].

Innogy Gas Storage. Natural gas storage of Innogy. Available at https://innogy-gasstorage-nwe.com/en/storage-marketing/capacities-and-booking [Last accessed 11 Sep 2018].

Jonsson, O Polman, E Jensen, JK Eklund, R Schyl, H Ivarsson, S 2003 *Sustainable gas enters the European gas distribution system*. Raport Danish Gas Technology Center. Available at www.dgc.dk/publikationer/konferen-ce/jkj_sustain gas.pdf [Last accessed 17 Nov 2017].

Kostowski, W and Górny, K 2010 *Analiza możliwości mieszania biogazu z gazem ziemnym z uwzględnieniem limitów wymaganej jakości gazu sieciowego*, Instal, nr 3.

Rasi, S et al. 2007 *Trace compounds of biogas from different biogas production plants*, Energy 32.

Schweitzer, J and Formanski, T 2017 *Toward New Technologies for the Gas Market*. Available at http://www.dgc.eu/sites/default/files/filarkiv/documents/ A0811_new_gas_technologies.pdf [Last accessed 17 Nov 2017].

Schweitzer, J and Persson, P 2014 *Do we need new gas technologies for the domestic and small commercial space heating market?* Available at http:// www.dgc.eu/sites/default/files/filarkiv/documents/C1402_IGRC2014_ Schweitzer.pdf

Skorek, J and Kalina, J 2003 *Gazowe układy kogeneracyjne*. WNT, Warszawa 2005.

Spiegelhauer, B, Persson, P and Kildsig, M 2017 *A Study of Corrosion in Balanced Flues Depending on Operation Conditions*. Available at http://www. dgc.eu/sites/default/files/filarkiv/documents/C0302_corrosion_flues.pdf [Last accessed 16 Nov 2017].

Thyssengas. Thyssengas Biogas. Available at http://www.thyssengas.com/en/ biogas/ [Last accessed 17 Nov 2017].

Thyssengas. Thyssengas Info. Available at http://www.thyssengas.com/en/ infothek/#power-to-gas [Last accessed 17 Nov 2017].

Valladares, M R and Jensen, J K 2011 *A Global Perspective on Progress and Politics in R,D&D Cooperation*, 4th World Hydrogen Technologies Convention, 2011, Glasgow, U.K., Paper ID: 0099. Available at http://www.dgc.eu/sites/ default/files/filarkiv/documents/C1103_global_perspective_hydrogen.pdf [Last accessed 17 Nov 2017].

Waterleau. Waterleau selected as biogas plant commissioner for region's energy recovery transformation project. 2016. Available at http://www.waterleau. com/en/news-events/news/commissioning-of-new-biogas-plant-in-bergheim-paffendorf [Last accessed 17 Nov 2017].

Wit, J 2006 *Safety matters, experience with the operation of gas engine CHP units*, Cogeneration and On-Site Production, September–October. Available at http://www.dgc.eu/sites/default/files/filarkiv/documents/A0613_safety_ matters.pdf [Last accessed 17 Nov 2017].

Wit, J and Andersen, S D 2012 *Open gas markets, experience gained during gas import/export for gas fired CHP plants*. Available at http://www.dgc.eu/ sites/default/files/filarkiv/documents/C1201_open_gasmarkets.pdf [Last accessed 17 Nov 2017].

2.2

The Problem of Utilization of Agricultural Enterprises' Biowaste: The LLC "Leader" Case Study (Zaporizhzhya Region, Ukraine)

Olena Borzenko (Slozko)*, Oleksandr Rogach†,
Oleksandr Pidchosa‡ and Olexiy Kravchun§

*Doctor Habil.oec., Professor, Head of the Department of
International Financial Research Institute of Economics and
Forecasting National Academy of Sciences of Ukraine
†Doctor of Economics, Professor, Head of the Department of
International Finance, Institute of International Relations of
Taras Shevchenko National University of Kyiv
‡PhD (Economics), Assistant Professor, Department of
International Finance, Institute of International Relations of
Taras Shevchenko National University of Kyiv
§PhD (Public Administration)

Introduction

The problem of management and utilization of the agricultural enterprises' biowaste in Ukraine is rather urgent given the increase in agricultural production and the absence of an integrated approach to solving the current problem. Other important factors are the lack or complexity of financing of these projects, as well as the incomprehension on the part of the owners of the enterprises on the benefits of biowaste recycling.

How to cite this book chapter:
Borzenko (Slozko), O., Rogach, O., Pidchosa, O. and Kravchun, O. 2019. The Problem
of Utilization of Agricultural Enterprises' Biowaste: The LLC "Leader" Case Study
(Zaporizhzhya Region, Ukraine). In: Gąsior, A. (ed.) *Pro-ecological Restructuring
of Companies: Case Studies*, Pp. 75–95. London: Ubiquity Press. DOI: https://doi.
org/10.5334/bbk.g. License: CC-BY 4.0

Taking the above mentioned into consideration, the main objective of the proposed case study is to develop the project of constructing and commissioning a biogas collection and utilization complex, followed by production of electricity and heat on the LLC "Lider" pig farm. It also should be noted that in this case study we used the actual data of the enterprise and the developed project could be implemented in practice.

General Description of the Pig Farm

LLC "Lider" is a full-cycle livestock complex (Table 1) of 1100 breeding sows with the capacity of about 26 thousand commercial pigs annually *(LLC Lider, n.d.)*.

Pig Farm Product Characteristic

The farm produces meat and breed pigs of salable live weight of 105–110 kg.
    Landrace and Duroc breeds are presented on a pig farm, they are characterized by high feeding quality, high fleshiness and good reproductive capacity.

Location of the Project

The pig company "Lider" is located near the village of Veselyi Gai (farm geographical coordinates are 47°59'10" N 35°48'24 E), which is the administrative center of Veselogaisky Village Council, Zaporizhzhya region in the southeastern part of Ukraine (Figure 1).

Fig. 1: Location of the pig farm LLC "Lider" on the map of Ukraine.

Source: developed by the authors.

Table 1: Key Features of the Pig Farm.

Facilities in the Structure of the Pig Farm	Key Features
Pig farm: 1. Pigsty No.1. The breed shed 2. Pigsty No. 2. Completing of growing shop 3. Pigsty No. 3. Feeding shop 4. Pigsty No. 4. Feeding shop 5. Pigsty No. 5. Feeding shop 6. Pigsty No. 6. Feeding shop 7. Pigsty No. 7. Feeding shop 8. Sanitary inspection room 9. Sanitary slaughter 10. Manure pit with cage 11. Manure liquid fraction pit 12. Manure solids pit 13. Storage of solid manure 14. 440 kWt Transformer substation	• Land plot area – 6 hectares • The total number of pigs on daily maintenance – 12,000, sows – 1200 • Built-up area – 10600 m² • The number of employees – 27 people
Emergency power supply system	• Diesel Generator – Power 300 kW • Fan-load switching system
Boiler room	• Fuel Type – mainly agricultural pellets (sunflower husks) • Thermal power – 500 kW (can consume wood pellets and coal)
Water treatment system	• Artesian wells – (total debit up to 10 m³/h) • Reverse osmosis (water treatment) – capacity up to 100 m³/day
Warehouses for storage of fodder ingredients	• Land plot area – 2.5 hectares • Grain storage area – 5720 m² • The volume of grain storage – 6 thousand tons • Technological equipment for cleaning of grain
Fodder production shop	• High-tech complex for production of premixes, AMVA, and complete fodder • Production capacity – up to 5 t/h
Agricultural fleet	• Tractors – 2 • Feed carriers – 2 • Universal loaders (3 ton) – 2

Source: developed by the authors.

The Project Base Line (Current Situation)

Overview of the current situation with waste on the pig farm and waste management system

Removal of manure from the "Lider" pigsty is carried out through the use of a water wash system followed by separation of manure (moisture content of about 93.7%) into the solid fraction (about 40.7% moisture) and a liquid fraction (90–100% humidity).

The water wash system on the pig farm involves the accumulation of pig faeces (dung and urine) through the trash gaps in a separate bath, followed by the periodic supply of industrial water and gravity flush of faeces into a separate underground tank. Manure from the underground tank is sent to the "SEPCOM" separator, where it is subsequently separated into liquid and solid fractions *(SEPCOM Horizontal, n.d.)*.

The solid fraction after separation is transported to a storage tank in a tractor trailer and applied into the fields after 8–10 months of fermentation.

The liquid fraction after separation is transferred from the separator into the rubber bladder (anaerobic pond/tank), from which it is taken out to the field in barrels after 6 months of fermentation.

The distemper is frozen and transported to the recycling plant, where the pig farm obtains a certificate of the delivered distemper weight.

In case of the absence of the proposed project:

a. The manure from the farm will be kept in the anaerobic pond and storage tank. In this case, the storage of manure in such conditions, the pig farm will have problems associated with the storage and handling of waste, which will lead to different kinds of penalties in the framework of the Ukrainian legislation. In addition, the waste will result in the emission of methane into the atmosphere, thus having a negative impact on the environment.
b. The pig farm will spend funds for waste disposal, as well as energy, thermal and electric power whose production and consumption leads to emissions of greenhouse gases into the atmosphere.

Summary and Scope of the Project

This section provides a detailed description of the proposed concept and design for the production of biogas and its combustion technology for power generation, which are widely used on pig farms around the world (the process of anaerobic digestion in digesters of methane tanks) and describes the approaches and modes of project equipment.

In many of the EU countries (Germany, Austria, the Netherlands etc.), the problem of disposing of manure is solved by biogas plants *(Holm-Nielsen et al.,2007; 2009)*. The output of these plants provides farmers with environmentally friendly liquid or solid bio-fertilizers without unpleasant odors, helminth eggs, weed seeds and nitrates.

In Ukraine, the introduction of biogas technology is associated with high capital costs and does not have a systemic nature. However, this problem can be solved by production of heat and electricity from biogas at cogeneration plants, as well as sale of electricity to the electric power network of Ukraine under the special "green tariff"[1], which is 2.07 times as expensive as the cost of electricity for businesses.

Large pig farms with capacity of 5000 heads or more or dairy farms built on modern technology with the number of cows from 1000 heads are attractive in terms of implementation of such projects. These farms usually store manure in anaerobic lagoons or pits, which contributes to production of the greenhouse gas methane. The raw material for the production of biogas are encouraged to use liquid manure, death loss, as well as such other organic additives/coenzymes (additional substrates) as maize silage, sunflower production waste, sugar beet pulp etc. to increase the productivity of biogas.

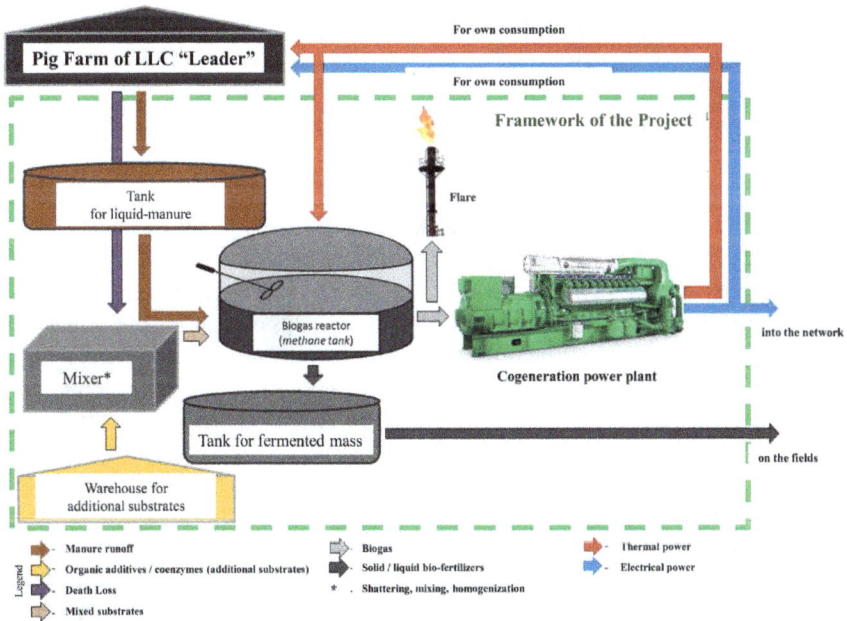

Fig. 2: The Framework of the project.

Source: developed by authors.

As part of the project, instead of manure storage in anaerobic ponds and storage tanks, we propose using the tried and proven biogas technology of anaerobic digestion in the biogas reactor (digester). The biogas digesters substrates will fermentate with the help of methanogenic bacteria at mesophilic temperature (20–40°C) or at thermophilic temperatures (50–60°C) (*Angelidaki & Ellegaard, 2003*). These temperature modes have their pros and cons, and they will be analyzed in detail in Section 5 "Optimum Modes and Configuration of the Project" in order to determine the optimal treatment for this pig farm.

Fermentation is carried out in a biogas reactor (digester) under a sealed gasholder, where methane will be accumulated as a component of biogas. The product obtained after the biogas fermentation (composed of 60% methane and 40% carbon dioxide) will be supplied to the cogeneration plant for heat and power and/or flared to reduce the emissions of greenhouse gases.

In addition to sale of electricity to the electric power network of Ukraine under the special "green tariff" (which is the main activity of the project), the pig farm will also be able to replace the consumption of heat and electricity, the energy produced from alternative sources, in particular, the energy of the resulting biogas in the cogeneration power plant.

As a complement to all the above, the pig farm will be able to use fermented substrate as fertilizer.

Based on the data of the pig farm provided by LLC "Lider", we propose introducing a biogas plant processing about 36 thousand m³ of substrate per year and providing the output:

		Unit of measurement	Amount
1	**Biogas total**	m³	**4 001 000**
2	**Liquid fertilizer total**	thousand ton	**46.25**

Under these terms the proposed biogas plant pays off for 5.7 years (9.7 years of the discounted payback period). This project solves the problem of recycling and efficient use of pig waste. The project pays for itself at the expense of what went to pay monthly bills for the power purchase, waste disposal costs and fines related to waste management in the enterprise. In addition, the profitable part of the project will be mainly provided by the sale of the produced biogas in the electricity network at "green tariff", as well as through applying fermented substrate as fertilizer. These funds will go to repay the loan raised for the project.

The proposed basic project configuration consists of the reactor (volume of 2250 m³) with an additional supply of dry substrates (including death loss waste) and cogeneration power plant (capacity of 1000 kW of electrical power and 1500 kW of thermal power). The cost of such turnkey facilities is 3,200,000 EUR.

Availability and Preparation of Raw Materials

Manure

Liquid manure (moisture content of about 93.7%) from farm buildings is supplied by a water wash system through the receptacle to the fermentor, where the liquid manure, together with additional substrates, is kept with simultaneous heating and stirring to produce biogas.

Death loss

Biogas production technology from death loss waste is already used on some pig farms around the world. The thermophilic mode should be used for slaughter waste, or the crushed waste should be pasteurized or sterilized before being fed to the fermenter.

Additional substrates

Crops of wheat, barley, corn, sorghum, sunflower and soybean are grown on an area of 4000 hectares around the pig farm.

Barley, corn, sorghum, soybeans – these crops are used for production of animal fodder for pig farm. Wheat and sunflower seed are grown for sale. These agricultural areas are not under control of the pig farm. Livestock and crop management is clearly separated in the enterprise structure. Still, this agricultural waste can be used as additional substrate for biogas production.

Corn silage. Plant biomass (stems, leaves and cobs of corn, sorghum, and miscanthus, grains of cultures at the start of the grain maturation, when the plant is still green) is traditionally used, which does not require additional pretreatment, except for silage.

As for corn, its harvest technology now common in Ukraine does not provide for the collection of plant residue. Leafy mass is crushed and scattered across the fields. In this case, the following options can be suggested: collection of shredded residue in vehicles and/or stationary cob threshing. After that, the collected waste is used for biogas production.

Despite this, there is low efficiency of raw vegetable fermentation after maturation because of the too-high carbon-to-nitrogen ratio and some micronutrient deficiencies. Most often, the plant biomass is fermented with animal manure wastes and this positively affects both the efficiency of biogas formation and qualitative characteristics of fertilizers *(Li et al. 2009; Pöschl et al. 2010).*

Sunflower production waste. As in the case of corn, given the high natural moisture content of waste, sunflower stalk silage can be recommended as the strategic direction with certain restrictions, followed by the production of biogas. It is necessary to collect the crushed sunflower residue to be able to use sunflower production wastes for biogas production.

There are no examples of use of sunflower plant residues for biogas production in Ukraine yet, but it is practiced abroad.

Optimum Modes and Configuration of the Project

Main Technological Aspects

Anaerobic fermentation technology is developed for organic substances, but its use is limited to organic wood substrates as lignocellulose cannot be processed using anaerobic processes. Anaerobic digestion technologies have the following advantages:

1) Sustainable energy production through biogas production and reduction of CO_2 emissions on a continuous basis;
2) The low level of odor emission (completely closed fermentation systems, mechanical machining in the halls) and low overall emissions into the environment; and
3) Compact units.

A wide range of technologies is offered for anaerobic digestion of waste. The main part of the biogas plant is an anaerobic digester (or reactor /methane tank) and it has various operating modes. Furthermore, all the components required for the anaerobic digester are chosen in accordance with the particular fermentation technology and operating mode. As a result, mass balances, energy balances and installation diagrams are specific to each project.

Regardless of this, the biogas plant comprises the following main components, which are discussed in detail below:

1) Reception (including measurement) and storage of raw materials
2) Pretreatment (in some cases), depending on the type of raw material
3) The anaerobic digester (or reactor / methane tank) including:
   - Equipment for feed supply
   - Stirring equipment
   - Heating equipment
4) Storage and use of biogas
5) Access to the electricity network
6) Pumping equipment and pipelines for liquids and sludge
7) Equipment for the transportation of solid waste (in some cases), such as conveyor belts and wheel loaders
8) The equipment for process control
9) Storage, processing and sometimes further processing of the fermented product

To ensure the smooth flow of the anaerobic digestion process the biogas plant, as well as a fermenter, the components described below are needed. The requirements for these components depend on the type of substrates *(De Bere, 2000)*.

Reception area and warehouse for storage of additional substrates

Additional substrate reception. Reception includes the appropriate measurement of the amount of the delivered substrates (corn silage, other silos, beets etc.), by weighing them (for hard substrates) or by flow measurement (for liquid substrates). In addition, quality control of raw materials should be applied.

Storage of substrates. Storage volumes should be sufficient to ensure a continuous digester load balancing daily and seasonal volume fluctuations if they occur for each substrate. Depending on the substrates, storage includes the following:

• tanks for storage of liquids and sludge (above or below the ground level);
• receiving hopper for solid substrates; and
• sites for storage of solid substrates (open, covered or closed).

Pre-treatment of substrates and fodder. Sometimes pre-processing is necessary in order to:

1) remove contaminants and inert materials; and
2) decompose, crush and/or mix different substrates (special installations for mixing and supplying additional substrates), including addition of water (if necessary) to ensure the substrate bioavailability and constant fermenter load. Liquid substrates can act as solvents for solid substrates.

To follow sanitary standards (for example, in treatment of animal waste), the respective substrate is pretreated by pasteurization. Pasteurization of the substrate can be achieved by heating to 70°C for at least 60 minutes. Anaerobic digestion at thermophilic temperatures can also ensure that the hygiene requirements set for substrates are met.

Areas for receiving a substrate and pretreatment have to be separated.

Anaerobic digestion in the bioreactor (digester)

Anaerobic technology is varied depending on general parameters of the process, operating conditions and types of fermenters, which have their own individual advantages and disadvantages, but none of them has been recognized as a technology leader. Substrate characteristics also affect the choice of anaerobic technology *(Vandevivere, et al., 2002)*.

Types of fermenters. Various types of fermenters (or reactors) may be classified according to the types of structures, namely:

- vertical or horizontal reactor design
- reactors made of concrete or steel
- reactors built above or below ground

Thermal insulation requirements for reactors depend on the type of fermenters and heating system designs.

The concept of the biogas plant is designed for fermenter volume of 2250 m³ (reservoir of round shape, which has an inner diameter of 22 m and an internal height of 6 m) with daily volumes of loading the substrate at the level of 98.74 m³ per day.

Various technological options of anaerobic digestion process.

Temperature

Depending on the range of operating temperatures, the anaerobic digestion process can be done in different temperature conditions, among which are:

1) psycrophilic mode – fermentation at a temperature below 20°C, but this is hardly used in practice (used in landfills).
2) mesophilic mode – fermentation at temperatures of 20–40°C (optimum temperature 35–37°C), which is characterized by a high level of process stability, however, a longer fermentation process (30–60 days) than in thermophilic mode (long retention time in the digester).
3) thermophilic mode – fermentation at temperatures of 50–60°C, which is characterized by an accelerated fermentation process (15–30 days), has substrate disinfectant properties and uses a smaller volume of the reactor, but this mode is more sensitive to various fluctuations in the biogas formation process.

Water Content

For biological anaerobic decomposition of organic material, it is always necessary to have certain water content. A minimum of 60% water content ensures proper anaerobic digestion process.

There is no definite difference between the terms "wet" and "dry" anaerobic fermentation in practice. They differ depending on the solid content of the substrate. Thus, the substrate used for biogas formation (fermentation) can be in two consistencies depending on the dry solid content (moisture), among which are:

1) Dry texture – dry solids content of more than 20% (humidity less than 80%). Such consistency is rarely used in the biogas practice.

2) Wet texture – dry solids content below 15% (over 85% humidity). Such consistency is typically used in the practice of biogas production.

Most operating biogas fermenters use the wet method, when solid substrates are fermented together within certain limits. Accordingly, the dry method is used in certain fermentation processes for solid substrates, e.g. organic waste or energy crops (organic agricultural waste).

<u>Operating Modes</u>

1) There are different modes of delivery (supply) of substrates[2]:
   a) in batches (technically used only with solid substrates in the mixing percolation system)
   b) semicontinuous
   c) non-stop
Supply systems differ depending on the consistency of the substrate:
   – Liquid slurry substrates can be pumped from the pre-processing/mixing tanks or directly loaded into the fermenter;
   – Solid substrates are loaded into the fermenter:
     • through a receiving hopper;
     • through the mixing tank as the joint substrate;
     • directly to an incoming pipeline of the fermenter;
     • by direct lateral loading to the fermenter using a membrane lid for biogas storage; or
     • by immediate top fermenter loading if it is equipped with a concrete cap.
2) There are different modes of mixing substrates:
   a) mechanical
   b) hydraulical
   c) pneumatic
   d) percolation
In order to prevent formation of a crust on the surface of the fermented substrate and to maintain its uniformity, each fermenter is equipped with mixers at certain angles.
3) There are different modes of heating substrates: external and internal (heat exchanger in the fermenter). In practice, these solutions are used as heating:
   – submerged heaters, through which the hot water runs (internal heat exchangers);
   – heaters mounted on the wall of the digester;
   – stirring hot water or steam; and
   – injection of the substrate through an external heat exchanger.

The necessary heat is obtained through the use of biogas.

The number of stages of fermentation process

The substrate has to be fed into the fermenter in regular portions several times during the day, which ensures stable production of biogas. The biogas storage (gas tank) is located above the ceiling of the digester. The gas tank is a rubber dome (membrane) for the accumulation of biogas production. The biogas proceeds from the fermentation tank through the annular opening in the ceiling of the fermenter. To protect the rubber dome, the outer protective dome is installed.

With the single step of anaerobic fermentation, all four stages will simultaneously occur in the fermenter with their mandatory balance in order to ensure the overall stability of the process.

Some contractors perform the process in two steps, when the first step is focused on hydrolysis and the second on the formation of methane, where the conditions can be provided more accurately: for example, the optimal PH value for the acid phase is from 5.2 to 6.3 and it ranges from 6.8 to 7.2 for the methane phase. Two-stage processes are aimed at increasing the conversion yield and reducing the biogas reactor volumes *(Demirer & Chen, 2005)*. However, one-step processes require less equipment.

In addition, it is possible to use the storage tank for further fermentation of the substrate and storage of biogas in a separate gas holder.

Biogas has the following content of gases:

• methane – 55–75%;
• carbon dioxide – 21–41%;
• nitrogen – 1–3%;
• hydrogen – 0.01–0.03%;
• hydrogen sulphide – 0–3%.

The calorific value of biogas is 5000–6500 kcal/m^3.

Storage tank for fermented substrate

Fermentation is 20% dry and 15% wet. With wet fermentation, substrates are pumped.

Two-reactor biogas plants (post-fermenter with the storage of the fermented substrate – two stages of fermentation) are used very rarely in the world. Biogas plants with one reactor (digester) where the fermentation process is carried out are mainly used. Despite this, the fermented substrate is usually sent into a special tank for its storage; it can also work for further eventual fermentation. In this case, a tank is equipped with a stirrer, and biogas is drawn here similarly to a biogas reactor (digester).

The fermented substrate is separated into solid and liquid fractions or used as a liquid fertilizer without fractionation through direct additional substrate transportation from the tank to the fields.

Fertilisers

The organic wastes contain the necessary elements for plant growth; their correct processing transforms toxic waste into expensive fertilizer. The company can use these fertilizers both for their needs (at their farmland) and sale.

The fermented mass is brought to fields using liquid-manure tankers. The liquid mass is poured over the surface of the soil proportionally and then the soil is re-plowed.

Cogeneration power plant

The produced biogas (after desulfurization in the desulfurization system and drying) enters the cogeneration plant. Cogeneration plants convert the biogas energy in electrical and thermal power using generators that are powered by internal combustion engines. The cogeneration plant consists of a gas engine and electric generator. The generated heat is used to heat the biogas plant and for other purposes, and the generated electricity is sold to the national Ukrainian electricity network on a "green tariff" and is also used for their own needs.

The mechanism of stimulation by a "green tariff" is the world incentive of the energy use of biogas by means of electricity production in mini-BPP (cogeneration plants).

The Potential of Production of Biogas, Electricity and Heat

Biogas production

Based on the LLC "Lider" pig farm data, we propose building a biogas plant that processes about 36 thousand m³ of substrates per year and provides the following output:

	Unit of measurement	Amount
Biogas total	m³	4,001,000

Manure runoff. The pig farm of 1100 sows and 26,000 fattening pigs produces 26,000 tons (71.3 tons/day) of manure annually.

In accordance with the physical and chemical analysis of the farm, the dry matter content of manure is 6.3% (with a moisture content of 93.7%). The dry content of the organic matter in dry matter of manure at the entrance to the biogas installation is 74.4% (respectively, the ash content is 25.6% of the total dry matter of manure).

Accordingly, the pig farm produces 1638 tons per year (4.5 tons/day) of manure, based on dry matter and 1218 tons (3.3 tons/day), based on the organic dry matter, respectively.

Only 49% of dry matter decomposes, forming biogas and biogas output level of 0.748 m³ of biogas per 1 kg of the decomposing dry matter. On this basis, the level of output of biogas from manure runoff is estimated at 600,350 m³ per year.

Mortality loss. The average annual mortality is estimated at the level of 42 tons (115 kg/day).

In accordance with the average content of bone at 11% for one pig carcass, waste from the sanitary slaughter is estimated at 37.4 tons per year (102 kg/day).

The yield of biogas is estimated at 0.3 m³ of biogas per 1 kg of slaughter waste (mortality without bones). On this basis, the level of output of biogas from pig mortality is estimated at 11,217 m³ per year.

The dry matter content in the slaughterhouse waste is 12% (at 88% humidity). The dry content of organic matter in dry matter of slaughterhouse waste at biogas plant inlet is 80% (respectively, the ash content is 20% of the total dry matter of slaughterhouse waste). Based on this, as well as a minor amount of mortality waste compared with the volume of manure, mortality loss can be mixed/homogenized with manure wastewater without additional water while maintaining the required level of dry matter content of maximum 5–15% in the total substrate weight for the process of fermentation and biogas production.

Additional substrates: The case of corn silage. The amount of necessary additional substrate is calculated based on the need to achieve the installed cogeneration plant capacity to 1000 kW with a view to further attraction of international funding for the project.

The pig farm will be able to additionally produce about 3,389,400 m³ of biogas a year by the addition of 18,830 tons (6017 m³) of corn silage, which can be harvested at 401 hectares planted with corn (Table 2).

Besides, it is necessary to additionally add about 1384 m³ of water a year to the total weight of the substrate in order to maintain the dry matter content at 10% level.

Table 2: Additional production.

№	Parameter	Value	Unit of measurement
1.	Corn silage yield of biogas	180	m³/ ton of silo
2.	Biogas yield from 1 ha of silo corn	7800–9100	m³/ha
3.	Silo volume	10–20	m³ of silo/ ha
4.	Dry matter content	33	%
5.	Dry organic matter content in the dry matter	95	%

Source: developed by the authors.

Power Generation

The combustion of 1 m³ of biogas can produce about 2 kW of electricity.

In this regard, the pig farm will be able to consume the produced biogas to produce 8,002,000 kW of electricity per year, and subject to the standard number of hours of operation of the cogeneration plant – 8000 hours/year – the required installed capacity of the cogeneration unit will just be at 1000 kW.

Our calculations show that the biogas plant installed on the pig farm will require the installation of an electricity generator in the range of 150–200 kW of installed capacity for the efficient utilization of existing waste (manure and death loss).

If about 20% of the processed product waste composition, providing a higher biogas yield (silage corn at this stage), the required installed electric power generator should be 1000 kW in this case. This capacity will provide a biogas plant and the pig farm with heat and electricity, as well as give an opportunity to sell electricity to the network at the "green tariff".

Heat Production

The combustion of 1 m³ of biogas can produce about 3 kWh of thermal power. In this regard, the pig farm will be able to consume the produced biogas for additional production of 12,003,000 kWh (10,322 Gcal) of thermal power per year, and subject to the standard number of hours of operation of the cogeneration plant – 8000 hours/year – the established thermal power capacity of the cogeneration unit will be at the level of 1500 kW.

Heated production halls and office buildings, nearby manufacturing plants, drying plants, housing and social infrastructure buildings, and small towns can become potential consumers of heat, and the generated heat may even be used for refrigeration.

The Socio-economic Impact, Environmental Protection and Ecology

The socio-economic impact of introduction of biogas plants includes:

• reduced dependence of national economy on imported power and increased energy security of the country;
• solving problems of sustainable energy supply for the agricultural sector of the economy with its own renewable energy source with high environmental and technical parameters of its consumer qualities;
• high levels of occupational safety and health;

- use of organic waste at agricultural enterprises;
- energy savings due to replacement of the electricity taken from the network by energy produced from alternative sources;
- improving the global environment (combating global climate change by reducing emissions of methane and carbon dioxide in the atmosphere);
- obtaining high-quality organic fertilizers, without helminth eggs, weed seeds and nitrates; and
- creating jobs in installation and construction of biogas plants as well as during their operation (3–4 workers for each unit).

The Cost of the Project

Capital expenditures

According to various estimates, the cost of capital expenditures may vary in the range of 250–900 euros per 1 m³ of the installed reactor or 2000–6000 euros per 1 kW of installed capacity.

Capital expenditures cover the following units:

1) land;
2) construction work, including infrastructure;
3) mechanical components;
4) electrical components and process control;
5) accession to the electric power grid systems and the possible distribution of heat; and
6) design.

In addition, an important factor is the added capital expenditure following unforeseen capital expenditures related to the development and implementation of the project:

1) The pre-feasibility study stage. About 15–20% of capital expenditures.
2) The feasibility study stage. About 10–15% of capital expenditures.
3) The design stage. About 5–10% of the capital cost.

Accordingly, the average capital costs are at a level of EUR 3,200,000.

Operating Costs

Annual cost of operation and maintenance includes the following components with indicative ranges:

1) Maintenance and repair;
2) Insurance and administration;
3) Purchase and delivery of additional substrates;
4) Feed water for additional substrates;
5) Start-up fuel to run the cogeneration plant;
6) Personnel; and
7) Selling fertilizers.

Accordingly, the average operating costs are at EUR 606,000 per year.

The Revenue Part of the Project

The revenue part will be provided by:

1) sales of electricity of its own production;
2) saving power consumption from the network;
3) saving energy for heating a pig farm and ensuring its hot water supply; and
4) sales of liquid fertilizers.

The produced electricity can be sold in a network at a "green tariff" at a price 2.07 times higher than the market rate of electricity for businesses. With the deduction of energy required for the operation of the pig farm as a whole, as well as the biogas plant, the electricity sale on a "green tariff" will give 932,000 euros annually.

Substitution of network power consumption by electricity of its own production will lead to saving 71,000 euros annually.

Saving fuel (coal, pellets) for heating the pig farm and ensuring its hot water supply will lead to saving 63,660 euros annually.

Income from the sale of liquid fertilizer (based on the price of 6–7 euros per ton of liquid fertilizer) is estimated at 323,750 euros annually.

Accordingly, the income part is estimated at EUR 1,390,406 annually.

On top of that, the pig farm will receive additional benefits by reducing costs and penalties associated with waste disposal.

Under these terms, the proposed biogas plant pays off for 5.7 years (9.7 years of discounted payback period). This project solves the problem of recycling and efficient use of pig waste. The project pays for itself at the expense of what went to pay monthly bills for power purchase, waste disposal costs and fines related to waste management in the enterprise. In addition, the profitable part of the project will be mainly provided by the "green tariff" sale of electricity produced by the biogas plant, as well as through the implementation of fermented substrate as fertilizer. These funds will go to repay the loan raised for the project.

Table 3: Results of Financial Analysis.

Parameter	Unit of measurement	Value
Lifetime of the project	years	25
Costs		
Capital expenditures (CAPEX)	euro	3,200,000
Operating costs (OPEX)	euro/year	606,000
Depreciation costs (20 years)	euro/year	160,000
Revenue		
The profitable part	euro/year	1,390,406
Additional Parameters		
Credit (financing 60% of the project, 15 years, the rate of 5% per annum)	euro	1,920,000
Tax on profits	%	19
Payback Indicators		
Net profit	euro/year	557,581
Simple payback	years	5.7
Discounted payback period (10% discount rate)	years	9.7
Net present value (NPV)	euro	11,651,160
Internal rate of return (IRR)	%	17.30
Net Present Value (NPV), with discount	euro	1,995,111
Internal rate of return (IRR), discount taken into account	%	6.63

Source: calculated by the authors on the basis of the data provided by LLC "Lider".

Under aforementioned terms, the proposed biogas plant pays off for 5.7 years (9.7 years of discounted payback period). This project solves the problem of recycling and efficient use of pig waste.

The project pays for itself at the expense of what went to pay monthly bills for power purchase, waste disposal costs and fines related to waste management in the enterprise. In addition, the profitable part of the project will be mainly provided by the "green tariff" sale of electricity produced by the biogas plant, as well as through the implementation of fermented substrate as fertilizer. These funds will go to repay the loan raised for the project.

Table 4: Project Implementation Schedule.

	Stage/month	1	2	3	4	5	6	7	8	9	10	11	12	13	14	15	16	17
1	Development and preliminary feasibility study	▓	▓															
2	Feasibility study			▓														
3	Development of the project implementation plan				▓													
4	Development of design documentation					▓	▓											
5	Tracking and obtaining permits						▓	▓										
6	Earthwork							▓	▓									
7	Building of structures								▓									
8	Insulation and cladding									▓								
9	Laying pipelines								▓									
10	Construction of machinery hangar										▓							
11	Pumping and mixing equipment											▓						
12	Heat distribution network												▓					
13	Installation of a cogeneration unit													▓				
14	Biomass supply system													▓				
15	Monitor/control system														▓			
16	Connecting to a network															▓		
17	Additional unforeseen work																	
18	Commissioning																▓	
19	Training																	▓

Source: developed by the authors.

Notes

[1] "The Green Tariff" policy is a feed-in tariff (FIT) scheme for electricity generated from renewable energy sources, introduced in Ukraine in 2009. The scheme will be open until 1 January 2030. "The Law on Electrical Energy Industry" of 16 October 1997 created a legal framework for the "Green Tariff" scheme.

The National Commission for State Energy Regulation (NERC) is responsible for management of the scheme, modification of the tariffs, granting and distributing financial support to the eligible parties. Support from the "Green Tariff" scheme can only be obtained upon the completion of a power plant. **Technologies eligible for the support:** solar PV; wind; hydroenergy (with capacity no larger than 10MW); biomass energy (International Energy Agency 2016).

[2] The sharp and substantial increase in bioreactors loading is not good, since it can slow down the biological process and, in some cases, stop biogas emission. The same can happen with a substantial change in the quality characteristics of the raw materials.

References

Angelidaki, I, & Ellegaard, L 2003 Codigestion of manure and organic wastes in centralized biogas plants. Applied biochemistry and biotechnology, 109(1-3), 95-105.

De Bere, L 2000 Anaerobic digestion of solid waste: state-of-the-art. Water science and technology, 41(3), 283-290.

Demirer, G N, & Chen, S 2005 Two-phase anaerobic digestion of unscreened dairy manure. Process biochemistry, 40(11), 3542-3549.

Holm-Nielsen, J B, & Oleskowicz-Popiel, P 2007 The future of biogas in Europe: Visions and Targets 2020. University of Southern Denmark, Esbjerg, 14-16.

Holm-Nielsen, J B, Al Seadi, T, & Oleskowicz-Popiel, P 2009 The future of anaerobic digestion and biogas utilization. Bioresource technology, 100(22), 5478-5484.

International Energy Agency 2016 Green Tariff (Feed-in Tariff). Retrieved from International Energy Agency, Policies and Measures, Ukraine, Available at http://www.iea.org/policiesandmeasures/pams/ukraine/name-38470-en.php

Li, X, Li, L, Zheng, M, Fu, G, & Lar, J S 2009 Anaerobic co-digestion of cattle manure with corn stover pretreated by sodium hydroxide for efficient biogas production. Energy & Fuels, 23(9), 4635-4639.

LLC "Lider" (n.d.). Retrieved from LLC "Lider Ltd" official website, Available at http://lider-agro.com/en/

Pöschl, M, Ward, S, & Owende, P 2010 Evaluation of energy efficiency of various biogas production and utilization pathways. Applied Energy, 87(11), 3305-3321.

SEPCOM Horizontal (n.d.). Retrieved from WAMGROUP official website http://wamgroup.com/en-GB/corporate/Product/SEPCOM%20Horizontal/Solids-Liquid-Screw-Separator-Press

Vandevivere, P, De Baere, L, & Verstraete, W 2002 Types of anaerobic digesters for solid wastes. Amsterdam: IWA.

2.3

The HS Company – Restructuring the Processes and Improving Organizational Excellence: Role of Top Management in Strategic Reorientation

Barbara Czerniachowicz

Dr, Department of Enterprises Economics, Institute of Management and
Investment, Faculty of Economics and Management, University of Szczecin

Introduction

The aim of this paper is to present the selected aspects of proecological strategic reorientation in the HS Company. The company is a producer of parts
for machines used in several industrial sectors of the Polish economy. The HS
company is the manufacturer with a more than 100-year-old tradition of offering high-quality products, construction and design, market suppliers, extensive
knowledge of gear production, and technological support.

In order to achieve the aim of the article, the following objectives are formulated: (1) presenting the history and characteristics of the HS company; (2)
introducing the concepts of strategic reorientation in the HS company; and
(3) identifying how the company implemented the approved strategy by using
contemporary tools of strategic management.

Nowadays, the HS company is a reliable manufacturer aiming at continuous development and creating opportunities for personal development of its
employees. The company attaches great importance to its customers' satisfaction and the newly adopted profile of the HS brand. It also strives to gain the

How to cite this book chapter:
Czerniachowicz, B. 2019. The HS Company – Restructuring the Processes and Improv-
    ing Organizational Excellence: Role of Top Management in Strategic Reorientation.
    In: Gąsior, A. (ed.) *Pro-ecological Restructuring of Companies: Case Studies*,
    Pp. 97–107. London: Ubiquity Press. DOI: https://doi.org/10.5334/bbk.h. License:
    CC-BY 4.0

appreciation of the local society and all its customers. All the groundbreaking changes were possible due to the strategic reorientation that was started in 2012.

Methodology

A strategy is a concept of systemic action based on the formulation of a set of long-term goals and their modifications depending on changes in the surrounding business environment. It requires the determination of the resources, the means necessary to achieve these objectives and the procedures for optimal distribution and their use. The aim of such activities is to react flexibly to market challenges and to ensure that the company operates in conditions conducive to its development (Penc 1994; Filipiak-Dylewska & Szewczuk 2000). The concentration strategy aims to choose a specific market segment – generally a geographically close market – and a consumer or a product type. This strategy is based on the assumption that a company can thus better and more efficiently service its narrow strategic segment of the market than its competitors. Due to such measures, a company is either able to achieve diversification by the effective fulfillment of its segment's needs or to lower the costs of service, or both (Moszkowicz 2005). This strategy is particularly favored by companies with limited production resources, insufficient possibilities for flexible operation or the ones unable to adapt rapidly and effectively to a changing market situation (Stróżycki 1999).

The instruments used to implement the overall strategy of a company can be either functional strategies that focus on how the organization approaches its basic functional activities (Pierścionek 1997) that are prepared for such areas as marketing, finance, manufacturing, research and development, human resources or logistic processes or production strategies relevant to those elements of a company's strategy that influence its manufacturing activity (Griffin 1997; Griffin 2015; Stabryla 2000; Krupski 1999; Urbanowska-Sojkin 1998; Urbanowska-Sojkin 2011). This strategy focuses on the quality, performance and technology and it is an integral part of the marketing strategy and a company's human resources. Due to the fact that it is dependent on the aforementioned factors, it is often very difficult to be distinguished from others and thus it is contractual in nature. The decisions included in the production strategy generally relate to issues included in the overall strategy, focusing, however, on their operational details (Filipiak-Dylewska & Szewczuk 2000; Kaleta 2010). Changes in the production strategy influence the reorientation of other functional strategies of a company (Krajewski 2009; Kaczmarek et al. 2005).

The presented case study carried out on the HS company in 2012 discusses the strategic reorientation associated with the necessity of introducing changes allowing the company to adapt to the changes in the environment. The restructuring mainly focused on the areas of production, employment, logistics and marketing (Czerkas & Teisseyre 2016; de Sousa 2014). The changes in functional strategies implemented from the years 2012 to 2015 aimed at improving organizational excellence (Recardo & Heather 2013; Crooks 2012).

The analyses were carried out on the basis of the original source material collected from the entities belonging to the HS company. The study used detailed, in-depth personal interviews, expert interviews, observations and the author's own survey. The scope and the depth of the study faced serious difficulties due to the inaccessibility of reliable data and problems with interviewing a sufficient number of employees. Independent observations, direct measurements and in-depth group and personal interviews were conducted in the period between 2012 and 2015.

History and Characteristics of the HS Company

The HS Sp. z o.o. (limited liability company) was founded in 1905 by a master of casting and operated as a family business. After the Second World War it was nationalized. Since its inception, the company prospered on the market very well. However, beginning in the early 1980s, it produced worse financial results, and the collapse of the Russian market resulted in the most difficult period for the company. In 1993, the company acquired a strategic investor to recapitalize the company, thus giving it a chance to gain new markets for manufactured gears and to expand the production of new products. On 4 December 1997, the Sipma S.A. (Holding) became the owner of 70% of the shares in a tender. Internal restructuring was carried out, redundant assets sold and agreements with creditors signed, which allowed the company to repay its debts. On 28 December 2010, Sipma Company sold all its shares to Grupa Kapitałowa Complex (Complex Holding), which has since become the main shareholder of the company.

The company had 42 shareholders. The share capital of the HS company amounted to 2,118,750 zlotys, which covered a total of 41,965 shares with a nominal value of 50 zlotys per share.

The organization constantly expands the product offer for its customers, along with technical advice. The company specializes in hydrodynamic transmissions, brake pumps for construction, road and mining and angular and cylindrical gears, as well as in hydraulic cylinders for agricultural machinery.

A constantly modernized machine park with proecological sozotechnical devices and experienced staff allow the company to take on new challenges related to production and services and to cooperate with partners in accordance with the wishes of domestic and foreign customers. Experience in the industry, a unique high-quality offer and availability of individual components, subassemblies and complex hydraulics and transmission, allow the company to be a key partner for demanding customers, all the while preparing a sales program to meet the needs of its customers in all industries.

The company's mission is to create and deliver comprehensive, innovative and systemic solutions for power transmission and energy. Their promoted values are associated with honesty (related to integrity), customer satisfaction, reactivity and continuous improvement.

Top managers realize proecological goals through the implementation of the following principles:

- ensuring continuing suitability, adequacy and effectiveness of the Quality Management System
- constant monitoring of customer satisfaction and taking actions to increase satisfaction
- constant tracking and application of the current legal requirements, standards, trends and technological progress
- systematic workers' qualifications deepening their awareness of their role and responsibility in meeting customers' requirements, legal requirements and standards
- maintaining a constant satisfaction of all the stakeholders of the organization
- conducting business in a manner friendly to the environment and health and safety at work

Management in the HS Company and Strategic Reorientation

In 2012, the HS Company experienced a crisis caused by a significant reduction in orders from the largest client – Sipma Holding. Discussions with the top management of SIPMA revealed that the crisis was expected to last for two quarters of 2012. Sipma had a number of orders from the Eastern European market that ceased to come and the company was forced to seek new customers. Similar events had occurred in the past; thus the company limited its production in order to last for the period. But for the HS Company, the situation was serious and required a huge effort on the part of the management and employees of the company in order to survive and look for new customers.

Sales potential was insufficient for a given mode of operation. Employees had extensive knowledge and experience in their field, but their effectiveness to attract new orders was limited. Therefore, the managers hired young workers to take advantage of the synergy of youth and experience in order to stimulate proper dynamics of the sales department (Karaszewski & Lis 2013).

Revenues from new orders were clearly too small, and there was no chance for an increase without financial support in order to change the manner and methods of sales department activity. The top management planned to use the crisis to "clean up" the company's problems and achieve higher revenue.

A big challenge for managers was to transform the organization into a profitable company. It was also a very costly operation due to redundancy payments, among other things. Organizational measures taken in May 2012 and consistent implementation of new solutions brought positive financial results in October 2012. In subsequent years, Sipma Holding, as the biggest client, increased orders for products from the HS company, which positively influenced the improvement of financial results of the company.

The main goal of the recovery program was to re-establish a profitable financial position of the company through cost cutting. In the opinion of the managerial staff, the difficult situation was temporary; thus they planned employment restructuring, cost reduction, change in working methods of the sales and production departments, and other organizational units.

The process of transformation was very expensive, and the workers were resistant as it forced them to work harder in order to improve the situation of the company. From May 2012 the lay-offs began, and this had a negative impact on the atmosphere and organizational culture.

HS Company focused on reducing operating costs, while maintaining a strong market position of angular gears and hydraulic systems. The company had fewer clients than before because it was now in a specialized market.

In 2012 the managers adopted a new strategy, which had to be verified due to the crisis. Its redefined assumptions were as follows:

1. adjustment of employment to the optimum level of capacity of production and the structure of realized sales
2. reducing costs, shortening lead times, optimum utilization of the machine park
3. verifying all agreements concluded by HS at lower prices used and determining reasonableness of their further continuation and reducing the operating costs of the company
4. increasing productivity and efficiency
5. increasing the level of services and manufactured goods
6. activation of new markets
7. modification of the machinery for proecological and efficient execution of orders

HS clarified its strategic advantage that was based on a more than 100-year-old tradition of offering products for several industrial sectors, high-quality products, extensive knowledge of gear production, market suppliers, customers and technological support, construction and design.

The managers also formulated product strategies focusing on market and product development strategy and market penetration strategy. They clarified the strategic product groups. Strategy for market and product development was related to the desire to become the leader among producers. The measures taken to achieve this aim included an increase in sales of existing products and offering new or improved products for existing and newly acquired markets. The main objectives of this strategy were:

- quality improvement;
- shortening lead times within the Customer Relationship Management (CRM); and
- reducing purchasing cost of materials by 10%.

The market penetration strategy was associated with an increase in the market share due to intensified sales activities, promotion and acquisition of new distribution channels.

Strategic objectives for the year 2012 were:

- generating net profit of 500,000 zlotys.
- increasing sales by 21%.

The main objectives for the sales and marketing department that year were:

- achieving total sales of 14 million zlotys (in Poland – 12 million zlotys, a 16% increase; abroad – 2 million zlotys, a 100% increase).
- acquiring at least two new customers (expected total turnover next year of at least 4 million zlotys).

For the long-term, the following goals were pursued:

1. creating tools enabling comprehensive customer service, primarily through expanding the product range, mainly thanks to the cooperation with Chinese companies;
2. acquiring new customer segments; and
3. introducing new products of unique technical solutions.

As part of the marketing strategy the managers assumed, among others, modernization of the graphic image of the brand, supporting direct sales with a series of gadgets with the company logo, using the Internet to reach a wider group of customers, positioning pages and web banners on industry-specific portals, and raising standards of packaging to the level of market leaders.

Changes in the sales promotion were mainly focused on creating a modern Internet platform (i.e. and online store offering delivery of products in 48 hours) and the introduction of loyalty programs for regular customers. The changes entailed the introduction and promotion of new products – preceded by market research and a demand forecast – preparation of promotional materials and a database of potential clients, and the launch of information and promotional campaign before the introduction of products into the market.

In determining the strategy for customer service, the managers of the company considered increasing the sales force productivity to be the most important issue. Thus, the country was divided into three sales regions, whilst the foreign or external market was divided into two regions (close to the customer). The company hired new regional sales managers and provided them with the tools necessary for fieldwork (i.e. a company car with a GPS, mobile phone, marketing tools). It also developed and implemented a training system for the sales department and introduced high labor standards based on a control-incentive system of Customer Relationship Management (CRM).

Orders were processed and fulfilled according to higher standards than those of domestic and foreign competition. The total delivery time was reduced to the best level in the industry, all the while maintaining quality standards. The company reduced the time associated with offering and preparing orders for production – the development of CRM (e.g. an efficient information-flow system between clients and the HS company, checking inventory online, offering standard products within several minutes, the process of completion of orders for standard products, issuing a manufacturing order within one hour).

Professional presales service for the HS clients related to technical advice on the selection of products, home demonstrations and customer training on the preparation and the proper use of products offered by the company. The professional service provided by the sales department was associated with after-sales service based on managing complaints and organizing technical training of managers and sales representatives. The strategy of customer service also included the development of distribution channels, both indirect distribution (boosting the sales and improving the quality of service by the managers and sellers and developing the sales network on foreign markets), as well as direct distribution to manufacturers with a focus on increasing sales of new products, through professional advisory services and an individual approach to customers and the launch of an online store. The company also introduced a system of foreign customer service.

The production strategy focused on joining the three production departments into one called Jotes Business Park. The main aim was to ensure that the production took place at a lowest cost, while maintaining the quality of products and punctuality in fulfiling orders to increase competitiveness on the market and achieve a high sales margin. The activities planned and implemented by the management in this area included:

- reorganizing production in order to reduce the cost of manufactured products and increase proecology;
- reducing production costs by 15% for each of the three production departments;
- increasing productivity by 20%;
- shortening production time by 20%;
- increasing production capacity while reducing the machinery park by 40%;
- eliminating mismanagement and preparing weekly reports and calculations;
- achieving competitive advantage; and
- creating a modern and international image of the company.

The tasks of the production strategy were carried out through the creation and implementation of a plan for relocating machinery, equipment and technology among the three departments and implementation of ecological solutions on production. The level of quality meeting the needs of target markets was maintained, and the production of orders was quicker and timely. The management also introduced production services and implemented procedures for Quality Management System ISO 9001 for the joint production plants. The company increased production capacity through the introduction of new production technologies and aimed to cooperate with the Technical University (University of Łódź) to pursue research and development activities and increase production.

In the logistics department, the managers strove to ensure timely deliveries and reduce purchasing costs, working time of warehouses, labor costs, stock levels and the cost of storage, the amount of complaints due to poor quality of purchased materials and poor work organization of the purchasing department.

The managers primarily introduced indicators to check and verify timeliness of completed deliveries, late deliveries or advertised deliveries, and to assess the efficiency of delivery, the loss of production due to lack of supply, productivity and operating efficiency. Within these tasks, the company also created a bonus system based on the indicators, introduced new solutions for supplying materials and raw materials to the company. It partnered with new shipping companies and providers of supplies necessary for the production of materials and semi-finished products, thereby reducing purchasing costs. The company changed the way it purchased materials, i.e.:

- the purchasing department bought smaller batches of materials.
- deliveries were divided proportionally to the demand sufficient to maintain production.
- the company renegotiated the minimum levels of purchase or signing contracts favorable to the company.
- the company used suppliers' warehouses to store materials.

The expected results came very quickly and were mainly noticeable in the more efficient management of human resources due to the ability to monitor the work of people allowing the company to make instant adjustments necessary to maintain production. Another result was the reduction of costs associated with delegating workers to the current material supply, reducing costs of storage and costs of leasing other transport companies on Polish territory (Gąsior 2015).

Reducing the working time of warehouses resulted in limiting overtime and other related costs and shortening working time of warehouse workers when giving out components for installation on the production line. Other benefits included shortening the time spent searching for parts and providing better quality of service both for internal and external customers by reducing the number of mistakes.

Reducing labor costs was mainly based on the implementation of the Kanban system in terms of shopping queues, inventory and the occupied space. The company also established close cooperation with the production department in order to develop a production plan for meeting deadlines. Another important element of the strategy was the continuous improvement of the 5S system together with the Lean Manager. The results of these activities were on-time availability of the necessary tools ensuring the continuity of production; simultaneous reduction of the need for machinery refitting caused by the lack of materials, thus shortening the time of making job lot; the possibility of better control over employee working time; and increasing the income of the company by selling redundant items, stock and scrapping obsolete tools, which resulted in reducing the occupied space by 36%.

The task posed by the management aiming to reduce inventory and storage costs was based on selling products in stock for more than six months and excluding costs of cutting process of materials from inventory costs. The close cooperation between the purchasing and sales departments and a good flow of information on suppliers in order to sell surplus stock were important here. The expected results came very quickly and in subsequent years resulted in the reduction of inventory, warehouse space and in a better control of inventory and warehouse costs.

The managers took up the challenge to reduce the amount of complaints due to poor quality of purchased materials. For this purpose, they made a ranking list of suppliers, dividing them into categories of materials, on the basis of a list of materials requiring qualification and a register of current and potential suppliers. The company also prepared a register of current and potential suppliers and the purchasing department defined a quality indicator of suppliers. These measures reduced the number of complaints arising from poor quality of parts fitted to the products. At the same time, the company improved the quality of products and acquired new clients, which had a positive impact on its image.

Conclusion

The difficult market situation in 2012 forced the managers of the HS company to implement proecological strategic reorientation. The managers introduced a number of changes and modifications in the organization and its functioning. The employment restructuring required funds for redundancy payments for employees laid off for economic reasons.

The managerial staff also changed the organization of production in order to reduce the costs of manufactured products. The company created a new organizational structure for the joint production department and introduced new management methods. The company also defined competence matrix for its employees and developed a training program for production workers.

Additionally, the managers applied the just-in-time and Lean Manufacturing concepts, the analyses and statistical methods for production and set targets for specific processes. As for the logistics department, they reduced the costs of logistic processes by 20% in 2012 compared to 2011. In subsequent years, the company still strove to reduce these costs. The managers eliminated all inefficient operations and activities and introduced restructuring that allowed them to improve the functioning of the entire organization. Constant improvement and organizational changes have since become the main strategic objective of the HS company.

References

Crooks, S 2012 Managing a successful organisation restructure. Available at https://www.plushr.com/plushr-performance-management-roundtable-dec-2012/ [Last accessed 10 October 2016].

Czerkas, K and Teisseyre, B 2016 Restrukturyzacja zadłużenia przedsiębiorstw. Od ugód bilateralnych do postępowań restrukturyzacyjnych i upadłościowych, Ośrodek Doradztwa i Doskonalenia Kadr Sp. z o.o., Gdańsk.

de Sousa, J 2014 Organizational restructuring and change management using a neuroscientific approach. Available at https://www.linkedin.com/pulse/20140810231843-2117408-organizational-restructuring-and-change-management-using-a-neuroscientific-approach [Last accessed 15 November 2016].

Filipiak-Dylewska, B and Szewczuk, A 2000 Zarządzanie strategiczne, Fundacja na rzecz Uniwersytetu Szczecińskiego, Szczecin.

Gąsior, A 2015 Salaries as a Determinant of Restructuring Large Companies in Poland. *Transformations in Business & Economics,* 14(3C)(36C): p. 389–406.

Griffin, R W 2015 Podstawy zarządzania organizacjami, PWN, Warszawa.

Griffin, R W 1997 Podstawy zarządzania organizacjami, PWN, Warszawa. p. 256.

Kaczmarek, J, Krzemiński, P, Litwa, P, and Szymla, W 2005 Procesy zmian w okresie transformacji systemowej. Prywatyzacja, restrukturyzacja, rynek kapitałowy, Wydawnictwo Akademii Ekonomicznej w Krakowie, Kraków.

Kaleta, A 2010 Dylematy wyboru strategicznego współczesnych przedsiębiorstw, in: Zarządzanie współczesnymi przedsiębiorstwami. Uwarunkowania strategiczne, innowacyjne i kulturowe, ed. T. Falencikowski, WSB, Gdańsk. pp. 37–49.

Karaszewski, R and Lis, A 2013 The Role of Leadership to Stimulate Pro-developmental Positive Organisational Potential, In: Stankiewicz, M J (ed.) *Positive Management: Managing the Key Areas of Positive Organisational Potential for Company Success.* , Dom Organizatora TNOiK: Toruń. pp. 59–87.

Krajewski, S 2009 Prywatyzacja, restrukturyzacja, konkurencyjność polskich przedsiębiorstw, PWE, Warszawa.

Krupski, R (ed.) 1999 Zarządzanie strategiczne, Akademia Ekonomiczna, Wrocław. p. 207.

Moszkowicz, M (ed.) 2005 Zarządzanie strategiczne. Systemowa koncepcja biznesu, PWE, Warszawa. pp. 137–161.

Penc, J 1994 Strategie zarządzania, Perspektywiczne myślenie – systemowe działanie, AW Placet, Warszawa. pp. 142–143.

Pierścionek, Z 1997 Strategie rozwoju firmy, PWN, Warszawa. p 185.

Recardo, J R and Heather, K 2013 Ten best practices for restructuring the organization. *Global Business and Organizational Excellence*. January/February. Pp. 23-37. DOI: https://dx.doi.org/10.1002/joe.21470.

Stabryła, A 2000 Zarządzanie strategiczne w teorii i praktyce firmy, PWN, Warszawa-Kraków. p. 69.

Stróżycki, M (ed.), 1999 Podstawy zarządzania przedsiębiorstwem. Szkoła Główna Handlowa, Warszawa. p 169.

Urbanowska-Sojkin, E 1998 Zarządzanie przedsiębiorstwem, AE, Poznań. p. 149.

Urbanowska-Sojkin, E (ed.) 2011 Podstawy wyborów strategicznych w przedsiębiorstwach, PWE, Warszawa.

Reducing Environmentally Harmful Activities of the Company: PJSC "Obolon" (Production of Beer, Soft Drinks, Mineral Water, Spent Grain etc.)

Iryna Fedulova[*] and Tetiana Iakymchuk[†]

[*]PhD Economics, Department of Management, Kyiv National University of Trade and Economics, Kyiv, Ukraine
[†]Senior Lecturer, Department of Management and Administration, National University of Food Technologies, Kyiv, Ukraine

Introduction

The goal of PJSC "Obolon" is to meet the demands and expectations of customers and, as a result, to hold a leading market position. Their strategy includes constant attention to the preservation of the environment and takes into account the interests of all stakeholders. The basis of the strategy of "Obolon" is growth based on sustainable development principles.

As part of the strategy, "Obolon" implements innovative and energy-saving technologies, improves the environmental performance of production, minimizes harmful emissions into the environment, and reuses and recycles resources. In recent years, many investment projects aimed at reducing environmental impact were implemented – on the collection and recycling of PET bottles, processing of brewer's wet grains to get animal feedstuff for agriculture needs, reducing harmful emissions and ensuring prudent use of resources.

How to cite this book chapter:
Fedulova, I. and Iakymchuk, T. 2019. Reducing Environmentally Harmful Activities of the Company: PJSC "Obolon" (Production of Beer, Soft Drinks, Mineral Water, Spent Grain etc.). In: Gąsior, A. (ed.) *Pro-ecological Restructuring of Companies: Case Studies*, Pp. 109–120. London: Ubiquity Press. DOI: https://doi.org/10.5334/bbk.i. License: CC-BY 4.0

It has caused not only significant reduction of the impact on nature but also increased the eco-awareness and eco-culture of workers.

The company demonstrates a responsible attitude to environmental issues in Ukraine. The company is aware of its impact on the environment and, takes full responsibility towards the community, employees and shareholders. The corporation constantly improves production processes for resource conservation, and this creates considerable positive environmental effects as well as positive economic benefits.

The Objective and Method

According to the UN Global Compact in Ukraine, which is a voluntary initiative of socially responsible companies, "Obolon" regularly provides information on corporate social responsibility as a social report (Obolon Corporation, 2015). The social reports of the company were used in order to write the paper.

The objective of the paper is to determine the impact factors and discuss the environmental initiatives that were realized by "Obolon" to reduce the environmental impact, reduce the hazardous waste of production and to improve the reuse of materials. Analysis is the main method that should be used to obtain the objective. General scientific methods of analysis, such as methods of epistemology (analysis and synthesis); economic and logical methods for general analysis, such as methods of averages, methods of complex evaluation; and heuristic methods, such as questionnaires, were used in the paper.

After analyzing the environmentally harmful activities of the company, the most significant impact factors among economic, political, socio-cultural, technological, international and ecological factors were determined for "Obolon".

Short History and Performance of the Company

The establishment of the enterprise was dedicated to the Olympic Games in 1980. Czech professional men were engaged as experts, the world-famous masters of brewing. They chose the place for the new brewery. The main factor for the location of the building was the presence of huge reserves of soft and crystal clear water. Soon the company formed the largest corporation in Ukraine for the production of beer, low alcohol and soft drinks, and mineral water.

The structure of the corporation formed over many years under the influence of a development strategy aimed at diversification of production, switching to raw materials of its own production, innovation, absolute environmental safety and full social responsibility. The company "Obolon" incorporates the main plant, two separate workshops, two subsidiaries and four companies with corporate rights. Overall, the corporation employs approximately 7.5 thousand people. In 2014, the corporation entered to the top 20 of the largest employers in the agro-industrial complex.

Table 1: Production indicators, million dal.

Indicators	Year					Difference (+/-) of 2014 against 2010	2014 against 2010, %
	2010	2011	2012	2013	2014		
Beer	98.7	87.3	88.9	78.4	69.4	−29.3	70.31
Low-alcohol drinks	2.2	2	2.3	2.3	2.25	0.05	102.27
Soft drinks	18.4	18.5	18.1	15.8	15.9	−2.5	86.41
Mineral water	9.0	7.2	6.8	5.5	5.5	−3.5	61.11

Source: Constructed by the author according to Obolon Corporation (2015).

The brewery has been making beer that has gained wide popularity. In 1989, "Obolon" became the first company among Soviet enterprises to export beverages to Europe and the USA. Its trademark, "Obolon", became recognized as traditional Ukrainian beer around the world. Nowadays, the share of "Obolon" in beer exports from Ukraine is 64.5%.

Today, the beer market in Ukraine includes more than 400 species and varieties of beer, 90% of which are produced by the market leaders AB InBev, Carlsberg Ukraine and "Obolon". On the Ukrainian beer market, the market share of "Obolon" is about 21–25%. The production indicators of the company from 2010 till 2014 are presented in Table 1.

The product portfolio of the corporation includes 10 name brands of beer, seven low-alcohol beverages, seven soft drinks, six waters etc. In the structure of domestic production, 49% of the products are manufactured in PET, 35% in glass bottles, 12% in kegs and 4% in metal cans.

The activities of the company in recent years allowed the company to obtain some financial results (presented in Table 2) that have contributed to the implementation of measures to preserve the environment.

The company has confirmed compliance with the management systems that operate in the corporation "Obolon": Quality management system (ISO 9001: 2008); Food safety management systems (ISO 22000: 2005); Environmental management systems (ISO 14001: 2004); and Occupational health and safety assessment scheme (OHSAS 18001: 2007).

Reducing Environmentally Harmful Activities of the Corporation

The basis for the continuous improvement of environmental protection is environmental programs that are the part of the enterprise's policy. The main environmental programs of the company are connected with gradual reduction of discharge (emissions) into the air; rational usage of resources; and the

Table 2: Financial and economic performance of the corporation, UAH thousand.

Results	Year					Difference (+/-) of 2014 against 2010	2014 against 2010, %
	2010	2011	2012	2013	2014		
Net income	3,352,095	4,861,378	4,075,269	3,877,633	4,073,461	721,366	121.52
Net profit	89,476	3,577,451	223,878	195,309	−538,985	−628,461	−602.38
Equity	817,605	489,062	1,103,460	1,323,165	762,116	−55,489	93.21
Assets	3,151,266	918,547	3,595,732	3,661,749	3,795,133	643,867	120.43

Source: Constructed by the author according to Obolon Corporation (2015).

maximum possible recycling of production waste. The main environmental programs of the company and their results are considered below.

Gradual reduction of emissions into the air and other pollution

There is yearly reduction of emissions by the corporation (Table 3).

Atmospheric emissions were reduced by 14% in 2014 compared to the previous year. In particular, nitrogen compounds, grain dust and carbon oxide were reduced in 2014 compared to the previous year.

There is a constant reduction of pollution in the environment at the corporation, including waste water (Table 4).

Waste water was reduced by 24% in 2014 compared to 2010 and by 7.9% compared to the previous year.

Rational usage of resources

As a result of the implementation of a number of energy efficiency and savings measures, the corporation's impact on the environment has been continuing to decline. The corporation's consumption of natural gas in 2012 was equal to 26,826 thousand м³; in 2013 it was 23,708 thousand м³; in 2014 it was 18,544

Table 3: Reduction of atmospheric emissions, tons.

Year	Emissions			Total
	Nitrogen compounds	Grain dust	Carbon oxide	
2010	29.95	12.6	0.42	44
2011	29.6	11.3	0.51	45
2012	24.04	9.9	0.45	37
2013	18.6	10.79	0.76	33
2014	17.3	9.5	0.64	30

Source: Constructed by the author according to Obolon Corporation (2015).

Table 4: Reducing pollution of the company, million litres.

Indicators	Years				
	2010	2011	2012	2013	2014
Waste water	2198	2121	2175	1810	1667
In % to previous year	–	96.5	102.5	83.2	92.1

Source: Constructed by the author according to Obolon Corporation (2015).

thousand м³. Thus, consumption of natural gas was reduced by 27% in 2014 compared to 2013. It is enough volume for cooking and heating for 1247 Ukrainian families throughout the year. In addition, beverage production of all categories decreased by 10% in 2014 compared to the previous period and by 30% compared to 2010. Accordingly, this decrease in production has reduced usage of resources.

In order to reduce the dependence on energy resources, regional enterprises of "Obolon" in Okhtyrka (Sumy Region) and in Fastiv (Kyiv Region) set up solid fuel boilers. Wood waste (sawdust, broken pallets, boxes and so on) are used as the fuel. Three to four kilograms of burned wood waste give 0.008 Gcal of heat as well as 1 м³ of gas. The system of solar collectors for water heating in the administrative building was established at the "Obolon" brewery and at production sites of Zibert's Brewery Subsidiary in the city of Fastiv.

On a global average, five litres of water are used to produce one litre of beverages. The company "Obolon" requires 2.7 litres of water for the production of one litre of beverages and no more than 3.5 litres for beer production. Water consumption in the corporation was equal to 3781 thousand м³ in 2012; in 2013 it was 3241 thousand м³; in 2014 it was 2633 thousand м³. Thus, water consumption decreased by 23% in 2014 compared to 2013. This volume is equal to 242 standard Olympic-sized swimming pools. Repeated consumption of water used for washing equipment and glass bottles was equal to 1074 thousand м³ in 2012; in 2013 it was 3241 thousand м³; in 2014 it was 2998 thousand м³.

Steam consumption in the corporation was equal to 201,094 Gcal in 2012; in 2013 it was 179902 Gcal; in 2014 it was 149650 Gcal. By using an energy conservation system the secondary steam is formed during the boiling of beer wort and returned to the production cycle. Thus, the usage of steam decreased by 20% in 2014 compared to the previous period. The usage of secondary steam was equal 2630 tons in 2012 year; in 2013 it was 2140 tons; in 2014 it was 1807 tons.

Electricity consumption in the corporation was equal to 309,046 GJ in 2012; in 2013 it was 275,832 GJ; in 2014 it was 195,397 GJ. Thus, "Obolon" reduced electricity consumption by 30% in 2014. For this purpose, the company implemented the following measures:

- Installed equipment for additional utilization of heat in the boiler-house.
- Installed 197 LED-lamps.
- In 2010, joined the global eco-initiative "Earth Hour" of the World Wildlife Fund for Nature (WWF). The company has showed concern for environmental problems more than five years. In 2014, the company saved about 300 kW of electricity in the frame of the initiative.

Maximum possible recycling of production waste

Today there is no legislative framework that would stimulate the recycling of waste in Ukraine. There are no effective incentives in the state for people to sort waste; there are no conditions for waste recycling and there is no waste management system. So "Obolon" launched its own program of recycling of plastic waste in 2003. The plastic waste (PET bottles) is the main threat to the environment because the decay period of plastic in nature is more than 400 years. Specialists state that the popularity of products in PET packaging (beer, beverages, household chemicals, etc.) is growing – this segment grows by 10–12% every year. The specific waste formation of the company is presented in Table 5.

Specific waste formation was reduced by three times during the manufacture of beverages from 2010 to 2014.

Recycling of waste at the company includes: internal recycling and reuse, waste disposal and third-party recycling (Table 6).

Internal recycling and reuse of materials as secondary raw materials in the production include: realisation of organic waste for feeding animals (brewer pellet, bran), plastic waste and so on. The examples of projects on recycling of waste that were realized by the company are considered below:

1. The company recycles carbon dioxide (CO_2) from gas fraction to liquid and then uses it in production. CO_2 is formed during brewery fermentation. Processing plants to get CO_2 are in Kyiv ("Obolon") and in Fastiv, Kyiv region (Zibert's Brewery). Re-use of CO_2 was equal to 11,922 tons in 2012; in 2013 it was 11,674 tonnes; in 2014 it was 11378 tonnes.

Table 5: Specific waste formation of the company.

Indicators	Year				
	2010	2011	2012	2013	2014
Useful product, tons/thousand dal	99.56	99.65	99.65	99.83	99.87
Specific waste formation, tons/thousand dal	0.44	0.35	0.35	0.17	0.13

Source: Constructed by the author according to Obolon Corporation (2015).

Table 6: Wastes of the Company and their Distribution.

Indicators	Year				
	2010	2011	2012	2013	2014
Recycling waste by the company, tons	169,200	170,300	156,592	134,614	129,839
Distribution of waste depending on recycling, %:					
Internal recycling and reuse	94.1	94.8	94.5	94.1	95.2
Waste disposal	4.3	3.7	3.6	4.1	2.9
Third-party recycling	1.6	1.5	1.9	1.8	1.9

Source: Constructed by the author according to Obolon Corporation (2015).

2. The innovative line on recycling of PET packaging has been established in Alexandria (Kirovohrad region). The Kirovograd region was the ideal location for the project in terms of logistics and equidistance from major cities.

Today "Obolon" independently collects raw materials (in production units installed over a hundred containers to collect used bottles) and buys used PET packaging from suppliers. The company's project to recycle of PET packaging has been going on for 12 years in Alexandria. Nine thousand tons of used bottles were recycled in the first 10 years of the project. Thirty million units of PET containers annually come to recycling and 2.5 million PET bottles are processed at the enterprise every month.

The effects from the project to recycle of plastic bottles include the following:
   - Proceeds from the sale of binding band were equal to 10.2 million UAH in 2013.
   - Provides recycling of plastic bottles.
   - Improves the environment through reducing the accumulation of plastic in nature.
   - Allows for production of new materials from waste.
   - Creates new jobs – more than 350 jobs.
   - Promotes eco-culture among the production companies.

The problems at hand include low culture of the collection of plastic waste among the population and some problems connected with collecting of plastic waste.

3. One of the main problems of the beer industry is the utilization of organic waste generated in the production process. Thirty million tons of such waste are produced in the world each year.

Most organic waste (brewer pellet, malt sprouts and yeast) traditionally are used in agriculture. The shelf life of most organic waste, for example brewer pellet, is short and because of it their logistics are limited. However, in the environmentally responsible companies, waste can go from costly budget items to income-generating items if they properly organise the issue of recycling.

The corporation "Obolon" was the first company in Ukraine to begin processing brewer pellet. The equipment for production of dry pellets can process up to 700 tons per day without harmful effects on the environment. The corporation "Obolon" had difficulties for some time with processing brewer pellet through large volumes of its formation. In 2008, the company introduced a project to dry brewer's wet grains. It solves the main problem – to increase the shelf life of brewer pellet to six months and expand its logistics.

The drying process requires a significant amount of energy. Therefore, the corporation implemented the project on reconstruction of a heat supply system in 2011 in order to reduce the energy intensity of production. So, now "Obolon" partly uses secondary pairs with 100% return condensate to the boiler for drying of brewer's wet grains. It saves about 35 thousand м³ of natural gas per month. "Obolon"'s main brewer pellet customers are the dairy farms of Ukraine (Association of milk in Ukraine) as well as farmers from the EU and Israel.

The effect from the project on processing of brewer pellet includes the following:

- – Significant reduction of waste formation of brewer's wet grains – by91 % in five years.
- – Improvement of the sanitary state of the territory.
- – Reduction of emissions into the air (exhaust gases) from automobile transportation as a result of reducing the number of shipping operations of brewer's wet grains.

Thus, every year the company works to improve its efficiency and responsible use of resources, financing measures for environmental protection. Recently there was decline in production, and as a result "Obolon" suffered a reduction in its economic indicators. In particular, in 2014 the company received a loss – 538,985 thousand UAH. However, the work on improving the environmental performance of the enterprise does not stop. This is shown by the costs for environmental activity (Table 7).

The costs for environmental protection in the corporation include:

- – operating costs for environmental protection: purchase of raw materials for maintenance of environmental protection equipment;
- – capital investment to install the equipment of high efficiency; and
- – fees for the services of environmental character on recycling of certain types of waste.

Environmental impacts that are caused by the introduction of new activities, products and processes are assessed in advance and are always minimized.

The influence of corporations on the environment is constantly monitored, documented and analyzed. According to the company's data, the proportion of reused water at "Obolon" is growing, and now more than 70% of

Table 7: The costs for environmental protection in the corporation.

Year	2010	2011	2012	2013	2014
Investments in environment protection, million UAH	23.6	15.3	19.5	16.0	10.0
The costs for environmental activity, in % of net income	0.70	0.31	0.48	0.41	0.25

Source: constructed by the author according to Obolon Corporation (2015).

the water is used again. "Obolon" recycles and reuses more than 96% of the production residue.

Introducing measures to reduce the harmful impact of activities on the environment was related to the following:

- Reliable relationships with suppliers and customers with the absolute performance of regulatory, legal requirements and contractual obligations.
- Desire to be the best in the field of quality, product safety and attitude towards the environment and to reduce occupational risks for staff and the people on the spot.
- Ensure increasing degree of employees' motivation and satisfaction of customers and other stakeholders.
- Use of modern equipment minimizes harmful emissions into the environment and decreases some production costs.
- The ability to save and to release additional resources.

Conclusions

"Obolon" seeks and uses innovative ways to minimize the harmful effects of their activity on the environment every day. They achieve this by reducing costs from saving energy, water and other resources, and increasing amounts of recyclable waste in their factories.

Table 8 demonstrates the influence of factors on the corporation "Obolon" in the context of reducing environmentally harmful activities and its ability to implement a restructuring process.

The above economic factors determine the financial condition of the enterprise and the impact on the restructuring process; it is not possible for other beer companies with a weak market position to participate in environmental programs and projects without financial support.

Among the political and legal aspects of the international market, "protection of the environment" impacts the company because "Obolon" is a modern enterprise that seeks to meet the international standards of activity, product quality and environmental protection.

Among the socio-cultural factors the biggest impact was made by factors 24 and 26. Today there are some changes in the population's awareness and attitude towards the environmental situation in the country. It is a gradual and slow process of changes connected with different factors and with the educational level too. The level of education in Ukraine is high, and there is environmental education at all levels of learning, from the first class to masters' course. More and more information is emerging about protection and preservation of the environment in other countries and the consequences that may occur if we consciously avoid such activities.

Table 8: Impact factors on the restructuring processes of the enterprise.

No	Determinant	Impact
1	2	3
Economic factors		
2	Inflation rate	10
3	The national currency exchange rate	10
8	Competition on core market	8
9	Consumer confidence	7
Political and legal aspects of the international market		
22	Protection of the environment	8
Socio-cultural factors in both the national and international sense, and the relationships between them		
24	The civilization progress (lifestyle and its changes, knowledge of the living standards in other countries)	5
26	The level of education	5
The technological factors		
35	The level of technological modernity industry	6
36	New inventions and development of science	6
International factors		
42	The international agreements and regulations	7
Ecological aspects		
49	Permanent monitoring of water consumption (e.g. control of leaking taps)	7
52	Ecological innovations	6
53	Encouraging environmental awareness of employees and business's stakeholders	7

Source: Constructed by the author.

Among the technological factors, the most important for the company are the factors 35 and 36. The company is engaged in scientific research and development but there is no research laboratory. Therefore, monitoring domestic and international developments that can be effectively used for restructuring and reuse of resources and usage of alternative energy sources and increasing waste production is important for the company. The achievements of modern science and technology in this direction are an impetus for the environmental activity of the company.

Among international factors, "international agreements and regulations" are significant, because the company carries out export operations and adheres to international business standards. Among the environmental aspect factors, 49, 52 and 53 are important, as the environmental initiatives of "Obolon" are connected with effective use and reuse of resources, alternative sources of energy and increasing level of waste-free production.

Future prospects of environmental focus for "Obolon" will be connected with increasing volumes of PET bottles processing at the company; with further reduction of air emissions and waste water, reduction of specific waste during the manufacture of beverages.

References

PJSC "Obolon", Sustainable Development Report of Obolon Corporation, 2015. Available at, http://report.obolon.ua [Last accessed 20 September 2016].

Learning by Engaging in Pro-Environmental Behaviour at Work

Alina Irina Popescu
The Bucharest University of Economic Studies, CCREI

Introduction

Environmental policies and strategies have rapidly become a common feature of the corporate landscape, as firms acknowledge that integrating sustainability in their business operations has a significant potential for substantial gains. However, developing and implementing environmental policies and strategies are not enough for effectively incorporating sustainability into the business practices. A cultural transformation that fosters employee engagement in environmental sustainability through pro-ecological behaviour is also required. In order to achieve sustainability goals, firms are turning to one of their greatest resources – the employees. In this context, employee engagement in pro-environmental behaviour at work emerged as a prerequisite for effectively mainstreaming organisational sustainability.

This case investigates the actions taken by the PwC Romanian entities, part of the Pricewaterhouse Coopers (PwC) global network, one of the largest professional services networks in the world. A sound environmentally friendly strategy was developed at the global level, part of the corporate responsibility strategy, which is implemented at different degrees by the local firms of the PwC network. In Romania, the goal of environmental stewardship creates a working environment that fosters the pro-ecological behaviour of the firms'

How to cite this book chapter:
Popescu, A. I. 2019. Learning by Engaging in Pro-Environmental Behaviour at Work.
    In: Gąsior, A. (ed.) *Pro-ecological Restructuring of Companies: Case Studies*,
    Pp. 121–133. London: Ubiquity Press. DOI: https://doi.org/10.5334/bbk.j. License:
    CC-BY 4.0

employees. Actions and measures were investigated using the framework proposed by PwC at the global level. We argue that learning by engaging in pro-ecological behaviour at the workplace in an environmentally aware and environmentally friendly context has a high potential to be transferred by the employees to their households, spinning off towards society.

Methodology and Area of Discussion

The focus of paper is to investigate the measures taken to implement at local level in Romania the environmental stewardship goal, part of the corporate responsibility strategy, formulated at the global level by the Pricewaterhouse Coopers global network of professional services firms; to gain a better understanding of the pathways to instil the pro-ecological behaviour to employees; and to examine environmental sustainability strategy implementation in an emerging market context.

The case study was prepared according to the qualitative research methodology. Data collection was done in the following ways: direct observation of the working environment by the researcher, face-to-face discussions with company representatives, and literature and mass-media reviews.

Pro-environmental behaviour (PEB) was defined also in relation to its impact on the environment, as "any action that enhances the quality of the environment, either resulting or not resulting from pro-environmental intent" (Steg et al. 2014); or, "a kind of behaviour that consciously seeks to minimise the negative impact of one's actions on the natural and built environment" (Kollmuss & Agyeman 2002).

In principle, according to the **goal framing theory** proposed by Lindenberg and Steg (2007), people are motivated to engage in pro-environmental behaviour for three different types of reasons: for normative reasons (because they think protecting the environment is the right thing to do), for gain reasons (because it saves money) or for hedonic reasons (because it is enjoyable). However, involvement in pro-environmental behaviour may generate conflicts between the normative reasons on the one hand and the hedonic and gain goals on the other hand (Lindenberg & Steg 2007). Acting pro-environmentally is largely considered to be the right thing to do, but often it proves to be more time-consuming, less profitable, less enjoyable or more effort than acting in a way that is harmful to the environment.

Measures were proposed to reduce or even remove the conflict between the three different types of goals described above (Steg et al. 2014). Examples in this respect include: making pro-environmental actions fun (e.g. games) or convenient (e.g. increasing the availability of trash bins), making environmentally friendly products financially attractive, increasing the cost of environmentally harmful actions through taxation, or by making the environmentally harmful options less pleasurable. In addition, engagement in the pro-environmental behaviour can be leveraged through strengthening the normative goals by creating and promoting the awareness of acting appropriately, in spite of cost and effort – for the benefit of the environment, of future generations and of other people. Many people buy organic food, engage in recycling or in the selective collection of garbage (Czajkowski et al. 2013) or support pro-environmental organisations.

But how to convince people to engage in pro-environmental behaviour? One of the most commonly referenced theories in the field of environmental studies that seeks to explain individual behaviour is the **theory of planned behaviour** (Azjen 1991). The theory of planned behaviour was applied in the context of pro-environmental behaviour by Rioux (2011) and also applied in both household and workplace contexts by Nye and Hargreaves (2010). Their findings showed that individuals have a higher propensity to engage in pro-ecological behaviours in their households than in workplaces. Furthermore, in workplaces it seems harder to change old behaviours and to adopt new roles given the organisational culture, and that there is a need for strong evidence to justify new actions in line with pro-ecological behaviour.

Also, it has be argued that the **social exchange theory** is one of "the most influential conceptual paradigms for understanding workplace behaviour" (Cropanzano & Mitchell 2005). According to this theory, social exchange occurs when something considered to bear value is exchanged between an organisation and its employees (Schaninger & Turnipseed 2005). Related to pro-environmental behaviour, evidence showed that organizations value employee loyalty and extra effort beyond the job requirements and that employees value support from their organization. Evidence also showed a positive relation between employees feeling supported by the organisation and their commitment to the organisation and job satisfaction; that generates a context in which employees are likely to reciprocate by performing behaviours valued by their organization (Lavelle et al. 2007).

According to the social exchange theory, the employees are more likely to engage in pro-environmental behaviour at work if they perceive that their organization attributes value to the cause of environmental sustainability. Pro-environmental behaviour adoption is positively correlated to their job satisfaction and their commitment to the organisation, and the last two are correlated to the perceived organisation support (i.e. employees' beliefs that their employer aims to foster a work environment that is conducive to well-being) (Paillé & Boiral 2013).

Factors that affect the adoption of pro-ecological behaviour at work can be divided into internal (individual) and external (organisational) factors, as proposed by Blok et al. (2015). The internal factors were the following: general values, personal norms, social norms, perceived behavioural control, attitude towards PEB, environmental awareness, and environmental values. The external factors identified were: situational factors, leadership support to PEB, and leadership boss (exemplary behaviour by leaders). Transformational leadership plays a significant role in employee motivation to engage in pro-environmental behaviour at the workplace. The adoption of an environmentally friendly strategic orientation requires firms to lead important changes in employee behaviour. This is effectively done through the inspirational and value-based nature of transformational leadership that motivates employees to accept these changes and to engage in pro-environmental behaviours at the workplace.

Background on PwC Romania

Pricewaterhouse Coopers (PwC) is one of the largest professional services networks in the world. It is present in 157 countries around the world, employing more than 223,000 people (PwC global website). The firms from the PwC network offer a wide range of professional services, including assurance, advisory and tax services. It is well-known as one of the so-called Big Four firms along with Deloitte, Ernst & Young and KPMG.

PwC entered the Romanian market in 1991 being, at that time, the largest professional service firm that established an office in the country, at Bucharest. During the past 25 years, PwC Romania has been actively involved in major projects for the Romanian economy, from involvement in the preparation of various legislative proposals to the establishment of several professional associations and institutions (including The Bucharest Stock Exchange, The Chamber of Financial Auditors from Romania, The Chamber of Fiscal Consultants, ANEVAR, UNPIR). They have been continuously promoting Romania as a place for foreign investment, and they managed to gradually attract foreign investors to the country (e.g. Unilever, SAB Miller, Ford, Enel, Heildelberg Cement). At the same time, they also focus on promoting Romanian entrepreneurship by being involved in the creation of a strong community for Romanian entrepreneurs within the Business Champions project. Last but not least, they support the economic higher education sector through their involvement in a series of projects in partnership with The Bucharest University of Economic Studies and The Babes-Bolyai University of Cluj (Simion 2016).

At present, PwC Romania offers a wide range of services in the fields of: assurance services (financial audit, risk assurance solutions, financial accounting advisory services), advisory services (consulting, deals and business recovery), tax services (taxation, human resource advisory), and legal services. They have regional offices in Bucharest, Cluj, Timişoara, Constanţa, Iaşi – in Romania – and Chişinău – in the Republic of Moldova – employing over 650 people (PwC Romania website; Daily Business 2015). On the Romanian market, PwC faces both the international competition, especially the competition coming from the other Big Four firms, and the competition of local professional services firms, which tend to specialize in one or few services.

Among the Romanian network of PwC firms, PwC Management Consultants SRL holds the ISO 14001 Environment Management System (EMS) certification. This standard provides a systematic framework to manage the environmental impact of an organisation's services and processes. This certification is an additional assurance to stakeholders that the environmental management system at the firm meets international industry-specific environmental standards.

The Environmentally Friendly Initiative at PwC

The PwC network adopted a corporate responsibility approach, aware of the need for the sustainable development of our world. By using corporate responsibility as a societal lens, PwC is better able to understand societal trends and stakeholder expectations, to align corporate activities to them, to help other businesses in their efforts towards greater sustainability, and to invest in positive societal change (PwC global website).

Four focus areas were envisaged by the corporate responsibility strategic orientation:

- **Responsible business** – Being a responsible business and contributing to society is essential to the PwC purpose. This is represented by building trust in society and by solving important problems, purposes that align corporate values and behaviours (Kelly 2016).
- **Community engagement** – PwC shares their international skills and experience to maximize the potential of local communities and of their individuals, of the social enterprises and of the NGO sector across the globe.
- **Diversity and inclusion** – Diversity and cultural dexterity are seen as essential to the PwC business, not only within the network, but also when working together and interacting with their clients. Inclusion leverages the power of differences, and the inclusion of a diverse workforce ensures high potentials for innovation and leadership.
- **Environmental stewardship** – This area of focus envisions the responsible use of resources and the protection of the natural environment through sustainable practices undertaken by PwC.

Fig. 1: Total gross emissions (tCO2e) per employee.

Source: http://www.pwc.com/gx/en/about/corporate-responsibility/environmental-stewardship.html.

Note: These figures relate only to the 21 largest firms in the PwC network.

PwC's environmental stewardship is implemented in two directions: reducing their own environmental impact, and working with clients to achieve environmental friendliness and sustainability.

1. Reducing their own environmental impact
At the global level, PwC committed to respect the environment by understanding and reducing their business operations' impact on the environment. The development of the Network Environmental Statement guides the operations of member firms from the 157 countries from across the globe in terms of improving their environmental performance.

According to the Network Environmental Statement, PwC member firms are expected to comply with all environmental regulations and requirements to which they are subject, and more precisely, they are encouraged to:

- Continuously improve their performance and aspire to integrate environmental management good practice in business operations;
- Use resources efficiently and minimise the generation of waste;
- Consider environmental and social issues in the procurement of goods and services;
- Consider environmental issues and energy performance in the acquisition, design, refurbishment, location, management and use of buildings; and
- Consider how to reduce the environmental impact of business travel. (PwC Network Environmental Statement).

The analysis on key environmental indicators showed a reduction of total CO_2 emissions per employee (t CO_2e) of 8% in FY 2016 as compared to FY 2014 (Figure 1). The greenhouse gas (GHG) emissions are also investigated by scope, as follows: i) gas, diesel and fuel for company-owned vehicles; ii) purchased electricity; iii) air travel. Efforts were also made to reduce the energy usage from offices and air travel and will continue to reduce gross and net emissions partly through making greater use of technology.

2. Working with clients to achieve environmental friendliness and sustainability
By working with clients to improve their environmental outcomes and to find new innovative solutions to environmental challenges, PwC gains their greatest impact on the environment.

Through the practice of Sustainability and Climate Change, PwC developed the Total Impact Measurement and Management (TIMM) tool. The tool helps businesses assess their total impact (social, environmental, tax and economic impacts), to identify and evaluate trade-offs, to make optimal decisions and to accommodate stockholders' interests.

The environmental impact of a business is assessed, taking into consideration greenhouse gases (GHG) and other emissions, water pollution, waste, land use and water use implied by the performance of the business operations. For a

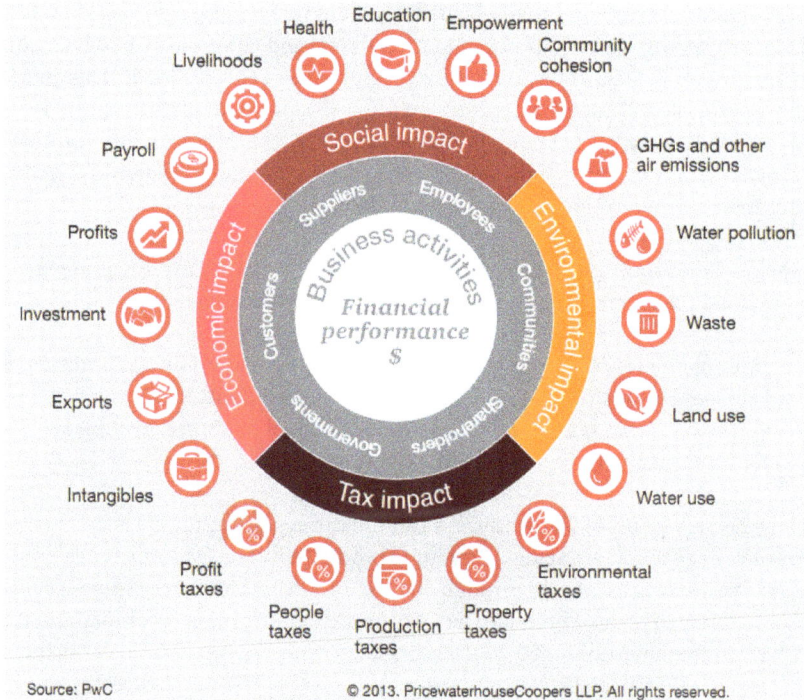

Fig. 2: Illustrative dimensions of impact considered within TIMM.

Source: PwC (2013) Measuring and managing total impact: A new language for business decisions, p.23.

detailed presentation of the other impact dimensions, please see Figure 2. The environmental impact measurement methodology quantifies the changes in the ecosystem resulting from the performance of value chain activities by using business data, public information and econometric modelling. Furthermore, the tool converts these impacts into monetary terms and tracks them over time.

Implementation of Environmental Stewardship in Romania

Encouraging pro-ecological employee behaviour at work emerged from the broader sustainability agenda of PwC. Incorporating sustainability into the business operations, meaning the practice of monitoring, measuring and reducing the environmental and social costs of doing business, requires the support of employees, who can make a significant contribution in terms of improving the environmental performance of PwC through engaging in environmentally sustainable work behaviour. The incorporation of environmental sustainability makes PwC able to provide clients with the most efficient, cost-effective and high-quality services and to distinguish itself on the Romanian professional services market through environmental friendliness and community involvement.

The pro-ecological behaviour of PwC employees is ensured and, at the same time, promoted through measures that, for the purpose of this study, were investigated using the framework proposed by the PwC Network Environmental Statement because they offer a common standard for all PwC network firms. The goals and the actions taken are the following:

Goal 1: Continuously improve their performance and aspire to integrate environmental management good practice in business operations:

- Holding the ISO certification for the ISO 14001 standard on environmental management system for PwC Management Consultants SRL.
- Electronic systems and sensors in place to control lightning, heating and air conditioning, printing, water consumption etc.

Goal 2: Use resources efficiently and minimise the generation of waste.
Resource efficiency, also called "resource productivity" or "eco-efficiency", provides cost-saving methods through the use of limited resources in a sustainable manner in order to reduce the environmental impact of a company. With regard to the environmental impact, primary resource inputs to any business are materials (especially paper), water and energy. Their use directly affects the environment, though extraction, pollution and waste generation. Other resources are also indispensable to the business activity – labour, money, time – but their environmental impact is generally more indirect.

Two directions are followed as regards resource efficiency at PwC Romania offices:

1. Resource saving:
   - Use of equipment that minimizes the amount of resources
   - Minimizing the waste of water by using sensor water taps
   - Use of an intelligent lightning system that adapts light's intensity to exterior conditions
   - Energy efficient heating, ventilation and air-conditioning system
   - Use of motion sensors to automatically shut off lights when the office is not in use
   - Use of energy star appliances and lightning
   - Turning off the laptops or using energy saving settings when not in use
   - More use of electronic newspapers and other media
   - Adoption of new business practices that reduce resource consumption
2. Recycling and reusing for waste reduction:
   - Recycling shredded paper, batteries
   - Replacement of the plastic kitchenware with reusable utensils made of glass, ceramic and iron, for both employees and guests

• The use of recycled or environmentally friendly toiletry supplies as disclosed by the supplier

Goal 3: Consider environmental issues and energy performance in the acquisition, design, refurbishment, location, management and use of buildings.
The use of environmentally friendly buildings provides a series of benefits in: resource efficiency, improved occupant health, improved occupant satisfaction and productivity, and reduced environmental impact through lowering the consumption of energy and other material resources (Lotspeich et al. 2003; Parker 2012).
PwC Romania's offices are located in an eco-friendly building, designed according to BREEAM standards, although the final certification was not pursued by the building owner. Established in 1990, BREEAM is the longest established method of assessing and certifying the sustainability of buildings.

Goal 4: Consider how to reduce the environmental impact of business travel.
Business travel is linked to the ability of serving PwC's clients. Visiting clients' locations for on-site discussions and documentation is often a prerequisite for delivering high-quality services. The efforts to reduce the environmental impact of business travel currently challenge the internal business travel policy in terms of decisions regarding the need, frequency and mode of travel. Two directions for action were identified in this respect: i) establishment of regional offices in major cities across Romania, to reduce the travel of the employees from the Bucharest main premises; ii) avoiding business travel by the organisation of virtual meetings and teleconferencing – internal or with external participants – whenever possible, instead of travelling to different locations by plane, company cars or rentals.

Goal 5: Consider environmental and social issues in the procurement of goods and services.
The procurement activity of a professional service firm has, in general, a lower impact on the environment than that of a manufacturing company. The PwC orientation in this respect is to buy products with environmental credentials whenever possible. In selecting the new providers and suppliers, an increasingly important role has been attributed to the ecological and social factors. PwC Romania is recognizing the importance of sourcing office supplies that have a lower impact on the environment. Examples include: no plastic kitchen materials (cutlery, glasses, plates etc.) and 100% recycled paper towels and toilet paper as reported by supplier.
PwC Romania is supporting their clients that look to make a difference in their environmental and social impacts and to embrace sustainability demonstrated by trustworthy and credible reporting. Services rendered to clients fall into the following categories: i) environmental compliance audit, aiming at establishing the level of compliance with the legal applicable environmental

requirements (e.g. identification of the legal applicable requirements, establishing the impact of the current activities upon the environment and the level of the risk and potential environmental liabilities, identification of the main non-compliances and of remedies); ii) environmental due diligence, identification of the environmental risks caused by non-compliances with the environmental law and quantifying the associated material exposure; ii) environmental impact assessment; iii) environmental site assessment; iv) waste management audit; v) development and implementation of environmental management systems in accordance with the requirements of SR EN ISO 14001; and vi) issues related to the environmental fund (PwC Romanian website).

The improvement of the environmental legislation in Romania is actively supported through discussions and by providing opinions within first rank advocacy and business growth professional associations (e.g. American Chamber of Commerce in Romania, Foreign Investors Council). Priorities formulated by the American Chamber of Commerce in Romania aim at: helping Romanian central public environmental authorities in transposing and implementing the communitary acquis related to environment and solving non-compliance issues, strengthening institutional capacity, offering technical support, improving the environmental legislation in Romania (AmCham website).

Employee support is a key driver of implementing environmental policies and strategies within business organisations. Employees are performing the business processes and operations, and their pro-environmental orientation is crucial to greening such processes and operations and transforming the business into a sustainable one.

Several measures were taken to raise employees' awareness on environmental issues, to increase employee engagement in voluntary pro-environmental behaviour and to promote employee health and wellness, such as:

- Minimizing or completely eliminating the use of paper through the insertion of the "Think before you print" signature at the end of each email
- Minimizing the use of paper and cartridges by using two-sided printing as the network standard; also use multiple-page printing when possible
- Sponsorship of various green initiatives (e.g. "Let's do it, Romania!", the largest voluntary initiative to collect and recycle waste from the natural environment)
- Encourage and financially support employee participation in various green initiatives
- Environmental awareness raising messages placed indoors (e.g. number of trees cut annually for paper production)

Through the implementation of environmentally friendly measures, PwC Romania provides its employees with an organisational environment in which they learn and practice pro-ecological behaviour. Employees' pro-ecological behaviour can be voluntary (e.g. dispose of waste in separate bins) or required (e.g. shred unneeded paper for confidentiality reasons, which goes to recycling). This pro-ecological behaviour, once adopted by the employees at the workplace, it is highly likely to be transferred to employees' households, spinning off into society.

Conclusions and Recommendations

Nowadays, the environmental context is challenging, raising concerns for businesses to meet higher and higher expectations coming from various stakeholders, shareholders and legislators. Environmental stewardship is one of the goals assumed by the investigated organisation, within the global corporate responsibility strategy.

A strong prerequisite for developing an environmentally friendly working environment is represented by the procurement of the ISO 14001 certification related to environmental management systems. This was done for only one firm of the PwC network in Romania, and it is recommended that it be achieved for other firms as well. This international standard with voluntary adoption provides that the organisation not only meets the legal environmental requirements, but goes beyond them by keeping with the expectations of their stakeholders and shareholders. In addition, this certification can be leveraged as a competitive advantage as the organisation is able to distinguish itself from other organisations through corporate communication. Last but not least, the ISO 14001 environmental management systems' standard is an organised way to get employees engaged in meeting the environmental commitments of the organisation.

Individual values, beliefs, motivations and attitudes clearly influence behaviour, but it is important to acknowledge that the social context (in this particular case, the workplace) alters them and has the power to change individual behaviour. Given the potential of the workplace to exert significant influence on individual values, beliefs and, ultimately, behaviours, we illustrated the adoption of the environmentally friendly orientation of a large professional services firm – PwC Romania. Working in an eco-friendly organisation has the potential to increase employee motivation and feelings of organisational support, and to change existing habitual behaviour into pro-ecological behaviour.

The implementation of the environmental stewardship commitment in Romania, part of the global corporate responsibility strategy, has been performed through a series of measures grouped by aim according the framework proposed by the global environmental statement. It was noted that some aims were better supported by implementation actions (e.g. resource efficiency), while others still present a large potential for improvement (e.g. business travel and procurement). The PwC requirements for the efficient use of resources not only create employee awareness of the environmental impact, but also assure employees of the company's support in adoption of pro-environmental behaviours.

Pro-environmental behaviour promotion has been developed according to the learning-by-doing principle. Learning from the experiences of one's own actions was widely believed to be the most effective way of learning. In addition, the use of employee environmental engagement methods is recommended. These may include: awareness-raising activities, education and training, creation of dedicated teams, contests and challenges, and providing of enabling conditions and effort recognition schemes, as discovered by a recently conducted study on employee environmental engagement practices in financial institutions (UNEP FI 2011). Employees' engagement in pro-ecological behaviour has the potential to stimulate employee passion and pride for working for a company that demonstrates good corporate citizenship behaviour, to increase employee productivity and retention, to better attract new employees that share the same values, and to create a working environment that stimulates creativity, diversity and innovation.

References:

Ajzen, I 1991 The theory of planned behavior. *Organizational Behavior and Human Decision Processes,* 50(2): 179–211.

American Chamber of Commerce in Romania 2016. Available at http://www.amcham.ro/index.html/committees?committeeID=97 [Last accessed 22 October 2016].

Blok, V, Wesselink, R, Studynka, O and Kemp, R 2015 Encouraging sustainability in the workplace: a survey on the pro-environmental behaviour of university employees. *Journal of Cleaner Production,* 106: 55–67.

Cropanzano, R and Mitchell, M 2005 Social exchange theory: An interdisciplinary review. *Journal of Management,* 31: 874–900.

Czajkowski, M, Kadziela, T and Hanley, T 2012 We want to sort! Assessing households' preferences for sorting waste (Working Papers 2012–07). Warsaw, Poland: Faculty of Economic Sciences, University of Warsaw.

Daily Business 2015 Ionut Simion va fi noul Country Managing Partner al PwC Romania. Availavle at http://www.dailybusiness.ro/stiri-cariere/ionut-simion-va-fi-noul-country-managing-partner-al-pwc-romania-106928/ [Last accessed 14 October 2016].

Kelly, C (2016): Who we are? Cole Kelly statement transcript. Available at http://www.pwc.com/gx/en/about/global-annual-review-2016/what-we-do/colm-kelly-video-transcript.html [Last accessed 14 October 2016].

Kollmuss, A and Agyeman, J 2002 Mind the gap: Why do people act environmentally and what are the barriers to pro-environmental behavior? *Environmental Education Research,* 8(3); 239–260.

Lavelle, J, Rupp, D and Brockner, J 2007. Taking a multifoci approach to the study of justice, commitment, and organizational citizenship behavior: The target similarity model. *Journal of Management,* 33; 841–866.

Lindenberg, S and Steg, L 2007 Normative, gain and hedonic goal-frames guiding environmental behavior. *Journal of Social Issues,* 63(1): 117–137.

Lotspeich, C, Fellow, B and Larson, A 2003 *Environment, Entrepreneurship, and Innovation: Systems Efficiency Strategies for Industrial and Commercial Facilities.* University of Virginia, Charlottesville, VA: DARDEN Business Publishing.

Nye, M and Hargreaves, T 2010 Exploring the social dynamics of proenvironmental behavior change. *Journal of Industrial Ecology,* 14 (1): 137–149.

Paillé, P and Boiral, O 2013 Pro-environmental behavior at work: Construct validity and determinants. *Journal of Environmental Psychology,* 36: 118–128.

Parker, J 2012 The Value of BREEAM, A BSRIA report. In Association with Schneider Electric. Available at http://www.breeam.com/filelibrary/ BREEAM%20and%20Value/The_Value_of_BREEAM.pdf [Last accessed 14 October 2016].

PwC Network Environmental Statement Available at https://www.pwc.com/ gx/en/corporate-responsibility/assets/pwc-network-environmental-statement.pdf [Last accessed 14 October 2016].

PwC 2013 Measuring and managing total impact: A new language for business decisions. Available at http://www.pwc.com/gx/en/sustainability/publications/total-impact-measurement-management/assets/pwc-timm-report. pdf, p.23 [Last accessed 14 October 2016].

PwC 2016. Environmental Studies. Available at http://www.pwc.ro/en/services/ tax-legal/indirect-taxation.html#Environmental_studies [Last accessed 22 October 2016].

PwC 2016. Megatrends. Available at http://www.pwc.co.uk/issues/megatrends. html [Last accessed 22 October 2016].

Rioux, L 2011 Promoting pro-environmental behaviour: collection of used batteries by secondary school pupils. *Environmental Education Research,* 17(3): 353–373.

Schaninger, W S, and Turnipssed, D L 2005 The workplace social exchange network: Its effect on organizational citizenship behavior, contextual performance, job satisfaction, and intent to leave. In Turnipseed, D L (ed.) *Handbook of Organizational Citizenship Behavior: A Review of 'Good Soldier' Activity in Organizations.* New York, NY: Nova Sciences Publisher, pp. 209–242.

Simion, I 2016 PwC: Noi credem în România, Ziarul Financiar Available at http://www.zf.ro/banci-si-asigurari/ionut-simion-pwc-noi-credem-in-romania-15075754 [Last accessed 22 October 2016].

Steg, L, Bolderdijk, J W, Keizer, K and Perlaviciute, G 2014 An integrated framework for encouraging pro-environmental behaviour: The role of values, situational factors and goals. *Journal of Environmental Psychology,* 38(2014): 104–115.

United Nations Environment Programme Finance Initiative (UNEP FI) 2011 If you ask us... Making Environmental Employee Engagement Happen: Results of a Global Survey, UNEP, Instaprint, Geneva, Switzerland.

2.6

Environmental Investments in New Technologies

Jarosław Korpysa

Dr hab., Department of Microeconomics, Institute of Economics, Faculty of Economic and Management, University of Szczecin

Theoretical Approach

Globalization processes, changing consumer expectations and increasing competition force businesses to vigorously search for new environmental technologies that will minimize pollutant emissions as well as save natural resources. In this sense, environmental technologies relate to all forms of creating and implementing production or services processes striving to acquire higher effectiveness and responsibility of a company in the field of using natural resources (Bocken et al. 2014). Therefore, actions for new environmental technologies leading to full exploitation of the environmental potential of particular solutions constitute an essential element of reinforcement of environmental protection policy for companies. The goal of these actions is to exploit the potential of a new technology in order to execute environmental challenges efficiently, while at the same time improving the competitiveness of the entities functioning on the market (Beltrán-Esteve & Picazo-Tadeo 2015). At this point it is important to bear in mind that the new environmental technologies industry includes mainly the sectors dealing with climate friendly technologies, controlling air pollution, waste water management and recycling. Currently, these sectors, whose annual value is EUR 600 billion, already comprise one third of the world's market (Bossle et al. 2016).

How to cite this book chapter:
Korpysa, J. 2019. Environmental Investments in New Technologies. In: Gąsior, A. (ed.) *Pro-ecological Restructuring of Companies: Case Studies*, Pp. 135–144. London: Ubiquity Press. DOI: https://doi.org/10.5334/bbk.k. License: CC-BY 4.0

The actions that are connected with new technologies for environmental protection include both pro-ecological investments (also called investment projects) and as various types of organizational and technical procedures reducing the negative impacts of entrepreneur's actions on the environment. Therefore, these investments may be defined as expenditure on creating new, enlarging the existing or restoration of used objects of tangible assets, whose goal is to conserve water, air, land, biodiversity and landscape as well as protection from noise and radiation. Some authors also include, in the category of pro-ecological investments, both investments whose goal is environmental conservation and those whose aim is to produce goods and services used in environmental protection, i.e. the investments in eco-industries (Wang 2015).

In the literature, it is assumed that the investments connected with environmental conservation might be divided according to the character of an investment. In this regard, so-called end-of-pipe or integrated investments may be distinguished. The specificity of the investments of the first kind is reduction or neutralization of the pollutions created in the production process. These investments do not limit the amount of produced pollution but limit their negative consequences (Zhang 2013). The second type of pro-ecological undertakings of new technologies are integrated investments, which, being part of the production process, reduce the amount of produced pollution at the source and change its quality to more environmentally friendly. As a result, the production becomes cleaner.

Some researchers identify investing in the creation of new technologies with creating eco-innovations. At this point it is important to bear in mind that the concept of eco-innovation exists in different forms in the subject literature. Therefore, eco-innovations lead to integrated solutions aimed at decreasing resources and energy expenditures, while at the same time improving the quality of products and services. Another definition is proposed by Triguero, Moreno-Mondéjar and Davia (2013), who define eco-innovation as changes in technology, organizational structure and managing the company which minimize the negative impact on the environment. However, according to Ghisetti, Marzucchi, Montresor (2015), eco-innovation is innovation integrating ecological features of a product and technology. Some researchers identify eco-innovation with each innovation that leads to the achievement of sustainable development by means of limiting the negative impact of production activities on the environment, increasing nature's resilience to environmental pressures or ensuring higher efficiency and responsibility in the field of use of natural resources (Beltrán-Esteve & Picazo-Tadeo 2015). Others claim that eco-innovations are new or significantly improved solutions (products, processes, methods of organization and marketing) whose goal is different than current management of natural resources, in compliance with the rules of sustainable development (sustainable development innovations) (Bossle et al. 2016).

In spite of the diversity of definitions, it should be stated that eco-innovations strive to develop new products and processes that not only provide values to the consumer and business, but also minimize the negative effects of the influence that market entities have on the environment. From such a perspective, the main feature of ecological innovation is creating new environmental technologies that contribute to reducing the environmental burden.

In the context of these reflections, it is worth remembering that creating new technologies for environmental purposes is connected with the concept of Best Available Technology (BAT). The concept of BAT refers to a set of technical facilities, methods of operation and organizational solutions – the best from the perspective of preventing, reduction or neutralization of pollutions, which became applicable on an industrial scale in the case of at least one manufacturer, without entailing excessive costs for adapting to the conditions and needs of another manufacturer. It means that the cost should be proportional to the accomplished effect (Loyon et al. 2016). Therefore, the concept of BAT is connected with utilizing low-waste technologies, using less dangerous substances, developing recovery and recycling of substances created and used in production processes, as well as wastes, improvements to their methods of operating that have been successfully tested on an industrial scale, technological progress and knowledge development (Wen et al. 2016).

In the USA and EU countries, the concept of BAT has been extended by a concept requiring the entities to use "best available technology not entailing excessive costs" (BATNEEC). BATNEEC, together with Council Directive 96/61/WE on integrated IPPC environmental permits, means increased pressure on entrepreneurs in connection with implementation of modern technical and technological solutions based on innovations and scientific research. As a consequence, these actions aim to put in practice the principles of permanent and sustainable development, in order to ensure the high level of entire environmental protection through integrated treatment of the whole process of preventing the emissions of pollutants and, where it is not entirely possible, reducing them to the greatest extent possible. The requirements of the IPPC directive are related to the activities carried out by entrepreneurs mainly in power, mineral, chemical, agriculture and food, paper, textile, tanning, production and processing of metals industries as well as in waste management (Evrard et al. 2016).

With regard to the characteristics of new environmental technologies, it should be stated that investments in new technologies are not only required by directives and legal regulations, but also by rarity of natural resources. Therefore, the environmental conditions creating and implementing new environmental technologies for companies contribute to minimizing negative external effects connected to the functioning of the company in the environment, on the one hand, yet on the other hand, they contribute to sustainable socio-economic development. In view of the above relationships, it is appropriate to present research results concerning the investments of Polish companies in new environmental technologies in the following part of this chapter.

Investments in New Environmental Technologies – Research Results

This section describes collective results carried out over the period 2012–2015 within the framework of the GreenEvo project of the Polish Ministry of Environment and the program of European Commission – The Environmental Technology Verification (ETV). The data concerning investments in new environmental technologies of Polish companies will be analyzed. According to the research results, among the factors determining the creation of new environmental technologies among Polish companies, results of a company's own research and development and identification of market needs are most commonly mentioned. A detailed breakdown has been presented in Figure 1.

Besides the results of a company's own research and development and identification of market needs, the client also has influence on creating new technologies. On the one hand, he orders the product and, on the other hand, he makes valuable comments concerning its functionality and performance. It is worth highlighting here that in some cases it was the clients who were the inspiration for the studied companies to create new environmental technologies; however, more often, the information from the clients contributed to modernizing already existing solutions. It should also be highlighted that new environmental technologies are created thanks to effective cooperation of business and science. It is important to bear in mind that the cooperation between the business and science sectors is playing an increasingly important role in the Polish economy as well as in the market of new environmental technologies. On the one hand, entrepreneurs discover possibilities of carrying out joint projects with scientific institutions. On the other hand, the scientists learn about the specific characteristics of the market and try to meet the expectations of its participants.

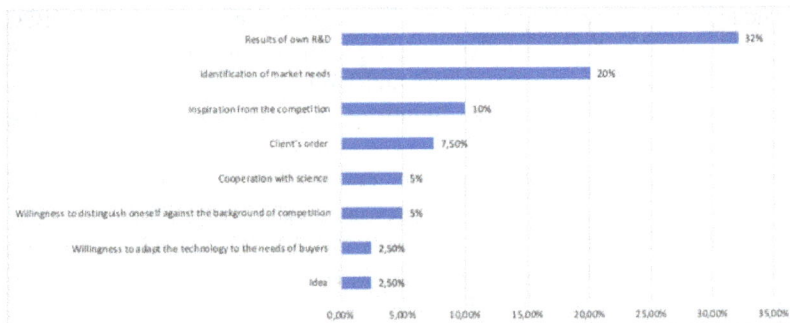

Fig. 1: Determinants of investments in new environmental technologies of Polish companies.

Source: Own study based on: Polski rynek nowych technologii środowiskowych, Warszawa, 2013 and Environment Technology Verification pilot programme, Brussels 2016.

Polish companies investing in new environmental technologies in 80% of cases declare their cooperation with universities and research institutes. Almost 20% explicitly acknowledge that they do not have any such cooperation. The cooperation with universities concerns various forms of collaboration. Particular forms of cooperation are displayed in Figure 2.

Among the forms of cooperation, practical student training and scientific internships occupy a unique position. Therefore, it should be assumed that it is the best way for the companies to obtain candidates for work as well as to acquire new scientific knowledge that may be commercialized.

By analyzing the subsequent results, it can be concluded that for companies creating new environmental technologies, the second-best form of cooperation with entities in the science and research sector is through science centers carrying out commissioned research concerning creating or improving technologies. In addition, 60% of companies contract projects, which are connected with improving existing technologies, to science and research sector entities. The cooperation chiefly concerns implementing particular elements of R&D that, according to respondents, are most often connected with the lack of equipment or scientific knowledge in companies. It is also important that half of the companies contract preparation of expert opinions and analyses to universities and research centers. Their goal is a verification of technical parameters of the offered solutions in order to authenticate them on the market. Another area of cooperation between universities and companies is renting laboratories belonging to the science sector, as well as didactic activities. In this respect, the didactics is connected with conducting seminars and presentations at universities by entrepreneurs and business representatives participating in scientific conferences.

In the context of cooperation between companies creating new environmental technologies with entities of science and research sector, it is also worth

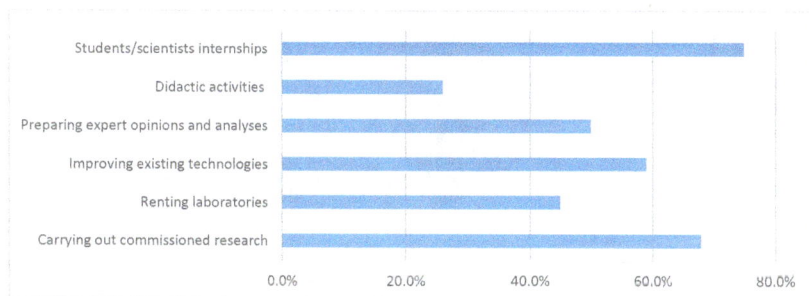

Fig. 2: Cooperation of companies creating new environmental technologies with science.

Source: Own study based on: Polski rynek nowych technologii Środowiskowych, Warszawa, 2013 and Environment Technology Verification pilot programme, Brussels 2016.

presenting the reasons for the lack of cooperation. Diverging goals of science and business (26%), costs of cooperation (24%), lack of trust (22%) and out-dated/lack of research infrastructure at universities (19%) were among the most common obstacles. While analyzing the most important obstacles, it should be noted that the divergence of particular goals may result from the fact that the science and research sector entities do not concentrate on the needs of the market as much as businesses do. It constitutes the main obstacle to undertake joint activities. Another problem is the lack of dedicated financial tools that may support the cooperation with the science sector, which in case of common (according to the entrepreneurs' declarations) overvaluation of research works constitutes a serious barrier. The lack of entrepreneurs' trust in research centers is another barrier. It is a result of entrepreneurs' concerns with possible leaks of their knowledge or universities misappropriating the rights to jointly devel-oped solutions. The last barrier is outdated or lack of research infrastructure at universities that might meet the demand of contemporary business.

Significant supplementing of the analysis concerning the cooperation of new environmental technologies companies with science would be the result of research in collaboration with other entities in the field of implementing new environmental technologies. Figure 3 presents the detailed results.

In the vast majority of cases, the implementations are carried out in collabo-ration with other companies or solely by external companies. This is primarily due to the size of these organizations, the cost of dedicated services, special-izing in performing specific activities, or an option of carrying out supervisory work. Taking into account the size of a company, one can observe that small and medium-sized enterprises mainly carry out independent implementation or in cooperation with external stakeholders. However, big entities usually del-egate the implementation to external companies. In terms of costs of dedicated

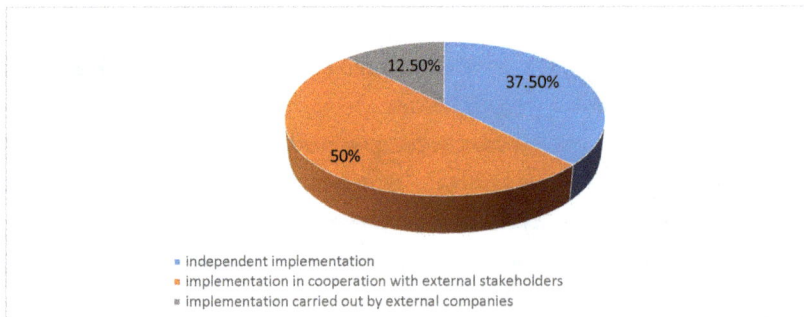

Fig. 3: Cooperation of companies creating new environmental technologies with other entities in the field of implementing new technologies.

Source: Own study based on: Polski rynek nowych technologii Środowiskowych, Warszawa, 2013 and Environment Technology Verification pilot programme, Brussels 2016.

services and specializing in performing specific activities, the delegation of implementation of new environmental technologies or cooperation with other entities depends mostly on the size of the project and its specific nature.

Analyzing the supervisory work of companies, it may be noticed that the implementation of new environmental technologies by partners with company supervision is carried out when the basic activities are carried out by external companies and the supplier mostly executes oversight over the correctness of the work done and integrates the system in such a way that the main project assumptions may be implemented in the end. However, when the implementations are carried out in cooperation with external companies, the companies share the range of implementation activities or, in certain circumstances, the entire workmanship with other entities. This remarkably often concerns creating the finished product, creating a project or configuration of machinery and equipment by external companies.

The results connected with identifying new environmental technologies with eco-innovations are another interesting aspect of the study. Over 70% of the surveyed entities identifies creating new environmental technologies with eco-innovations. Therefore, the entrepreneurs emphasize that the new technology is created as a result of research which frequently has all the traits of basic research. In addition, the entrepreneurs also notice that new technologies are connected with a so-called market destruction, which is reflected in introducing a new solution/product/service to the market. However, 25% of the entrepreneurs clearly state no connection with eco-innovations, arguing that the new technology is chiefly connected with the implementation of a new combination of the factors of production, resulting in the creation of a product or service that is already on the market, in the production and service process. Only 5% of manufacturers had no opinion on this matter, emphasizing that the process of creating new environmental technologies is of no importance to them.

When assessing the importance of financial and non-financial support for a company where a new environmental technology is created, it should be stated that approximately 80% of companies create a new technology based on the resources generated from current sales. Additionally, around 10% acquire money by means of credits or bank loans, whereas 3% obtain money from professional investors or the stock market.

In view of the fact that in the vast majority of cases, the companies creating new environmental technologies rely on their own financial resources, it is worth making a diagnosis of the size of the funding of these works (Figure 4).

The majority of studied companies (25.82%) spend between 3% and 5% of their annual income on creating new environmental technologies. The entities whose level of funding did not exceed 3% (21.74% of companies) as well as those between 5% and 8% (19.78% of companies) accounted for a substantial proportion. The companies spending over 8% on innovative activities constituted the least numerous group.

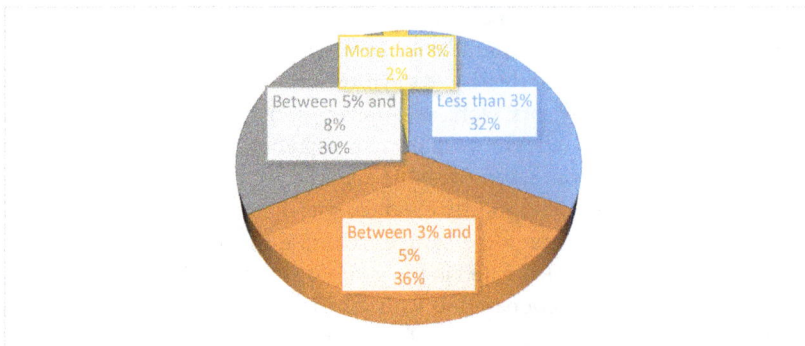

Fig. 4: The size of the funding from own financial resources of works connected with creating new environmental technologies by companies.

Source: Own study based on: Polski rynek nowych technologii Środowiskowych, Warszawa, 2013 and Environment Technology Verification pilot programme, Brussels 2016.

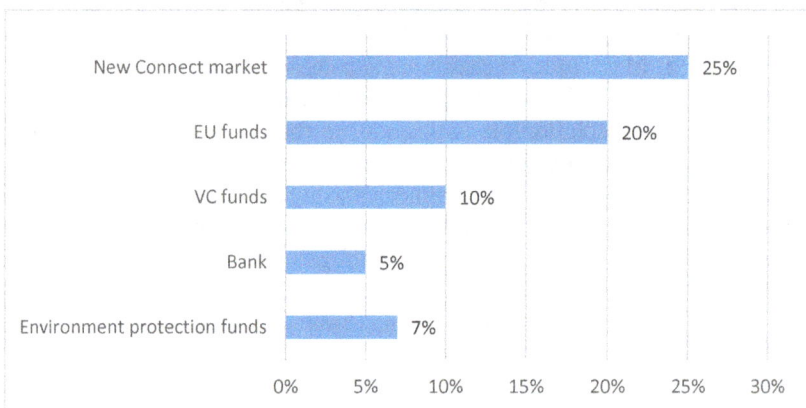

Fig. 5: Awareness with regard to obtaining financial support to create new environmental technologies.

Source: Own study based on: Polski rynek nowych technologii Środowiskowych, Warszawa, 2013 and Environment Technology Verification pilot programme, Brussels 2016.

Taking into account a very small percentage companies utilizing external capital to create new environmental technologies, it is worth making an analysis concerning respondents' awareness with regard to potential sources of financial resources from the market (Figure 5).

Among significant external sources of capital, NewConnect market is enumerated among other things. In this regard, there are a few significant reasons that encourage companies to enter the capital market. The most important

reason is willingness to obtain capital for development. Prestige is also important, as well as benefits resulting from company transparency, including facili-
tating tender participation. However, among the firms that are unwilling to
enter the NewConnect market, the low concern results in most cases from the
lack of need for additional capital in the context of creating new environmental technology and from willingness to preserve independence in managing
the company. What is more, entrepreneurs' unwillingness to enter the New-
Connect market results from the feeling of low and stagnant demand for the
products on the market and also from the fact that in spite of possessing modern environmental technologies, they would obtain low valuation on the stock
exchange market, which could contribute to acquiring too low sums for scheduled further investments.

According to the obtained results, the companies, besides acquiring financial
resources from NewConnect market, indicate EU funds or finding a strategic
partner who, besides capital, would also bring additional benefits, i.e. knowledge and technology transfer from one to the other entity. The smallest number
of respondents indicated obtaining funds for the development of new environmental technologies from the bank or environmental protection funds.

Taking into account the possibility of companies funding the environmental
investments from EU funds, it should be stated that 75% of companies applied
for such support. However, less than 20% of the respondents received funding.
Among the most common sources for which the companies applied were: the
Innovative Economy operational programme (50%), the European Commission's Framework Programme (20%) and the European Commission's LIFE+
Programme (15%). In this respect, one should bear in mind that the use of
European funds for research and development activities may be a source of
competitive advantage for the companies creating new environmental technology. However, big competition can result in a low success rate for a single
company.

Conclusions

Summing up, we must firmly emphasize that creating new environmental technologies is one of the main tasks of contemporary business. In this way, companies create new technological environmental solutions as a result of their own
research and development activities or market needs. Another important matter is also the cooperation of companies with science centers as well as other
entities in implementing new technologies. Thanks to this collaboration, not
only does the transfer of know-how and technology take place, but the companies also enjoy major economies of scale, which condition their growth and
market efficiency. In addition, there still exists quite substantial financing of the
investments connected with creating new technologies from companies' own
resources with a simultaneous dislike of financing the investment process from

external capital resources. Therefore, on the one hand, there is a need for intensifying actions of capital – investment market entities significantly increasing the funding for enterprises of creating new environmental technologies – while simultaneously for the cooperation of these very entities with other external stakeholders who contribute to the processes of companies creating new environmental technologies.

References

Beltrán-Esteve, M, and Picazo-Tadeo, A J 2015 Assessing environmental performance trends in the transport industry: Eco-innovation or catching-up? *Energy Economics*, 51: 570–580.

Bocken, N M P, Farracho, M, Bosworth, R and Kemp, R 2014 The front-end of eco-innovation for eco-innovative small and medium sized companies. *Journal of Engineering and Technology Management*, 31: 43–57.

Bossle, M B, de Barcellos, M D, Vieira, L M and Sauvée, L 2016 The drivers for adoption of eco-innovation. *Journal of Cleaner Production*, 113: 861–872.

Evrard, D, Laforest, V, Villot, J and Gaucher, R 2016 Best Available Technique assessment methods: A literature review from sector to installation level. *Journal of CleanerProduction*, 121: 72–83.

Ghisetti, C, Marzucchi, A and Montresor, S 2015 The open eco-innovation mode. An empirical investigation of eleven European countries. *Research Policy*, 44(5): 1080–1093.

Loyon, L, Burton, C H, Misselbrook, T, Webb, J, Philippe, F X, Aguilar, M and Bonmati, A 2016 Best available technology for European livestock farms: Availability, effectiveness and uptake. *Journal of environmental management*, 166: 1–11.

Triguero, A, Moreno-Mondéjar, L,and Davia, M A 2013 Drivers of different types of eco-innovation in European SMEs. *Ecological economics*, 92: 25–33.

Wang, Z L 2015 Triboelectric nanogenerators as new energy technology and self-powered sensors–Principles, problems and perspectives. *Faraday discussions*, 176: 447–458.

Wen, Z, Meng, F, Di, J and Tan, Q 2016 Technological approaches and policy analysis of integrated water pollution prevention and control for the coal-to-methanol industry based on Best Available Technology. *Journal of CleanerProduction*, 113: 231–240.

Zhang, W F, Dou, Z X, He, P, Ju, X T, Powlson, D, Chadwick, D and Chen, X P 2013 New technologies reduce greenhouse gas emissions from nitrogenous fertilizer in China. *Proceedings of the National Academy of Sciences*, 110(21): 8375–8380.

SECTION 3

Ecoinnovations

Introduction

Joanna Duda

PhD, AGH University of Science and Technology, Kraków, Poland

In the era of globalization, competitiveness of enterprises is of particular importance. It is determined by many factors both external and internal, but it is the innovation that is assigned a special place, because it is widely regarded as a factor determining the development of enterprises.

Schumpeter, who sees innovation in terms of transferring an innovation into material realities, is regarded as the pioneer of this discipline. It implies practical application of new ideas, specific usage of discoveries or inventions that stem from creative thinking. Schumpeter offers a very broad view of innovation without restricting it to merely technical solutions, and claims that innovation encompasses economic undertakings, e.g. acquisition of a new market or application of a new raw material, and is apparent in areas of organisation, management, marketing and interpersonal relations (Schumpeter 1939, p. 84).

Innovation also denotes introduction of a new or a markedly improved solution to process or product (commodities or services) practices of an enterprise by launching the solution in the market or application of a new or improved marketing or organisation solution to operations of an enterprise (Dworecka 2011, p. 10).

How to cite this book chapter:
Duda, J. 2019. Ecoinnovations: Introduction. In: Gąsior, A. (ed.) *Pro-ecological Restructuring of Companies: Case Studies*, Pp. 147–148. London: Ubiquity Press. DOI: https://doi.org/10.5334/bbk.l. License: CC-BY 4.0

These definitions imply that innovation can be understood as a tool or process for creating and using new ideas.

However, with increased awareness of environmental risks and the importance of innovation for the competitiveness and economic development, in the 1990s the concept of eco-innovation emerged. Because of the intensified environmental problems and the search for a new, more sustainable paradigm of economic development after the global crisis, eco-innovations are attracting growing interest from researchers and public authorities.

For eco-innovation we can take actions that improve the efficiency of the use of natural resources in the economy, reduce the negative impact of human activities on the environment or enhance resistance to environmental pressures.

This definition indicates that, in addition to the limitations of the harmful effects of economic processes on the environment, it is also important to ensure productive use of natural resources, and so in addition to the ecological dimension, an economic dimension is also important (cost reduction), as is security (reducing dependence on supplies of raw materials).

Therefore, in this chapter we touch upon six important topics, including environmental benefits created from products, energy use, pollution, international standards, state support of the ecoinnovations and state policy. The last chapter contains two examples of the final benefits for users.

The Benefits of Introducing Non-chromate Technology in Conversion Coating Applied to Aluminum Elements: The ABC Colorex Case Study

Agnieszka Czaplicka-Kotas[*], Mateusz Figiel[†] and Marzena Smol[‡]

*MSc Eng., AGH
†MSc Eng., COLOREX
‡PhD, Mineral and Energy Economy Research Institute,
Polish Academy of Sciences

Introduction

Environmental regulations attach great importance to the monitoring of production's impact on environment. Currently environmental policy in the European Union is governed by the strategies "Europe 2020", as well as "Sustainable Development", and the "7th EAP Environment Action Programme to 2020". Some postulates of these ideas include eco-design and sustainable design, which aim to minimize the adverse effects of production upon the environment. Due to the implementation of the principles of designing environmentally friendly products, it is possible to avoid high emissions and hazardous waste.

An example of an action that would reduce negative impact upon the environment is to switch from chromate to chromate-free conversion coating applied on aluminum elements. The coating's role is to increase corrosion resistance, reduce friction, increase adhesion of other coatings and obtain decorative effects. The benefits of the transition from chromate to chromate-free coating

How to cite this book chapter:
Czaplicka-Kotas, A., Figiel, M. and Smol, M. 2019. The Benefits of Introducing Non-chromate Technology in Conversion Coating Applied to Aluminum Elements: The ABC Colorex Case Study. In: Gąsior, A. (ed.) *Pro-ecological Restructuring of Companies: Case Studies*, Pp. 149–158. London: Ubiquity Press. DOI: https://doi.org/10.5334/bbk.m. License: CC-BY 4.0

leads to an improvement of both its technological roles as well as environmental factors. Technology chromate based on hexavalent chromium is usually used in the industry powder coating due to its very good corrosion-resistant capabilities. However, there is a potential danger of introducing chromium into the environment, because it can cause mutagenic changes and carcinogenic properties to exist within the environment. Therefore, the aim is to introduce a non-chromate treatment, for example, based on compounds of fluorides, titanium, zirconium and organic compounds that are more environmentally friendly.

The company in question, ABC Colorex Ltd., is a company operating in the field of powder coating and metal processing services. One of the company's strategic goals is to increase production capacity while minimizing the impact of the production on the environment. This plant is an example of the implementation of good practices in the field of production. It is a pioneer in the implementation of non-chromate technology based on titanium compounds.

Ecological Way in Product Design

One of the main horizontal objectives implemented by the European Commission is to increase the efficiency of raw materials in the Europe 2020 strategy. The measures focus on maintaining balance between environmental policy and demands of the market. Due to an innovative way related to the eco-production and services, as well as better estimation of the life cycle of products in the value chain, they can result in more efficient use of raw materials (Lacy & Rutqvist 2015). The main idea that stimulates the optimal management of raw materials and energy is the circular economy (CE). This concept relates to the closed-loop product lifecycle, which results in an increased re-use of waste.

A potential tool that may influence a more efficient implementation of the circular economy is eco-design, which is defined as "the integration of environmental aspects into product design with the aim of improving the environmental performance of the product throughout its whole life cycle"[1]. According to the European Comission[2] activities related to, among others, eco-design and waste prevention can result in minimizing the net expenses by 600 billion euros and reduce annual greenhouse gas emissions by 2–4%. The main purpose of eco-design is to reduce negative factors affecting the environmental life cycle of products (Burchart-Korol 2010). ISO 14062 is the main guideline which regulates relations between the environment and design at every stage of the process (Stachura & Karwasz 2007).

Designing products according to the principles of sustainable development pertains to two areas: eco-design and sustainable design. One of the conditions for the development of eco-design is sustainable product design. The difference between these two concepts results from the fact that sustainable design also takes into account the following aspects: economical, social and ecological, i.e. it aims for the "triple bottom-line" (Diegel et al. 2016). Vezolli and Manzini identified four fundamental aspects that influence the introduction of sustainable system design according to ecological factors, namely the choice of environmentally friendly materials, implementation of the design that brings less ecological damage, creation of a sustainable production-consumption system, promotion of sustainable lifestyle (Vezzoli & Manzini 2008).

Description of the Company ABC Colorex Ltd.

ABC Colorex Ltd. is a company operating in the field of powder coating services and metal processing. In 1992 the first headquarters was opened in Cracow in a two-storey building with the purpose of powder coating services.

In the same year, Technology Center Powder P.U.P.H. Colorex was founded in ABC Colorex Ltd. The company was developing dynamically, quickly acquiring new satisfied customers, and in a short time it has become the largest provider of powder coating services.

In June 2000, these very elements enabled the launch of new headquarters in Cracow, where a branch under the name ABC Colorex Ltd. was created, which met the standards of the twenty-first century in the field of metal coating. The new plant had more than 3500 m² of usable area. There were two lines created for hand painting details and chemical baths. The plant meets the most stringent global requirements in the field of chemical surface treatment as well as powder coating materials made of steel and aluminum.

On 21 August 2001, the plant became a member of the Association of Contractors Surface Treatment Aluminum QUALIPOL, which on behalf of Qualicoat from Zurich, conducts continuous monitoring of powder coating with the Quality Mark in terms of production and organization. In the same year, as the fifth company in Poland, it has been awarded a certificate of quality Qualicoat No. 1505 issued by the Association for Quality Control Powder Coating, Paints and Coatings QUALICOAT in Zurich.

Another significant document for the company is a certificate issued in June 2002 by IGP Pulvertechnik, a supplier of powder coatings. The supplier allowed ABC Colorex Ltd. to use paints from a unique series, namely IGP HWF 2001, for which the manufacturer gives 25-year warranty for coating durability.

The plant has also received other certificates from suppliers of powder coatings such as: Synthatec for HB Fuller lacquers with 25-year warranty period, Akzo Nobel with a 10-year warranty period, Jotun and many others.

In May 2006, ABC Colorex Ltd was certified ISO 9001: 2000 in the field of powder coating, which was issued by the certifying company DEKRA INTERTEK CERTIFICATION.

In 2004, the plant started the first fully automatic lacquering line with a nine-step surface preparation, including phosphorence zinc. It has been dedicated for customers from the household appliances market, who provided numbers of elements. A year later, in Krakow another fully automated line was launched, whose customers are mainly contractors from the automotive industry.

Further demand for this type of activity has led to the opening of new powder coating lines, both manual and automated ones. In December 2006, the first powder coating line in Poland was created with the process of preparing the surface for elements 15 m long, and, in exceptional situations, which can implement a technological process for profiles up to 16.8 m long.

Then, in 2008, a production hall was constructed that is adapted to the needs of a machine park; it was significantly expanded in January 2014. Currently, its total floor area is over 3000 m². There are machines for metal flashing, such as: laser, guillotine, bending, rolling mill and others related to a specific production. Thanks to this, the area of operations was expanded and customers are provided with comprehensive services.

In 2012, the event that helped the company to gain the leading position in Poland was building a modern production hall with a fully automated powder coating line for aluminum with baths for preparing the surface of chromate-free bathing process.

Currently, the plant has 15 powder coating lines in three locations, including three automatic lines on the area of over 12,000 m². On premises, there is also the first station in Poland for corrosion monitoring, which has been providing information about the properties of anti-corrosion powder coating for over 15 years.

What distinguished ABC Colorex Ltd. was the introduction in 2006 of innovative technologies in the field of powder coating associated with hot stamping. The execution of décor is based on transferring a pattern made from foil in the process of pigment sublimation on the metal surface covered by a special polyurethane powder by means of modern machinery. The result is a durable yet exceptionally decorative surface which can resemble wood, stone or any other pattern.

Comparison of the Chromate and Chromate-free Processes

Applying a conversion coating is a method for refining metals and their alloys. It is created in a specific chemical solution during the processes, such as immersion or spraying. The process is divided into two stages. The first one is an artificially induced and controlled corrosion process, followed by a reaction of the anion contained in the solution of the metal cation, which causes insoluble substances and creates a layer that is closely adherent to the element. Coating can be dived into phosphate, chromate, oxide, polymer and oxalate. Its role is to significantly increase corrosion resistance, reduce friction, increase adhesion of other coatings and obtain decorative effects. In the analyzed plant, three kinds of coating are applied: amorphous iron phosphate for steel and chromium and titanium dioxide for elements made from aluminum.

Iron phosphating process is based on a reaction on the metal surface submerged in a solution of phosphoric acid (V) and metal hydrogenphosphate, in this case trivalent iron. The second substance, which is water soluble, reacts with metal, which results in a shift of the chemical balance of a dissolved salt. A sparingly soluble salt, iron (III) hydrogenphosphate, is created which infiltrates the intercrystalline areas of the coating. The reaction is as follows (Gumowska, Harańczyk & Rudnik 2007):

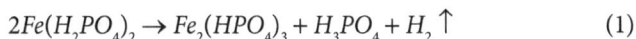

$$2Fe(H_2PO_4)_2 \rightarrow Fe_2(HPO_4)_3 + H_3PO_4 + H_2 \uparrow \tag{1}$$

Phosphating processes is preceded by the process of cleaning and degreasing. Immediately before it an additional washing in demineralized water must be executed to prevent neutralization of the phosphate solution. Phosphate coating has a crystalline structure, porous and thickness in the range of 1–20 μm.

Chromate (Cr +6) yellow – a process where during the electrochemical or chemical treatment for metal elements, the powder coating is immersed in a bath containing compounds such as chromic acid anhydride (VI) CrO_3, sodium chromate or potassium. The process may either take the form of immersion or spraying. It is a kind of metal passivation, which significantly improves anti-corrosion protection. The surface detail has been subjected to passivation by creating on it an oxide layer during the process of bathing. The process has to be shut down in a controlled way, and the metal needs to be assisted in the transition into ionic form, which means creating a chromate conversion coating. To achieve this effect, one has to add chemical substances consisting of anions such as sulphates or chlorides into a solution containing hexavalent chromium ions. It should also be noted that sulfuric acid (VI), which is a depassivating substance, is another compound occurring during the reaction. The following reaction takes place in the process (Drápala et al. 2007):

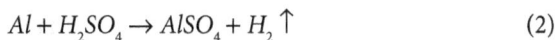

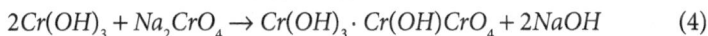

$$Al + H_2SO_4 \rightarrow AlSO_4 + H_2 \uparrow \tag{2}$$

$$12H_2 + 4Na_2Cr_2O_7 + 3O_2 \rightarrow 2Cr(OH)_3 + 2Na_2CrO_4 + 3H_2O \tag{3}$$

$$2Cr(OH)_3 + Na_2CrO_4 \rightarrow Cr(OH)_3 \cdot Cr(OH)CrO_4 + 2NaOH \tag{4}$$

The creation of the chromate coating is the transformation of aluminum into an ionic form and separation of hydrogen (Reaction 2). On the border solution, the pH of the metal increasing through the decrease in concentration of hydrogen cations and precipitate appears in the form of chromium hydroxide (VI) (Reaction 3), and then through the creation of layer of water soluble compound $Cr(OH)_3 \cdot Cr(OH)CrO_4$, which is the anticipated coating (Reaction 4) (ABC Colorex Ltd. External material).

Before this process, a preliminary preparation of the surface and rinsing in demineralized water is required. After that, the rinsing process must be repeated.

The acidity of the bath is pH 1.5-2.5, the temperature is 20–35°C and aluminum is immersed in the bath for 5–8 minutes. The time depends on the amount of previously digested aluminum. After chromate treatment, elements have a slightly yellow-green color. The coating is rough, has a thickness of 0.01–1.5 μm, it is watertight, easy to color, abrasion-resistant and has very good adhesion. This treatment (Chromate Cr (VI)) is toxic and its waste has a negative impact on the environment. Therefore, in the future, all companies will be obliged by the European Union to withdraw from using this method. For this reason, new alternatives for this treatment are currently being researched. So far, baths containing chromium (III), organic compounds, or inorganic compounds do not give as good final results as hexavalent chromium, therefore it is still widely used.

Titanium dioxide (TiO_2) conversion coatings is the second kind of chemical treatment of aluminum used in the described plant. It is a chromium-free process based on fluorides of titanium, zirconium and organic compounds. It was introduced on the new Hall X, where the line for powder coating is fully automatic, because of the need to withdraw baths based on hexavalent chromium in the future. This is an immersion process (there is also a spray process), wherein the pH is 3.1–3.4. The immersion time is 60–120 seconds at 25°C. The obtained coating is colorless, with a thickness of 10–30 μm and weight of 3–10 mg of Ti /m^2. The reactions are as follows (Błachowicz 2011):

$$2Al + 6H^+ \rightarrow 2Al^{3+} + 3H_2 \uparrow \tag{5}$$

$$Al^{3+} + Ti^{4+} + F^- + 4H_2O \rightarrow Al(O_2H)Ti(O_2H)F + 6H^+ \tag{6}$$

First, the process of digesting aluminum takes place, resulting in improved adhesion. Due to the presence of hydrogen cations, aluminum cations are released (Reaction 5), which then, reacting with cations of titanium, fluoride anions and water, form a protective conversion coating on the metal surface (Reaction 6).

One of the main goals of the ABC Colorex Ltd. enterprise is introducing efficient production systems as well as realizing the postulates of environmental policies. Implementation of the oxide conversion coating as a replacement for chromate coatings used for aluminum components is an example of their activities.

To obtain a conversion coating, formulations based on hexavalent chrome (Chromate 12 LC Repl) and a non-chromate treatment (Nabutan 810) can be used. The parameters of these two formulations have similar physical and chemical properties (Table 1). A significant difference was observed for treatment times used during spraying, which is related to coating thickness. After the chromate treatment the coating is 15 times thicker than after the chromium-free one. Parameters of the preparations differ also in terms of the value of pH. Chromium-free passivation shows a different acidity of the solution, and the product itself, which based on complexing compounds, titanium compounds and polymers, in a short time creates a durable metal surface layers of colored interference.

Based on the literature review and internal company research, it has been demonstrated that in terms of corrosion resistance chromate is a more effective technology than non-chromate (Kwiatkowski 2009; Winiarski & Szczygieł 2012; Rubel, Tomassi & Ziółkowski 2009; Landra 2002). However, chromate

Table 1: Comparison of physical and chemical properties of a preparation based on non-chromate treatment and on hexavalent chromium treatment.

Parametr	Chromate 12 LC	Nabutan 810
Temperature	20–35°C	20–35 °C
Processing time (spraying)	2–5 min.	15–60 sec.
Processing time (immersion)	45–120 sec.	60–120 sec.
Spray pressure	0.7–0.9 bar	0.5–1.0 bar
pH value	1.5–1.9	3.1–3.4

Source: The safety data sheet for preparation: Chromate 12 LC Repl, Nabutan 810.

treatment has many defects, mainly due to the presence of toxic compounds. In accordance with the principles of sustainable design, the aim is a highly effective product that is also environmentally friendly. Therefore, it seems appropriate to conduct research on increasing corrosion resistance using a non-chromate passivation. The possibilities can be discerned by improving pre-treatment or electrolytic processes (Kwiatkowski 2009).

Recent studies of ABC Colorex Ltd. have shown that the aluminum corrosion resistance associated with the use of non-chromate technology are comparable with those associated with the use of chromate technology. Corrosion tests were conducted on six pieces of 10-centimeter aluminum Machu and salt chamber. The Machu test (accelerated corrosion test) was performed on the three profiles slit on a metal cross (1 mm width) and immersed in a mixture based on NaCl, CH_3COOH, H_2O and then heated to 37°C. After the test, there were no signs of the appearance of corrosion, which proved the very good quality of the chemical preparation (Nabutan 810). The other three cut profiles were immersed in the salt spray for 1000 hours. This study was carried out in accordance with standard ISO 9227. After the test, no changes and approaches in excess of 1 mm in length were detected (Świerczek & Zając 2013).

A very important aspect of the process of powder coating is the adhesion of the applied paint coating. In order to compare the two variants of the chemical surface preparation prior to painting, ABC Colorex Ltd. performed an adhesion test according to EN ISO 2409. After a crosswise cut was made on the lacquered elements, there were no problems with the adhesion of the coating in both cases (Gt = 0). Comparing the characteristics associated with adhesion, much better results are obtained by processing based on titanium than chromium (VI). The process based on yellow chromate often results in an excessively thick chromium layer, which results in dusting and reduces adhesion. In the case of non-chromate treatment being applied it is possible to have more control over the coating thickness (Świerczek & Zając 2013).

Another disadvantage of the bath based on the compounds of Cr (VI) is a high share of carcinogenic compounds. In order to regulate the content of chromium (VI) in the European Union, the Directive Restriction of Hazardous Substances 2011/65/EU of 8 June 2011 is applied. Chromate baths, due to the high content of toxic substances, encounter limitations; for example, this type of treatment is banned in the food industry (Landra 2002).

In contrast, the chromate method's undoubted advantage is the low cost. Based on the financial analysis performed by ABC Colorex Sp Ltd., which compared the economic and technological factors, it was found that non-chromate processing technology is more demanding than chromate processing technology.

However, the cost may be increased due to the necessity of acid neutralization bath after chromated yellow. During the reduction of chromium it is necessary to acidify the bath; to this end a technical grade of sulfuric acid 94% is used (the annual consumption of 200 l.). This process is carried out by use of the reduction reaction of Cr (VI) to Cr (III) by sodium sulfate (IV) (Na_2SO_3) (1500 kg/year) or hydrazine (750 kg/year). By reducing hexavalent chromium to trivalent chromium Cr_2O_3 is precipitated. The colorimetric method is used to control sulfur content. As a result of the acid neutralization bath after the yellow chromate process a hazardous waste code is formed 11 01 05 "Acids not otherwise specified" (ABC Colorex Ltd. IPPC).

It should be stressed that it is much easier to dispose of waste water after non-chromate treatment. Technological sewage after processing yellow chromium has to be recirculated. This process is based on a demineralization water treatment after the yellow chromate is treated with ion exchangers (cation + acid anion). For the regeneration of the cations, hydrochloric acid technical is used (6000 liters / year), and for the regeneration of anions sodium hydroxide (1500 kg / year). During the process of setting on ion exchangers, leachate is produced, which is placed in containers and defined as hazardous waste code 11 01 09* "Sludges and filter cakes containing dangerous substances". Chemical baths after chemical treatment are considered liquid waste which is not taken into account in the balance. The next step is to exchange, and then neutralize. Recovery of water and concentrated salt concentrate takes place in a vacuum evaporator. The recovered water is reused in the process, and the concentrate is considered waste and collected in sealed containers. The amount of waste water in the Colorex plant is 220 m³ per year. Thanks to the recovery, the water is reused in the process (ABC Colorex Ltd. IPPC).

Conclusion

In recent years, sustainable design and eco design have grown in popularity. They are promoted by the European Union as environmental tools, which are designed to fulfill the demands of the "sustainable development" strategy or the idea of a "circular economy". One of the examples of companies that implement environmentally friendly production is ABC Colorex Ltd. This plant pays attention to the legal conditions as well as efficiency of production. The action that is intended to implement eco design is introducing non-chromate technology in conversion coating applied to aluminum elements.

Another important aspect in achieving the objectives of environmental policies are the principles of sustainable design. The product is considered in terms of three aspects, ie. economic, social and environmental. Considering the costs, processing based on the compounds of Cr (VI) is more profitable than non-chromate passivation. However, with reference to the long-term goals, which are associated with the development of innovative technologies that are environmentally friendly, investment in the alternative method of creating of chromate-free conversion coating appears to be better in view of economic factors.

The main reason associated with the reduced use of baths based on hexavalent chromium is their toxic effect on the environment. The yellow chromate process is burdensome for the environment because it emits carcinogenic and mutagenic compounds of chromium, leading to the formation of defects in the chromosomes of organisms. Based on previous studies it was found that regardless of the amount of Cr (VI) used in the process the reaction was still damaging to the environment.

In terms of technology a yellow chromate treatment undoubtedly has improved properties related to the corrosion resistance. However, current research shows that it is possible to increase the effectiveness of methods of corrosion protection in the chromium-free process. The big advantage of the use of chromium-free conversion coating technology is getting much better adhesion than by using yellow chromate. Non-chromate technology is also associated with easier control of thickness of the coating.

Based on the analysis, it was found that the company ABC Colorex Ltd. implements the principles of sustainable design in the powder coating industry. According to the policy of the European Union, which supports eco design as well as sustainable design, innovative solutions and improvements in production in this chemical sector should be striven for.

Notes

[1] Directive 2009/125/EC of the European Parliament and of the Council of 21 October 2009 establishing a framework for the setting of ecodesign requirements for energy-related products
[2] Communication from the commission to the European Parliament, the council, the European economic and social committee and the committee of the regions towards a circular economy: A zero-waste programme for Europe.

References

ABC Colorex Ltd 2008 Integrated Pollution Prevention and Control (IPPC) for Powder Coating.

Błachowicz, E 2011 *Proste i skuteczne metody. Chemiczna obróbka powierzchni w malarniach i w innych zakładach produkcyjno-usługowych*, Lakiernictwo przemysłowe, nr 3(71), maj – czerwiec, p. 72–74.

Burchart-Korol, D 2010 Ekoprojektowanie – holistyczne podejście do projektowania (Eco-design-holistic approach to design). *Problemy Ekologii (Ecological Issues)*, 14(3) p. 119-120, maj-czerwiec Available at http://yadda.icm.edu.pl/yaddaelement/bwmeta1.element.baztecharticle-BAR8-0005-0016/c/ httpwww_bg_utp_edu_plartpe1-32010burchart.pdf [Last accessed 30.09.2016].

Communication from the commission to the European Parliament, the council, the european economic and social committee and the committee of the regions towards a circular economy: A zero waste programme for Europe.

Diegel, O, Kristav, P, Motte, D and Kianian B 2016 Additive Manufacturing and Its Effect on Sustainable Design [in] *Handbook of Sustainability in Additive Manufacturing Volume 1*, Springer Singapore, p.77–78.

Directive 2009/125/EC of the European Parliament and of the Council of 21 October 2009 establishing a framework for the setting of ecodesign requirements for energy-related products.

Drápala, J, Kořeny R, Louda, P et al. 2007 *Aluminium Materials and Technologies from A to Z*, Adin, Prešov.

Gumowska, W, Harańczyk, I and Rudnik, E 2007 *Korozja i ochrona metali ćwiczenia laboratoryjne*, AGH Uczelniane Wydawnictwa Naukowo-Dydaktyczne, Kraków.

Kwiatkowski, L 2009 *Podatność na korozję i skuteczność aktualnych metod ochrony przed korozją stopów aluminium stosowanych w budownictwie*, Inżynieria powierzchni 4, p. 24–32.

Lacy, P and Rutqvist, J 2015 *Waste to Wealth: The Circular Economy Advantage.* London: Springer.

Landra, T 2002 *Przygotowanie powierzchni odlewów do malowania farbami proszkowymi*, Archiwum Odlewnictwa, Rocznik 2, Nr 3 PAN, Katowice p. 79.

Rubel, E, Tomassi P and Ziółkowski, J 2009 *Najlepsze Dostępne Techniki (BAT) - Wytyczne dla powierzchniowej obróbki metali i tworzyw sztucznych*, Instytut Mechaniki Precyzyjnej; Ministerstwo Środowiska, Warszawa, p. 26.

Stachura, M and Karwasz, A 2007 *Eko projektowanie w praktyce*, Zeszyty Naukowe Politechniki Poznańskiej, Budowa Maszyn i Zarządzanie Produkcją Nr 5, p. 54.

Świerczek, K and Zając, W 2013 *Opinia o innowacyjności bezchromowego procesu przygotowania aluminium do lakierowania proszkowego wykonana dla instalacji w firmie ABC Colorez Ltd*, Kraków 31 Lipca.

Winiarski, J and Szczygieł, B 2012 *Właściwości ochronne bezchromowych powłok konwersyjnych osadzanych z kąpieli na bazie związków Ti(IV), Mn(II) oraz kwasu fosforowego modyfikowanej dodatkiem organicznym*, Ochrona przed Korozją 5 p. 224–228.

Vezzoli, C and Manzini, E 2008 *Design for Enviromental Sustainability*, London: Springer London.

Pollutions - Social Responsibility and Green Banks as a Driver for Sustainable Development in Ukraine, on the Example of Privatbank

Ianina Tkachenko* and Liudmyla Huliaieva[†]

*PhD (Economic Sciences), The Head of Finance Chair of The Academy of Labor, Social Relations and Tourism (ALSRT)

[†]PhD (Economic Sciences), Scientific Secretary, Associate Professor of the Finance Chair of the Economics Department of The Academy of Labor, Social Relations and Tourism (ALSRT)

Introduction

One of the biggest domestic banks in Ukraine is interviewed within the research. Established in 1992, PrivatBank became a state-owned company (Statute 2018). This is the bank that owns 42.27% of assets, 32.72% of capital and 39.61% of credit and investment portfolios of the banking system the of Ukraine, as of 1 October 2016. According to market research carried out by Gfk Ukraine in the fourth quarter of 2015, 40.2% of individual clients considered PrivatBank to be their main bank. Privat is also the leader in the sphere of financial services for corporate clients. Thus, the share of corporate customers who use the services of Privatbank, is 42.6%.

The Bank's network in Ukraine comprises the following (PrivatBank 2016):

- 2.5 thousand branches
- 7200 ATMs

How to cite this book chapter:
Tkachenko, I. and Huliaieva, L. 2019. Pollutions - Social Responsibility and Green Banks as a Driver for Sustainable Development in Ukraine, on the Example of Privatbank. In: Gąsior, A. (ed.) *Pro-ecological Restructuring of Companies: Case Studies*, Pp. 159–169. London: Ubiquity Press. DOI: https://doi.org/10.5334/bbk.n. License: CC-BY 4.0

- 12,500 self-service terminal (SSTs)
- 1400 postamats

Overestimating importance of PrivatBank as that of an employer in the Ukrainian labour market would be difficult. More than 35,000 people are employed in this bank. PrivatBank is a socially responsible bank and employs people with disabilities (4% of the total workforce). Furthermore, PrivatBank offers a full social-benefits package, a paid annual vacation of 24 calendar days, a concession-lending system, participation in the private pension fund programme, and travel vouchers at discounted prices for adults and children. PrivatBank has been recognized as an innovator in the Ukrainian market and worldwide. Thi is despite the relatively low level of the financial market of Ukraine in comparison with European countries and the crisis situation in the banking system of Ukraine (in 2014–2016 84 insolvent banks were removed from the market; that is 45.6% of their total number).

According to NACE classification (KVED 2016) PrivatBank is universal bank and provides banking services to the population and legal entities; payment, depository services, equity account, securities brokerage and other banking services with the transition from servicing in bank branches to training of customers for application of remote banking instruments.

Company and Restructuring

The bank represents the quaternary sector of the economy. In general, the process of pro-ecological restructuring is very useful for a deposit corporation because it brings a lot of positive transformations to the bank, namely increasing the bank's clients, because of the innovative bank service with the transition from servicing in bank branches to training of customers in the application of remote banking instruments, operative cost reducing, increased profitability and so on.

The decision to enact pro-ecological restructuring in this deposit corporation was made by a manager of the company. The main reasons for it were the changes in technology, the need to improve the financial situation of the company and the qualitative changes.

PrivatBank has already achieved some objectives in this sphere, among which are improvement of organization, financial restructuring, ecological restructuring and employment restructuring. When discussing the socio-economical aspect, we should define the gained benefits: customer and local community loyalty, boost to the reputation and increased market share. Everything mentioned above was achieved by business planning, current asset optimization, program of development, corporate and social responsibility realization, optimization of operative process and implementation of strategies for social responsibility.

Detailed company information is given in Table 1.

Table 1: Pro-ecological restructuring of quaternary sector.

Company	Reasons for pro-ecological restructuring	Decision-maker (who has decided about this kind of process?)	Duration of restructuring (How long has this process taken?)	Made objectives	Advantage or disadvantage of socio-economical aspect of restructuring	Were pro-ecological activities taken as an objective of the restructuring?
			Quaternary sector (economy of knowledge)			
PrivatBank	The need to facilitate the financial situation of the company; low productivity / financial losses; improving the efficiency of the organizational structure	Board of directors	Less than 12 months	Organization improvement; ecological restructuring; employment restructuring	Employees' and customers' loyalty; image and reputation	Business planning; current asset optimization; current cost reducing; strategy implementation of corporative and social responsibility

Source: own calculation based on Privatbank official site information https://en.privatbank.ua.

PrivatBank is the leading banks in Ukraine in the implementation of environmental initiatives, focusing on the strategy development for the "green bank" model. The first step in this direction was the implementation of the practice of a "green office" in all divisions of the bank across the country. In a fairly short time, all documentation was transferred from the paper bank to the electronic one. The environmental technology cash collection was introduced into the bank. It is important to point out that the bank not only introduces environmental component to its business model, but also strongly promotes environmental and social responsibility of its corporate and private clients. PrivatBank promotes the emergence of new environmental trends in Ukrainian society, through numerous environmental and social orientation projects:

- The "green office". In 2016, thanks to the work of electronic document management systems and the electronic banking systems of PrivatBank, the bank employees and its customers have saved more than 473 tons of paper, which means a saving of 13.5 hectares of forest. Also, PrivatBank annually saves more than 20 tons of paper by introducing electronic services providing information and a digital system for processing incoming correspondence – letters and requests of customers. On admission to the bank, all external correspondence is transferred into electronic form, and the majority of responses to customer requests are provided by email or ATMs and bank terminals.
- The introduction of new technologies in banking leads to reduction in the use of material resources as well as accelerates the "greening" of the real economy.

PrivatBank is one of the most high-tech world banks. "SMS-banking" (1999), OTP passwords via SMS (2000), P2P, transfers between cards (2003), "Electronic rest" (2009), "Online –inkasatsiya" (2010) and others are among the technologies that PrivatBank has been first to implement in the world. PrivatBank has become one of the first banks to implement a contactless technology for customer service via QR codes. Using QR, PrivatBank customers can log into their online bank accounts to withdraw cash from ATMs, to fill the car at the gas station, as well as make orders and pay at restaurants using their cell phones. Nowadays every third client of the bank enjoys its services via the Internet and mobile applications.

Ukrainian Privatbank, which is among the leading innovative banks in the world, has become one of the heroes of the digital banking guru Chris Skinner's new book, *Value Web* (Skinner 2016). As Skinner says, financial markets are reassessing their business models now. While not everybody has understood yet what is happening, the banks' visionaries who are integrators, aggregators and creators of banking services, divided into components, have appeared in the world. A good example of this is PrivatBank in Ukraine. Skinner belives that the PrivatBank team showes how innovative a modern bank can be. PrivatBank has opened API and created a transparent IT architecture, which easily interacts with external developers. Moreover, the author calls PrivatBank one of the first banks in the world to offer services on the API base and hundreds of different APIs, on which base, as with blocks.

Ukrainian PrivatBank was one of the first in the world to establish commercial mass production of robots allowing companies and entrepreneurs to maintain communication with customers and sell products via smartphone without cost supporting of mobile applications and platforms. Over 205 thousand corporate clients of PrivatBank and 450 thousand entrepreneurs receive free robots in Privat24 Sender, which are ready to communicate with customers and accept payment by bank cards.

Users of iPhone Privat24 are the first in the world who are able to transfer money and fill in a mobile phone's account directly to their contact on iMessage, without needing to run applications and fill in the receiver's card number.

Privat24 became the first in the world with an iOs payment plan that uses new possibilities of the iPhone and iMessage messenger base, realized in the tenth version of the Apple OS. As communicated in PrivatBank, the updated version of Privat24 allows the owners of iPhone to make exchanges between them directly through Messenger. All payment transactions and services, including service ordering are available from computer or a smartphone using the Privat24 Internet banking system.

Implementation of new technologies gives concrete positive results in reducing the negative impact of people on the environment. Active usage of Internet Banking "Private 24" by customers, as well as mobile banking and massive response of customers to the bank's appeals to refuse the print paper check.

The PrivatBank gives Ukrainian business the opportunity for free usage of effective the electronic document management system "PryvatDok", which motivates (due to effective tools) customers to move to the "green offices" operating model. This modern and secure service allows any private company or public company to give up paper documents, reduce costs and increase business efficiency. The system of electronic document flow is a "cloud" technology that does not require the customer's bank expenses for the development of IT infrastructure.

Another innovative environmental initiative in the business process of the bank is an environmental project of recycling of lead seals. As a result of environmental monitoring of work conducted by specialists of Privatbank, it was found that used lead seals often fall in the waste, which could lead to further risk of contamination of soil and groundwater. Now, lead seals that are used by the bank in the process of cash collection are collected and directly transferred to recycling.

• The implementation of sustainable environmental initiatives in local communities. The systematic action of cleaning up the environment, with active involvement of employees and bank customers as well as local communities, is held. Banking units, along with local communities, hold "green" Saturdays all over Ukraine to make the country cleaner through their efforts. Bankers, bank clients and partners clean parks, gardens, promenades and recreational areas through joint efforts. For example, in 2015, the bank's initiative was supported by more than 150 thousand caring people from 1360 cities of Ukraine. Following the "green" initiative of the bank, 500 thousand hectares of urban parks and recreation areas were cleaned, 1500 tons of garbage were removed and nearly 20 hectares of forest were planted. Moreover, large enterprises, including hundreds of Ukrainian companies, government agencies, factories and football clubs spend their Saturdays together with the bank.

Another pilot project is the establishing of Ukraine's largest network of bike parking by PrivatBank. Nowadays there are more than 400 bike parkings near the bank branches, and clients of offices can comfortably park their bikes in large cities and in rural areas.

Travel by bicycle in the city is a fashionable trend and saves fuel, but in the Ukrainian villages, biking is one of the main means of transportation.
• Educational activities amongst Ukrainians on resource conservation and eco-technologies.

The PrivatBank has now launched a new educational project, "Saving together!" through which customers of the bank and all the people of Ukraine are able to share their experiences and tips on how to conserve energy and other resources, as well as effective usage of resources and favorable choice of banking services. As a result of such a project, the folk encyclopaedia of economic activity is planning to be created.

The project aims at encouraging people to consolidate and help each other in the difficult economic situation in Ukraine. At a special site of the project, everybody can share how to save on food, clothing, entertainment or household items. Site users can not only read, but also evaluate each benefit of advice and vote for it. The expert group of PrivatBank will select the best advice and give monthly prizes to authors.
• The implementation of sustainable environmental initiatives in the business system of customers. Privatbank launched kub.pb.ua – a service of national lending for Ukrainian businesses, which is expected to be a powerful investment platform for implementation. The service allows small business and entrepreneurs to involve money for its development from individuals and companies and let the residents of the country invest money in Ukrainian business. The project aims at helping entrepreneurs in Ukraine, giving small business and the population the opportunity to receive loans quickly and transparently. It should become a powerful impetus for the development of small businesses and self-employment in Ukraine, for the revival of the credit market and for increasing the number of jobs in the country, particularly in environmental initiatives and social entrepreneurship. Entrepreneurs and businesses (restaurants, bakeries, shoe shops, photo studios, clothing

stores etc.) interested in attracting investments will receive funding up to 300 thousand UAH at the site, and the application not only presents the business and plans for its development, but also offers additional bonuses and discounts for future investors. The online application "kub" will be active within two weeks: if the project collects the required amount, it will be recalculated to the owner of the company as the paid loan.

To best protect investments, the leading specialists of the bank hold a careful selection of projects for funding, based primarily on the characteristics of the current business and prospects of its development, rather than on collateral. To ensure protection, all attachments are also insured.

Within the new project, the incomes of investors will be higher than the deposits offered by bank, through direct investment in a business without the mediation of the financial institution. Investments can be counted from any bank card, and 25% of annual income will be paid monthly to the card. The PrivatBank, as the organizer of the platform, undertakes to relend the borrower in case he faces difficulties in loan repayment to investor, so the investor definitely gets their money back. Also, all loans in the "kub", and investments respectively will be fully insured by the insurance company.

The kub.pb.ua platform operates within the national program of small business development "Country of entrepreneurs", initiated by PrivatBank. This project will help everybody who wishes to start a business, and will help businesses to enjoy free advice and assistance.

• Increased transparency of the bank and its clients motivation to openness. Ukraine's largest bank, PrivatBank, was recognized as a leader in a rating of bank openness compiled by the Ukrainian credit rating agency (UCRA, 2015). It is worth mentioning the bank site, which is not only an important source of information where clients can get all the information about the bank and its services, but also an interactive channel of communication through which you can book a card deposit, make a transfer and use many other services with just a few clicks. In addition, PrivatBank's site is one of the most popular Ukraine Internet resources among the search engines and social networks.

• Charitable and social projects aimed at solving urgent problems in Ukrainian society. The bank takes an active social position, annually introducing dozens of measures of different scale and direction, including aid to soldiers of the antiterrorist operations, care and development of children, and help for temporarily displaced persons. Thus, PrivatBank became a partner of the international non-governmental organization GOAL under the new program of financial support for people affected by the conflict in Eastern Ukraine. Cash benefits are the most common form of humanitarian aid, protecting the life and dignity of people affected by crises, while ensuring that humanitarian aid is being used effectively.

In 2015 PrivatBank was recognized as the best among major benefactors of Ukrainian companies in the framework of the national competition "Charitable Ukraine". PrivatBank finances not only a large number of charitable projects, but actively engages the community in the bank's projects, forming new socially responsible trends in society. In particular, in 2015 320,000 citizens of Ukraine and around the world supported charitable projects organized by PrivatBank. To ensure transparency in the collection and control of expenditure of funds, a special blago.pb.ua has been created, which describes all the results of charitable programs that PrivatBank and its customers actively participate in.

For charitable projects, Privatbank has created its own charitable foundation, "It's Easy to Help", which regularly assists orphanages and boarding schools, children with cancer, as well as victims of natural disasters or terrorist attacks. The purpose of the fund is charitable activities on the behalf of public, individual groups, categories of persons who need care and protection; providing moral, material and financial support to individuals and legal entities; and promotion of education and culture. For this purpose, media enterprises, institutions, organizations, communities and Ukrainian diaspora are involved. Customers and employees of Privat-Bank have collected over $52,240,000 for charitable projects over five years (which is quite a noticeable amount of money for Ukraine).

An important factor in the success of charitable projects is the convenience and transparency of payments, so anyone can make a donation for any amount via PrivatBank, ATM or Internet banking through Privat24. The uniqueness of the fund and the program "It's Easy to Help!" is due to large investments of individual patrons or enterprises and through active involvement of society in solving social problems by the help of small amounts given by citizens. All people who transfer money will get a report on its use in e-mail or SMS.

The innovative character is embodied not only in the business processes of the bank, but also actively implemented primarily in the environmental and social responsibility of the bank. PrivatBank was the first Ukrainian bank to receive the Social Responsibility Mark award, assigned to the most socially responsible companies.

Pro-ecological Aspects of Undertaken Restructuring Procceses

This part investigates the factors of encouraging pro-ecological restructuring related to ecology and other issues (e.g. corporate social responsibility, stakeholders opinion, employment). Restructuring is mostly expressed in CSR implementation. Investigation also reveals the reason for it and shows the role and position of stakeholders in the process. The data is collected in following tables.

Table 2: Undertaken restructuring process of quarterly sector.

Name of the company	Factors of great influence on the company and their realization	Reason for implementation of the CSR (corporate and social responsibility)	Stakeholders and restructuring
PrivatBank	1) Political: International trade, tax policy, legal restriction; 2) Economic: consumer confidence, the bankruptcy of a large number of banks, rate of inflation, exchange rate; 3) Social: work, education, demography, income distribution; 4) Technological: Internet, development of information technology	New clients' involvement, competitiveness, corporate image, higher motivation of employees	There is a responsible coordinator for realization of the CSR (board of directors)

Source: own calculation based on Privatbank official site information https://en.privatbank.ua.

Tertiary and quarterly sectors are represented by PrivatBank. That is why the following factors (see Table 2) have the most visible effect. The reason for implementation of the SCR is, first of all, reputation, and so the deposit corporation struggles for value increasing and involving new clients.

To summarise all shown above, there are similar methods of restructuring in all sectors. Restructuring is mostly caused by the need to improve efficiency or competitiveness. The companies use the same instrument, and usually there is someone responsible for making restructuring and reacting to environmental turbulence.

Pro-ecological Employment

In this section, the purpose of our analysis is to determine the impact of undertaken ecological restructuring on employment in the company. All the processes related to the restructuring of the company have a huge impact on employment; of course, this also applies to ecological restructuring as well. Restructuring in this case includes the creation of new jobs (so-called green jobs) and modification of existing jobs in accordance with the new environmental standards, but often these processes lead to a reduction in staff. So it is quite natural that the attitude of workers towards the process of restructuring of the company cannot always be positive. Detailed company information about peculiarities of impact of pro-ecological restructuring on the employment are given below in Table 3.

Table 3: Pro-ecological employment of quaternary sector.

Creation of ecological/green jobs	Direct Activities	No
	Indirect Activities	Yes
Modification of work places		Yes
Existence of plans to create green jobs		No
Percentage of dismissed workers		0
Reaction of the staff to the restructuring process	Supporting	0.55
	Against	0.05
	Neutral	0.4
Involvement of local communities in the processes of ecological restructuring		Clients are interested in this process
Attracting of workers to the ecological restructuring		low level of involvement, workers were only informed about what was happening; workers forced to obey the processes

Source: own calculation based on Privatbank official site information https://en.privatbank.ua.

So the importance of ecological restructuring for sectors of economy depends on their market specialization and the chosen direction of corporate development. Almost all banks paid careful attention to professional training according to the implementation of the ecological restructuring. PrivatBank (apparently in order to save resources) didn't create new jobs (green jobs) and tried to train staff and upgrade and modify already existing workplaces for new ecological standards.

PrivatBank, due to their specialization, considers the problems of ecological restructuring to be very important for development of the bank. PrivatBank plans to create divisions related to environmental protection to implement some aspects of environmental management. That is why the company considers professional training according to the implementation of the ecological restructuring to be highly important.

The study shows that in Ukraine, ecological restructuring in the bank sector is at a sufficient level.

Summary of the Case Study

Thus, pro-ecological restructuring for a job is modern trend for sustainable development. It brings plenty of advantages to the companies that have implemented the process as well as to the whole economy. Generally, the most sufficient benefits are:

- saving the sources resulted in cost-cutting and
- growing reputation.

In the case of Ukraine, pro-ecological restructuring is considered and analysed according to the bank sector of the economy.

Quaternary sectors recognize the importance of pro-ecological restructuring and have made some sufficient steps in this direction. Basically, companies specialise in providing service, and that's why the main achieved objectives related to operating activity improvement, namely organization improvement, financial restructuring and employment restructuring. In terms of the socioeconomical aspect, gained advantages include: program of development, boost to the reputation, optimization of operative process, R&D department functioning, introduction of waste management, current asset optimization and increased market share.

There are ecological divisions created regarding new standards for the implementation of ecological restructuring. Modification of workplaces and special divisions related to environmental protection are also planned.

Due to the specialization of the quaternary sector, the problems of ecological restructuring aren't so important when comparing both primary and secondary sectors. Restructuring appears in professional training according to the implementation of the ecological restructuration.

References

KVED, Класифікатор видів економічної діяльності Available at https://kved.biz.ua

PrivatBank https://en.privatbank.ua [Last accessed 21 December 2016]

PrivatBank *Official site.* Available at https://en.privatbank.ua/individuals/branch-network/ [Last accessed 21 December, 2016]

Skinner, C 2016 *ValueWeb: How Fintech Firms are Using Bitcoin Blockchain and Mobile Technologies to Create the Internet of Value.* Published by Marshall Cavendish Business, Singapore.

Statute 2018, Статут акціонерного товариства комерційного банку Приватбанк.Нова редакція. 2018 Available at https://static.privatbank.ua/files/statut-new.PDF [Last accessed 21 August, 2018]

UCRA 2015, UCRA: исследование информационной прозрачности банков по результатам 2014 года Available at http:// https://news.finance.ua/ru/news/-/346060/ucra-issledovanie-informatsionnoj-prozrachnosti-bankov-po-rezultatam-2014-goda

3.3

Law Changes and International Standards in the Field of Ecoinnovation

Joanna Witczak

PhD, Poznan University of Economics and Business, Department of
Commodity Science and Ecology of Industrial Products

Introduction

Ecoinnovations are a fundamental area of activity involving economy, environment and society. They directly and indirectly affect the various fundamental aspects of human activity and, as a result, policy affairs. They are a requirement for increasing competitiveness that can be only reached in a synergic way between economic and ecological effects. Thus ecoinnovation should be based on resource productivity, efficiency, competitiveness and ability to safeguard the environment. It equally concerns profits made directly from decreasing environmental impact as well as social and economic profits arising indirectly. Introduction of ecoinnovation law and international standards is particularly important for creating organisation and consumer pro-ecological behavior. It allows companies to implement and develop more sustainable and eco-conscious solutions.

Ecoinnovations in Poland and EU

Recent years, mainly due to legislative and organizational changes in European Union, indicate ecoinnovations as a leading area of activity in the field of environmental protection for boosting greening the economy. The Ecoinnovation

How to cite this book chapter:
Witczak, J. 2019. Law Changes and International Standards in the Field of Ecoinnovation. In: Gąsior, A. (ed.) *Pro-ecological Restructuring of Companies: Case Studies*, Pp. 171–182. London: Ubiquity Press. DOI: https://doi.org/10.5334/bbk.o. License: CC-BY 4.0

Table 1: Ecoinnovation index in 2010–2015.

	2010	2011	2012	2013	2014	2015
EU (28)				100	100	100
EU (27)	100	100	100			
Belgium	114	115	118	101	96	97
Bulgaria	58	67	80	38	49	49
Czechia	73	91	90	71	92	99
Denmark	155	138	136	129	185	167
Germany	139	123	120	132	134	129
Estonia	56	74	78	72	74	80
Ireland	101	118	113	95	136	134
Greece	55	59	67	66	72	72
Spain	101	128	118	110	107	106
France	96	99	96	108	112	115
Croatia	0	0	0	57	87	67
Italy	98	90	92	95	99	106
Cyprus	64	71	74	43	59	60
Latvia	60	77	71	52	72	75
Lithuania	45	52	53	66	71	73
Luxemburg	94	130	108	109	188	124
Hungary	70	83	73	61	79	81
Malta	66	82	72	67	57	64
Holland	110	109	111	91	96	98
Austria	131	125	112	106	106	108
Poland	**54**	**50**	**54**	**42**	**63**	**59**
Portugal	72	81	84	79	99	102
Romania	52	67	78	63	76	82
Slovenia	75	109	115	74	91	96
Slovakia	48	52	54	47	68	72
Finland	156	149	150	138	135	140
Sweden	128	142	134	138	123	124
England	103	105	101	122	100	106
Iceland	no data	no data	no data	no data	no data	no data
Norway	no data	no data	no data	no data	no data	no data
Switzerland	no data	no data	no data	no data	no data	no data

*Index (EU=100)

Source: Eurostat Statistics 2016.

Index is a rating created on the basis of 16 indicators that depicts the position of each country within the scope of ecoinnovation in relation to the average of the European Union member countries. The number of ecoinnovations implemented in most countries is not high, especially in eastern ones. The Eurostat data show that in the Ecoinnovation Index 2016 Poland belongs to the group of low ecoinnovation (cf. Table 1).

In 2015 Poland has a significantly lower than average (59 out of 100) result in the index, in particular in reference to outlay and activities related to ecoinnovation, which reflects the generally low innovativeness of the country. Poland took the penultimate position ahead of Bulgaria only. This poor result is caused by small outlay linked with ecoinnovation activity, including research and development activity, R&D personnel, investment at early stages and investment in green technology.

The latest Central Statistical Office data indicate that Polish enterprises introduce not only a low number of ecoinnovations but also little innovation at all (GUS 2015). The number of innovative enterprises in Poland decrease from 27.9% in 2008 to 23% in 2012. The latest GUS data from 2015 indicate that within the group of industrial enterprises, there was a slight increase in the number of innovators. Their share increased from 17.7% in 2010–2012 to 18.4% in 2011–2013. However, in the group of service enterprises the share of innovative companies once again decreased from 13.9% in 2010–2012 to 12.8% in 2011–2013, which is a negative phenomenon as it causes the decrease of the innovative potential. In the case of countries like Poland, this trend creates large risk and may be difficult to reverse.

However, ecoinnovations in 2012–2014 were introduced more often than other process and product innovation. The study showed that in the analyzed years the ecoinnovations were introduced by 10.3% in industrial and 3.9% in service enterprises (it refers to both product, process, organisational and marketing innovations). The highest number of implemented innovations were process innovations in industrial enterprises (4.1%) and product innovations (1.7%) in service enterprises (cf. Figure 1).

The following factors are believed to be key elements of introducing ecoinnovation for companies in Poland: high operational costs, desire to reduce costs related to energy, water and materials, as well as readiness for the access to new market, for increasing competitiveness and improving the reputation of a given company. It is confirmed by the data of Central Statistical Office (GUS 2015), according to which the main factors that amount to the incentive to introduce ecoinnovation in 2012-2014 were (given below according to importance):

• high costs of energy, water and materials;
• improvement of the company's reputation;
• existing legislation related to environmental protection;
• voluntary initiatives for the environment and good practices in the sector;
• existing taxes and environmental fees;

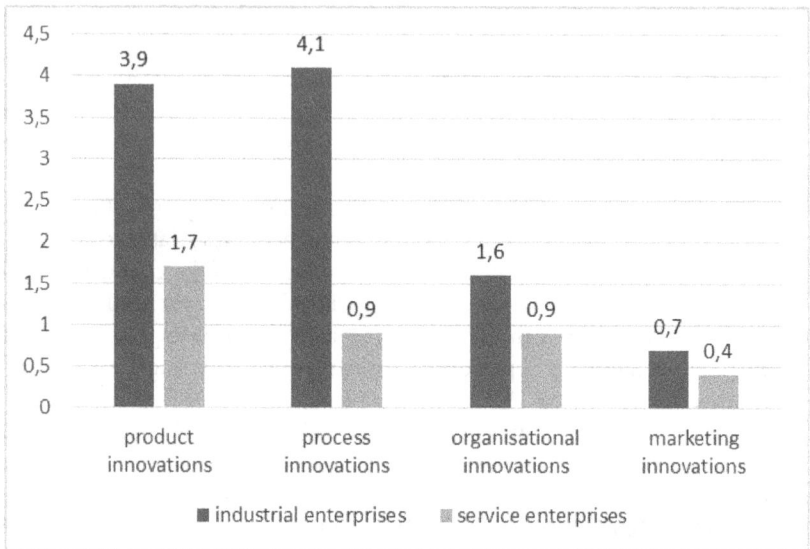

Fig. 1: Polish enterprises which introduced ecoinnovations resulting from types of introduced innovations as the share of total enterprises.

Source: GUS, 2015, Działalność innowacyjna przedsiębiorstw w latach 2012–2014.

- legislation related to environmental protection and expected taxes;
- fashion and expected demand for ecoinnovation;
- meeting requirements within the scope of public tenders; and
- governmental subsidies, subsidies and other financial stimulants for introducing innovation, which is beneficial for the environment (cf. Figure 2).

The importance of the three factors of highest importance is almost the same for industrial and service companies that have introduced ecoinnovation. High costs of energy, water and materials are very important factors for 36.7% of industrial companies and for 42.3% of service companies. Existing legislation related to environmental protection is the third most important factor for 19.8% industrial and 16.9% service companies. Polish enterprises are aware of environmental regulations or taxes expected in the future and perceive ecoinnovations through the prism of necessity for meeting requirements for public procurement contracts also.

Despite Polish enterprises' awareness of the importance of implementing innovations, private green investment at early stages were one of the lowest in the EU, however, they were at a similar level to other Central and Eastern European countries. Poland is above the EU average in the case of only one indicator – environmental industry income, as a percentage of total income in all companies. Nevertheless, the Polish market of green technologies and

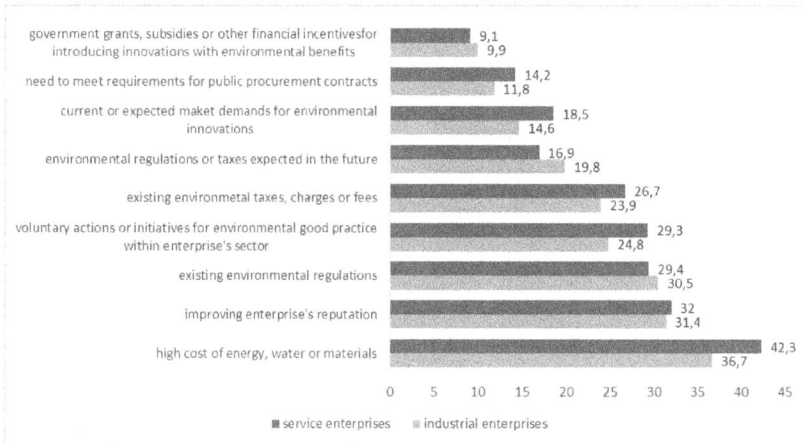

government grants, subsidies or other financial incentives for introducing innovations with environmental benefits 9,1 / 9,9

need to meet requirements for public procurement contracts 14,2 / 11,8

current or expected maket demands for environmental innovations 18,5 / 14,6

environmental regulations or taxes expected in the future 16,9 / 19,8

existing environmetal taxes, charges or fees 26,7 / 23,9

voluntary actions or initiatives for environmental good practice within enterprise's sector 29,3 / 24,8

existing environmental regulations 29,4 / 30,5

improving enterprise's reputation 32 / 31,4

high cost of energy, water or materials 42,3 / 36,7

■ service enterprises   ■ industrial enterprises

Fig. 2: Polish enterprises that rated importance of a given factor in driving an enterprise's decisions to introduce ecoinnovations as "high" as the share of enterprises which introduced innovations with environmental benefits in the years 2012–2014.

Source: GUS, 2015, Działalność innowacyjna przedsiębiorstw w latach 2012-2014.

ecoinnovation is still at the stage of development and shows its considerable potential for growth (Wrzesiewski & Miler 2010).

Fostering Ecoinnovation

Nowadays human beings face a range of environmental challenges that will impact on our future prosperity. These include resource depletion, climate change, increasing water scarcity, air pollution and biodiversity loss. Ecoinnovation and innovative environmental technologies can provide solutions to minimalise environmental impact of our industrial activity. Economic recovery and environmentally and socially sustainable economic growth were recognized as the key challenges for all countries (*Declaration on Green Growth* 2009). Thus the European Commission puts a lot of effort into supporting ecoinnovation as the most important factor of environmental protection activity.

In 2011 European Commission introduced The Eco-innovation Action Plan (EcoAP). The plan includes targeted actions both on the demand and supply side, on research and industry and on policy and financial instruments. The implementation of the actions will be supported by the partnering approach between stakeholders, private and public sector, and the European Commission. The key EcoAP drivers for the market uptake of ecoinnovation are the following:[1]

1) using policies and regulations in the field of environmental protection to promote ecoinnovation
2) supporting demonstration projects and establishing partnerships to introduce promising, smart and ambitious operational technologies to the market
3) developing of new standards to stimulate innovation,
4) mobilizing financial instruments and support services for SMEs
5) promoting international cooperation
6) supporting the development of emerging skills, creating new jobs and training programs for adapting to the labor market needs
7) supporting ecoinnovation through the European Innovation Partnerships foreseen under the "Innovation Union".

For supporting and promoting ecoinnovation the Seventh Environment Action Programme (EcoAP) was introduced. It is a continuation of the ETAP program, which takes a broader approach to the question of ecoinnovation and includes more actions aiming at strengthening stimulants and overcoming barriers to the implementation of original environmentally friendly solutions. EcoAP aims to increase the contribution of environmental policy in the transition to a resource-efficient, low carbon economy in which natural capital is amplified, and the health and welfare of the citizens are protected.

The Seventh Environment Action Programme will be guiding European environment policy until 2020 (including eco-innovation) and concerns the following priority objectives:[2]

(a) to protect, conserve and enhance the Union's natural capital;
(b) to turn the Union into a resource-efficient, green and competitive low-carbon economy;
(c) to safeguard the Union's citizens from environment-related pressures and risks to health and well-being;
(d) to maximise the benefits of Union environment legislation by improving implementation;
(e) to improve the knowledge and evidence base for Union environment policy;
(f) to secure investment for environment and climate policy and address environmental externalities;
(g) to improve environmental integration and policy coherence;
(h) to enhance the sustainability of the Union's cities;
(i) to increase the Union's effectiveness in addressing international environmental and climate-related challenges.

One of the results of ETAP and EcoAP is creating the Environmental Technology Verification System (EU ETV), which environmentally verifies enterprises in order to eliminate information gaps and market uncertainty related to the efficiency of the new environmental solutions. ETV is an initiative which aims to address the problem of credibility of information about the environmental performance of innovative technologies. Environmental Technology Verification (ETV) provides for third-party verification of the performance claims made by technology manufacturers in business-to-business relations.

The European Union has created support instruments focused on innovation and entrepreneurship, which are supposed to develop stimuli for investment in processes and technologies linked with the environment. One of the instruments is the EU Competitiveness and Innovation Program (CIP). It is used to propagate ecoinnovation in the form of various support actions, e.g. risk capital funding and actions for the development of the cooperation network.

The LIFE program is dedicated uniquely to co-funding projects within the scope of environmental and climate protection. It is a financial instrument of the European Union, which follows the LIFE+ program. Its main aim is to support the process of implementing the community environmental protection law, the realization of the EU policy within this scope, as well as the identification and promotion of new solutions for environmental problems.

In 2014–2020 the financial instrument of the "Innovation Union" project is the EU program for scientific research and innovation – "Horizon 2020". Its objective is to support research within the scope of new solutions, as well as the monitoring, presentation and market development of them.

In Poland a number of initiatives have been undertaken aimed at popularizing the knowledge of ecoinnovation. One of the projects focused on this objective is the national information and educational campaign entitled "Are you a creator? Become an ecoinnovator!" conducted in 2014–2015 by the University of Economics in Poznań, which in order to realize this undertaking, obtained funding from the National Fund for Environmental Protection and Water Management. The project was dedicated to widespreading information and knowledge about ecoinnovation among different target groups (entrepreneurs, administration, researchers, students). All tasks realized within the project and its results can be accessed at www.ekoinnowator.ue.poznan.pl.

The first Polish industrial program in the area of environmental actions is Gekon (Environmental Conception Generator). It was prepared and realized by two institutions: the National Research and Development Center and the National Fund for Environmental Protection and Water Management. The program supports projects from the private sector related to conducting scientific research and development, and then implementing the obtained results in the form of innovative environmental technologies.

A national support instrument is also the program of the Ministry of the Environment called GreenEvo – an accelerator of green technologies (Polish abbreviation: AZT). The initiative aims at helping Polish ecoinnovators to enter the global market. The help is realized in the organizational, technical and financial aspects.

Environmental Legislation

As one of the basic supporting instruments, environmental legislation is very important driver for ecoinnovation and for the industry development. The main areas involving are water and air pollution, waste management, recycling, and climate change mitigation. There are a number of regulations dealing directly or indirectly with ecoinnovations. In the area of Environment, Health and Safety, roughly 500 additional regulations were adopted in 2012 compared to 2009 (Shaffer &Hendel-Blackford 2013). Many of them have been a strong driver for ecoinnovation in a variety of sectors.

The REACH (Registration, Evaluation, Authorization & Restriction of Chemicals)[3] regulation is dedicated to chemical companies. It covers lists of substances of very high concern (SVHC) for which substitution is required when safer alternative substances or technologies become technically and economically feasible. The REACH validity forces an active search for more environmental friendly and safer substitutes as well as stimulates R&D activities. The regulation is also a very good example of driving innovation worldwide. On the one hand the chemical companies across the world must follow the REACH when developing products that should meet the requirements of EU markets. Inside the EU, the regulation affects a wide range of producers, importers and exporters across many sectors and impacts a variety of goods – from chemical components to finished products.

Product-focused environmental regulation is also the WEEE (Waste Electrical and Electronic Equipment) Directive.[4] It shifts the responsibility of the post-use phase to the producer. The first WEEE Directive (Directive 2002/96/EC) entered into force in February 2003. The directive provided for the creation of collection schemes where consumers return their WEEE free of charge. These schemes aim to increase the recycling of WEEE and/or re-use. The directive was revised in December 2008 in order to tackle the fast-increasing waste stream. The new WEEE Directive 2012/19/EU entered into force on 13 August 2012 and became effective on 14 February 2014. The directive related to electronic products is also Directive 2009/125/EC of the European Parliament and of the Council of 21 October 2009 establishing a framework for the setting of ecodesign requirements for energy-related products.

The RoHS (Restriction of the use of Hazardous Substances) Directive[5] restricts the use of certain substances in products. RoHS Directive 2002/95/EC entered into force in February 2003. The legislation requires heavy metals such as lead, mercury, cadmium, and hexavalent chromium and flame retardants such as polybrominated biphenyls (PBB) or polybrominated diphenyl ethers (PBDE) to be substituted by safer alternatives. In December 2008, the revision was done and the RoHS recast Directive 2011/65/EU was introduced on 3 January 2013.

The environmental issues are also present in ISO 14000 standards. The most important are these referring to ecodesign and life cycle assessment mentioned below:

- ISO 14001: Environmental management systems. Requirements with guidance for use. ISO 14004: Environmental management systems – General guidelines on principles, systems and support techniques.
- ISO 14030s: *Environmental management – Environmental performance evaluation.*
- ISO 14040s: Environmental management – Life Cycle Assessment.
- ISO 14020s: Environmental labels and declarations.
- ISO/TS 14067: Greenhouse gases – Carbon footprint of products –Requirements and guidelines for quantification and communication.
- ISO 14046: Environmental management. Water footprint – principles, requirements and guidelines (under construction).
- ISO/TR 14062 (2002): Environmental management – Integrating environmental aspects into product design and development.
- ISO 14006 (2011): Environmental management systems – Guidelines for incorporating eco-design.

The mentioned standards specify principles, requirements and guidelines related to products, processes and organisations based on life cycle assessment (LCA). They give the information and the structure of general LCA or design procedure and are dedicated for including the environmental aspects into whole life cycle.

The European Commission has taken actions aiming at supporting the green product market. In the communication to the European Parliament, the Council, the European Economic and Social Committee, and the Committee of the Regions "The Roadmap to a Resource Efficient Europe" the Commission obliged itself to establish a methodological approach, which will enable a thorough evaluation, presentation and comparative analysis of products, services and enterprises on the basis of the comprehensive evaluation of environmental efficiency throughout life. As a result of actions taken in 2013, the European Commission issued a recommendation on the use of common methods to measure and communicate the life cycle environmental performance of products and organizations (2013/179/EU). The aim of these actions is the development of a common methodology for qualitative evaluation of products' environmental impact in their whole life cycle as a way of supporting the credibility of the evaluation and labelling. The European Commission recommendations are not binding for member states nowadays. However, the methodology in the future may become a part of obligatory legislation within the scope of environmental protection, energy efficiency, green public tenders and other disciplines contributing to strengthening the competitiveness of green economy.

Nowadays the European Commission's strategy is to introduce and implement the conception of a "circular economy" into practice. It is based on a recycling society with the aim of reducing waste generation and using waste as a resource. It provides also life cycle thinking to achieve more efficient and more sustainable products and services. In 2015 the EU action plan for the Circular Economy[6] was introduced. The plan establishes a concrete programme of action, with measures covering the whole cycle, from production and consumption to waste management and the market for secondary raw materials. The proposed actions aim to "close the loop", which means recycling and re-use in product lifecycles.

Conclusions

Ecoinnovation is a combination of innovative solutions and the care of the environment. It is an essential part of the sustainable economy. Ecoinnovation provides opportunities for development and promotion, long-term welfare, as well as maintaining competitiveness. It calls for investment in both scientific research and human capital. Thus, the necessity of creating proper conditions for the green economic growth is very high. It means development favorable for entrepreneurs dealing with the implementation of environmental friendly scenarios. However, appropriate actions must be taken for creating and popularizing environmental behaviors and habits also. Therefore, it seems that launching various types of initiatives leading to increasing the knowledge of ecoinnovation, presenting concrete examples and solutions combined with legal actions may become a stimulus for the innovativeness growth. It creates the need for an ecoinnovation implementation strategy in enterprises. The right direction of future changes seems to be the environmental impact evaluation that may contribute to protect the environment as well as increase the economy's competitiveness. The main issue of introducing environmental legislation is bringing benefits for both the environment and the economy. International standards obligatory in all countries are one of the main factors contributing to improving producers' and consumers' practices to make environmental change in the way they think, to introduce the life cycle thinking.

Notes

[1] Communication from the Commission to the European Parliament, the Council, the European Economic and Social Committee and the Committee of the Regions, Innovation for a sustainable Future - The Eco-innovation Action Plan (Eco-AP), Brussels, 15.12.2011, COM(2011) 899 final.

[2] Decision No 1386/2013/EU of the European Parliament and of the Council of 20 November 2013 on a *General Union Environment Action Programme to 2020 'Living well, within the limits of our planet.*

[3] Regulation (EC) No 1907/2006 of the European Parliament and the Council on the Registration, Evaluation, Authorisation and Restriction of Chemicals (REACH).

[4] Directive 2012/19/EU of the European Parliament and of the Council of 4 July 2012 on waste electrical and electronic equipment (WEEE).

[5] Directive 2011/65/EU of the European Parliament and of the Council of 8 June 2011 on the restriction of the use of certain hazardous substances in electrical and electronic equipment.

[6] Communication from the Commission to the European Parliament, the Council, the European Economic and Social Committee and the Committee of the Regions, *Closing the loop - An EU action plan for the Circular Economy*, 2.12.2015, Brussels, COM/2015/0614 final.

References

Communication from the Commission to the European Parliament, the Council, the European Economic and Social Committee and the Committee of the Regions, *A resource-efficient Europe - Flagship initiative under the Europe 2020 Strategy*, Brussels, 26.1.2011, COM (2011) 21.

Communication from the Commission, *Europe 2020. A strategy for smart, sustainable and inclusive growth*, 3.3.2010, Brussels, COM (2010) 2020 final.

Communication from the Commission to the European Parliament, the Council, the European Economic and Social Committee and the Committee of the Regions, Innovation for a sustainable Future - The Eco-innovation Action Plan (EcoAP), Brussels, 15.12.2011, COM (2011) 899 final.

Communication from the Commission to the European Parliament, the Council, the European Economic and Social Committee and the Committee of the Regions, Roadmap to a Resource Efficient Europe, 20.9.2011, Brussels, COM (2011) 571 final.

Communication from the Commission to the European Parliament, the Council, the European Economic and Social Committee and the Committee of the Regions, *Closing the loop - An EU action plan for the Circular Economy*, 2.12.2015, Brussels, COM/2015/0614 final.

COM (2010) 2020, EUROPE 2020 A strategy for smart, sustainable and inclusive growth.

Decision No 1386/2013/EU of the European Parliament and of the Council of 20 November 2013 on a *General Union Environment Action Programme to 2020 'Living well, within the limits of our planet.'*

Declaration on Green Growth, adopted at the Meeting of the Council at Ministerial Level on 25 June 2009, C/MIN (2009)5/ADD1/FINAL.

Directive 2012/19/EU of the European Parliament and of the Council of 4 July 2012 on waste electrical and electronic equipment (WEEE).

Directive 2011/65/EU of the European Parliament and of the Council of 8 June 2011 on the restriction of the use of certain hazardous substances in electrical and electronic equipment.

Eurostat Statistics 2016.

Foltynowicz, Z 2009 *Ekoinnowacje szansą na rozwój*", Ecomanager nr 1 (in Polish).

GUS 2015 *Działalność innowacyjna przedsiębiorstw w latach 2012-2014* (in Polish).

Innovation for a sustainable Future - The Eco-innovation Action Plan (Eco-AP), European Commission, COM(2011) 899, Brussels 15.12.2011.

Regulation (EC) No 1907/2006 of the European Parliament and the Council on the Registration, Evaluation, Authorisation and Restriction of Chemicals (REACH).

Towards Green Growth, 2011, OECD.

Shaffer, V and Hendel-Blackford, T 2013 Then and Now: The Difference 4 Years Can Make in EHS Regulatory Focus around the World. 29 March 2013. www.ehstoday.com/safety/then-and-now-difference-4-years-can-make-ehs-regulatory-focus-around-world-slideshow

UNEP 2014, *The Business Case for Eco-innovation*.

Witczak, J (ed.) 2014 *Jesteś kreatorem? Zostań innowatorem!*, dodatek do Przeglądu Komunalnego 7/2014 Available at http://ekoinnowator. ue.poznan.pl/files/Biuletyn_nr_1.pdf (in Polish).

Wrzesiewski, T and Miler, R 2010, *Polski Rynek Technologii Środowiskowych*, Warszawa (in Polish).

3.4

Case 1: A professional online exhibition platform as an example of final user's benefits

Joanna Duda[*] and Łukasz Lelek[†]

[*]PhD, AGH University of Science and Technology, Faculty of Management, Krakow, Poland

[†]M.Sc. Eng., Mineral and Energy Economy Research Institute of The Polish Academy of Sciences, Krakow, Poland

Introduction

From the earliest times, human life has involved the exchange of goods and services. Even before the rise of civilization, people formed the foundation for the market of goods. In ancient Rome and Greece, the form of exchange of goods and services were fairs. Currently fairs developed on a massive scale. Every year, thousands of events are organized, which bring together thousands of exhibitors and visitors. Initially, they played only commercial function. But with time they also adopted the function of information and promotion, allow to reach genuinely interested clients in your offer. Additionally they offer the possibility of contact with customers in order to receive their opinions and reactions to products, especially for new ones that have yet to be subject to manufacturing or services. This interaction has many benefits, which don't provide other forms of marketing. They are also a form of communication and creating the image of the company and for many entrepreneurs are also a point of gathering information about the industry, competition, needs and customers' preferences. At the

How to cite this book chapter:
Duda, J. and Lelek, Ł. 2019. Case 1: A professional online exhibition platform as an example of final user's benefits. In: Gąsior, A. (ed.) *Pro-ecological Restructuring of Companies: Case Studies*, Pp. 183–198. London: Ubiquity Press. DOI: https://doi.org/10.5334/bbk.p. License: CC-BY 4.0

fair the latest innovative achievements are presented. Trade and business plays an important role not only in the life of companies, but also in the life of cities. Today's business events, trade fairs and conferences are very different from what was organized in the last century. Due to the strong specialization, they are mainly industry events on narrow topics, often combined with seminars and expert meetings, during which all kinds of novelties are present. The largest trade fair centers in Poland are Poznan, Kielce, Warsaw, Łódź, Gdańsk, Kraków and Lower Silesian agglomeration. Trade is popular not only in Poland but all over the world. The largest known centers include Hanover, Milan, Frankfurt, Cologne, Duesseldorf, Chicago, Valencia, Paris, Birmingham, Berlin, Nuremberg, Leipzig and Brno.

The dynamically changing global market currently puts new demands on businesses. Consumers expect from them not only competitive, but innovative products in terms of ecological and cost and activities that would be considered by society as responsible. According to the definition of the European Commission, corporate social responsibility is an including, on voluntary basis, by the enterprise, social and environmental issues in their business, going beyond the legal requirements and contractual obligations. Therefore, there are many areas of social responsibility, eg. economic, sociological, ecological, ethical, legal and philanthropic.

On the one hand, enterprises are forced to reduce the cost of business in order to be competitive in the market, and on the other hand, the attitude of customers are becoming strongly pro-ecological. Corporate social responsibility means that more and more companies treat environmental and social aspects not only as secondary activities, but as one of the main objectives of their strategy. It is not just to follow trends, but entrepreneurs also have begun to see a lot of benefits that result from environmental initiatives. Given the changes in the climate, these actions are becoming more important in business. Therefore, the aim of this paper is the presentation of an innovative platform for an online trade fair, which lowers the costs of participation in trade fairs, conferences and business meetings and is an example of good practice in environmental and social activities.

Business Tourism as a Tool for Supporting Business Innovation

In Poland, business tourism is a young but rapidly growing industry that is an important segment of the tourism market. Poland's accession in 2004 to the EU and central geographical position stimulate the number of business meetings in our country. Economic development and internationalization of the economy led to an increase in the number of foreign investors contributing to the need for the development of the Meeting-Incentive-Conferences-Event (MICE) industry. However, Poland as a place for international meetings, conferences and congresses for the European MCIE industry is still a new and attractive destination. According to the report prepared by Institute of Tourism in 2011, the number of arrivals business in Poland was estimated at 3.5 million, increasing the advantage over the arrivals for tourist-recreational purposes (about 3.1 million – the data for the first three quarters of the year). However, according to data published by the Association of Conferences and Congresses in Poland (2013) by business arrivals remained at the level of 4.3–5.2 million per year. Business purpose represents therefore 30% of all tourist visits in Poland, where more than 40% of them combine business with other aims. Therefore, at the European, national and regional level and national institutions, governments, businesses, hotels and convention centres compete with each other for the greatest number of customers in the field of organized events. To meet the market requirements, specific information is needed, including research and analysis of statistical data. Among the global institutions engaged in the evaluation and rankings of business tourism the following should be mentioned:

• UIA (Union of International Association)
• ICCA (International Congress and Convention Associations)
• UNWTO (World Tourism Organization)
• The Global Association of the Exhibition Industry

The data are collected mainly by the Poland Convention Bureau (PCB), Hotel Market Institute and the Institute of Tourism, whose statistics are based on data compiled by the regional convention bureaux and conference facilities. Depending on the assumptions and criteria, e.g. the number of participants and duration of the event (referred as conference or congress), the data may largely differ from each other (Table 1).

Poland has quite a high position at the forefront of business tourism, which is increasing every year (in 2010 – 32 with 98 meetings, according to a report by the ICCA). In addition, you may notice that the dominant places for meetings and congresses are Warszawa and Krakow.

Analysing the national data in this regard the number of included meetings, conferences and conventions is significantly higher than that resulting from international statistics. This is due the criteria, which take into account the typical national meetings. According to data published in 2011 (Table 2), the number of meetings amounted to a total of 24,843, and at the forefront of the cities where these meetings took place were Warszawa, Krakow and Trojmiasto. Warszawa has a predominance of hundreds of meetings over the Krakow. These meetings corresponded for a total of 88% of all identified events in the national ranking (Borodako et al. 2014).

It should be noted that in 2012 the standardized methodology for data collection in the field of national statistics on the tourism business was introduced, so these results are subject to a methodological lapse, e.g. the methodology of identifying the meetings in Krakow, differed from that used by the PCB for other cities.

Table 1: Poland and individual cities in the rankings of ICCA (International Congress and Convention Association) and UIA (Union of International Associations) in 2011.

International organizations	ICCA	UIA
The criteria for carried out rankings	• meetings are held periodically • focus a minimum of 50 participants • participants from at least 3 different countries	• meetings last at least 3 days • focus a minimum of 300 participants • participants come from a minimum of 5 different countries • At least 40% of the participants come from abroad
Place of Poland in the global rankings in 2011	21	23
Cities with the largest number of meetings	1. Warszawa – 65 meetings 2. Krakow – 40 meetings 3. Gdansk – 23 meetings 4. Wroclaw – 10 meetings 5. Poznan – 8 meetings	1. Warszawa – 40 meetings 2. Krakow – 30 meetings 3. Gdansk – 12 meetings 4. Wroclaw – 7 meetings 5. Poznan – 6 meetings

Source: N. Tomczyk, *Zarządzanie turystyką biznesową na przykładzie wybranych convention bureaux w Polsce*, Praca magisterska, Instytut Geografii Miast i Turyzmu, Uniwersytet Łódzki, 2013.

Table 2: The number of meetings within group business tourism in selected Polish cities in 2011year.

City	Number of meetings	Share [%]
Warszawa	8830	33.5
Krakow	8304	33.4
Trojmiasto	4773	19.2
Katowice	900	3.6
Poznan	766	3.1
Bydgoszcz	496	2.0
Wroclaw	440	1.8
Torun	334	1.3
Summary	24,843	100.0

Source: K. Borodako, *Turystyka biznesowa w Krakowie na tle wybranych miast polskich*, Prace Geograficzne, zeszyt134, Instytut Geografiii Gospodarki Przestrzennej UJ.

Analysing the tourism business in particular, regional data for 2012 show a slightly different situation from that presented directly for the cities. The business meetings in Poland reached the level of 22,300 events, of which 10,622 were congresses and conferences, 5305 were incentive events, 4657 were corporate events, and 1716 were fairs and exhibitions. The data presented by the PCB confirm the dominance of Warsaw, Mazowieckie region (Figure 1). However, the position of individual regions and cities in the rankings of business tourism is dependent on many factors, the following being the dominant factors:

• tourist popularity and recognisability of the city in the world
• popularity in various environments, i.e. the scientific, economic and administrative
• promotional activities of the region and the city

An available infrastructure is also important, including technical and formal background, such as the number of hotels in a given business segment, e.g. the standard of the 4- and 5-star, the number of available rooms, meeting rooms and convention centres. Another factor is accessibility, which is especially

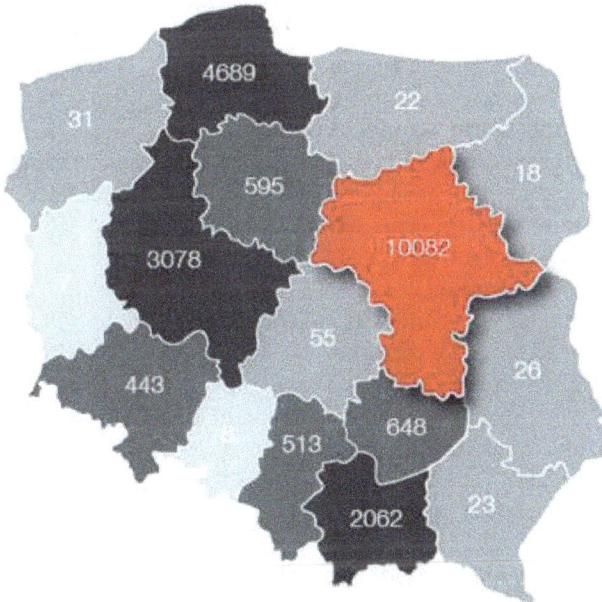

Fig. 1: The number of meetings and events with the division into voivodeships in 2012.

Source: K. Celuch, Raport „Przemysł spotkań i wydarzeń w Polsce – Poland Meetings and Events Industry Report 2013", PCB, Warszawa, 2013.

important in the case of international events. In this case, a complement of flights is important, and there also should be good bus, rail and metro lines. Additionally, each industrial sector is characterized by their own criteria, which determine the choice of the place of venues and events. For the research sector, which is an important segment of the meetings industry, mainly due to the popularity of conferences, congresses and conventions, an important factor is functioning in a place such as research institutes. This is due to the fact that this research centres are largely responsible for the organization of such events, and in most cases they choose their own technical facilities, including meeting and conference rooms. Many more factors, determining the popularity of the site, can be identified. They are also dependent on individual industries benefiting from the tourism business (Borodako et al. 2014).

Statistical data show that the MICE sector is an important segment of the national economy and that every year it becomes more and more important in the overall structure of tourism in Poland.

Economic Aspects of the Example of Krakow City

The economic importance of the meetings industry is closely related to the amount of events organized in a particular place. In the case of Krakow, in 2013, 3413 meetings took place there, of which three-quarters were held in hotels, and a quarter had an international character. For the most part these meetings were a conference or convention, and 70% of them were organized by the company in the technic and IT branch.

The cost of participation in conferences, congresses and training accounted for an average amount of 2098 PLNs (including all the costs, i.e. participation, accommodation, personal expenses etc.), while in fairs and exhibitions it was 1023 PLNs. The costs for the issuer of the trade fair stood at 15,791 PLNs and for the representing person 2439 PLNs, which accounted for individual spending. In 2013, the meetings industry generated 1,068.9 million PLN in Krakow, which accounted for 2.37% of Krakow's GDP. Proceeds to the city budget in the form of taxes and fees amounted to 89 million PLNs (2.4% of budget revenues of Krakow). This contributed to the creation of over 12 thousand year-round jobs and 316 million PLN of earnings for workers employed in this industry (Borodako et al. 2014).

Organisation of Ecological Business Events, and the Benefits for Users

The perception of the benefits from involvement in environmental initiatives and doing business with in a way that society considers as a responsible are becoming more frequent practice among Polish entrepreneurs. Companies are beginning pay attention to pro-environmental aspects of their activities and fit the principles of sustainable development in their strategy. In the case of the MICE industry, it is related to an increase in events organized in a sustainable and environmentally friendly manner, including conferences, exhibitions, workshops etc. The main idea of this approach is to minimize the environmental impact of the event at every stage of its implementation. An intermediate goal can be, for example, raising awareness of the participants in terms of pro-environment and effective management of resources and materials.

A change of approach and thinking in the field of environmental activities may contribute to measurable and visible benefits for the company. In the long term, taking care of the environment can contribute to cost savings and a positive image of a company, which can increase its competitiveness on the market (Kostecka, Pączka & Piękoś 2013).

Increasing economic and environmental efficiency by minimizing the use of resources and energy and reduce the amount of waste generated are actions that distinguish sustainable events. Reduced costs and waste generation can be achieved by, for example, the introduction of programs in the field of energy efficiency (hotels, conference centres), reducing the amount of printed materials, and the use of local or ecological food. In addition, eliminating the transport, such as by locating events within walking distance of the major transportation hubs, or the maximum use of daylight can contribute to further cost reduction.

The possibility of minimizing expenses associated with the organization of events, meetings and conferences in a sustainable way is undoubtedly a major factor in the growing interest in this approach. However, aspects of environmental and social responsibility should be taken into account at the same level. So, in order to treat an event as an ecological, there should be more segregation of waste or use of biodegradable cups. Such an event should be organized in accordance with the formal environmental standards, which take into account all factors that could have an impact on the environment. The concept that allows for an assessment of the services or processes in field of environmental impact is the Life Cycle Assessment (LCA). LCA is part of a broader concept known as lifecycle management (LCM). According to this idea the products and services should be designed, evaluated and compared with each other through the prism of all stages within their whole life cycle. This allows for a better understanding of a particular service or product, as it requires us to examine the issue of environmental, social and economic factors, which are associated with both before (supply chain) production and post-production stages.

A good example of cost reduction can be organized every year in the Vienna International AIDS Conference. In 2010, its organizers decided to change the organization system and take environmental activities into account and estimate the costs that could be saved thanks to them. The conference in 2010 attracted more than 19,000 participants, and achieved reduced costs of:

- 33,000 USD by eliminating the printing of invitations and brochures, for the benefit of electronic shipping,

- 20,000 USD by printing a summary book on request only,
- 500,000 USD by resignation of providing an airport transfer and encouraging the use of public transport (offering a 30% discount on the price of public transport tickets), and
- 50,000 USD by using tap water instead of bottled for delegates.

In total, these actions contributed to a savings of 603,000 USD in comparison to the conference in previous years (Sustainable Events Guide 2012).

Another good practice is developed by the UNEP model for estimating and budget management, travel and business delegations. Each time you purchase travel tickets, a model based on the means of transportation and details of the route generates the carbon footprint of the journey and calculates an additional fee, which is charged to the same budget lines as expenses. The money collected in this way is then sent monthly to the UNEP Climate Neutral Fund and used for environmental activities, in order to offset greenhouse gas emissions arising during the trips. In this case, it generates additional costs for meetings, but helps to improve the image of the company and in the long term can contribute to economic benefits, e.g. increased competitiveness.

A very interesting example of the environmental and economic benefits is also presented below innovative platform for online trade fair, built by Future Expo Sp. z o.o.

Event organisation

Each customer buying any package rents, for the duration of the fair, an e-stand, which is posted by its logo and which is matched to the supplied graphics, files and information. During the time of the fair, a customer receives at a unique Skype address by which they will be able to negotiate and present the company offer live. There is also the possibility of designing the stands in a foreign language opening the possibility for the international market. The online fair platform, Future Expo Sp. z o.o. offers various packages, which are presented in Table 3:

Table 3: Cost of participation in the online fair.

Package name	Description	Costs
BASIC	• e-stand • the table of contact details • box with a description of the business • box with a place on the content of the company's offer • database of companies taking part in trade fairs • Skype account integrated with e-stand • 3 links for outside the website • 1 GB of cloud storage for customers' files	600zł

Package name	Description	Costs
PRO	• e-stand • the table of contact details • box with a description of the business • box with a place on the content of the company's offer • database of companies taking part in trade fairs • Skype account integrated with e-stand • 5 links for outside the website • 1 GB of cloud storage for customers' files • business card in the catalog of enterprise • sending the offer/presentation to all participants of the fair	1200zł
PREMIUM	• e-stand • the table of contact details • box with a description of the business • box with a place on the content of the company's offer • database of companies taking part in trade fairs • Skype account integrated with e-stand • 5 links for outside the website • 3 GB of cloud storage for customers' files • business card in the catalog of enterprise • sending the offer/presentation to all participants of the fair • logo "Industry Leader" • page in the registry of Premium Companies • Advertising on the home page (advertising banner) • Certificate The Leader of Future Expo Fair	1800zł

Source: Elaboration on the basis of materials supplied by the Future Expo Sp. z o.o. company.

The organization of online trade fairs offers many benefits, the most common include:

- the ability to simultaneously present in the country and abroad,
- low costs of participation in trade fairs,
- building business relationships in a modern way,
- knowing the competition,
- expansion of the customer portfolio,
- modern forms of information cxchange,
- increased competitiveness,
- direct contact with client,
- strengthening of position,
- time savings resulting from staying at the office,

- financial savings related to the delegations of workers to traditional fairs, the costs of travel, accommodation etc., and
- no costs associated with renting facility, hiring technical staff, catering, printing promotional materials etc.

In addition, attention should be paid to the environmental benefits, which include the fact that:

- online fair does not generate waste,
- organization of meetings online generate significant less amounts of electricity than full infrastructure of direct meetings,
- online fair does not generate direct water use and do not require the services of catering and cleaning, and
- there is no need to use any way of transport – fuel savings and less pollution.

A more detailed economic analysis of the events organized in the traditional manner, taking into consideration environmental aspects as well as online, is presented below.

Economic analysis of ecological events organizing

The methods of economic analysis can include a number of financial indicators, ie. ROI, NPV, IRR, which are gaining use in assessing the efficiency of investment, not only financial, but also investments in the enterprises. However, in the case of ecological events we are not dealing with an ordinary investment, therefore it was decided to use profit and loss to account for economic analysis. It is a comparison of generated revenue, such as from grants, sponsorships, conference fees etc., in a given period with costs incurred during the organization of the event. According to the Accounting Act in the profit and loss analyses the financial result is determined in a "ladder", showing income and expenses and profits and losses separately. Table 4 presents a template showing examples of types of entries. Please note that the budget depends largely on the specifics of the event.

Table 4 presents costs that are expenses of one of the conferences organized by PAN MEERI.[1] The budget does not include the proceeds, since the aim was to show the possibility of reducing expenditure. In this example it is assumed that the costs were planned to actual expenditure. The table summarizes the reduction or increase in costs relating to the organization of the event itself, however, taking into consideration environmental and social aspects. The assumptions for the calculation are shown in Table 5.

Table 4: Comparison costs of events held in the ordinary way and taking into account the environmental and social aspects.

	Description	Expenditure ordinary event [PLN]	The possibility of reduction / increase of costs [%]	Expenditure ecological event [PLN]	On line event
INCOME					
1.	Subsidies, public funding	–	–	–	-
2.	Sponsors	–	–	–	-
3.	Conference fees	–	–	–	-
4.	Advertising stands	–	–	–	-
5.	Other income	–	–	–	-
6.	TOTAL INCOME	–	–	–	-
EXPENDITURE					
ADMINISTRATION					
1.	Administrative costs	6011	–	6011	5200
2.	Management costs	8363	–	8363	24,300
3.	Insurance costs	–	–	–	
4.	Delegations and accomodation	13,376	-38%[1]	8293	2400
5.	Salary and Fees	33,380	–	33,380	43,400
6.	Other administrative expenses	–	–	–	-
7.	TOTAL ADMINISTRATION EXPENDITURE	61,130	–	56,047	75,300
EXPENSES OF EVENTS					
1.	Costs of preparing requests for proposals / tenders	–	–	–	
2.	Cost of rental	17,404	–	17,404	0
3.	Other operating costs (rental of equipment, technical personnel, etc.).	16,922	–	16,922	
4.	Security and safety	–	–	–	
5.	Insurance	–	–	–	
6.	Catering costs/banquet/ dinner	63,641	+30%[2]	82,733	

Continued.

	Description	Expenditure ordinary event [PLN]	The possibility of reduction / increase of costs [%]	Expenditure ecological event [PLN]	On line event
7.	Transportation of participants	3234	-90%[3]	323	0
8.	Entertainment/artistic programs/study visits	–	–	–	
9.	Accommodation	11,000	+30%[4]	14 300	0
10.	Preparing invitations/ tickets	5754	−70%[5]	1726,2	0
11.	Other expenses	1230	–	1230	
12.	Translator	20,824	–	20 824	6150
13.	TOTAL	140,009	–	155 462	6150
MARKETING AND PROMOTION					
1.	Advertising - Media and PR	38,227	−50%[6]	19,113	9400
2.	Promotional gadgets	–	–	–	
3.	Design and implementation of electronic materials on CD, DVD, etc.	8790	−100%[7]	0	0
4.	Design and print promotional/technical materials	95,672	−100%[8]	0	0
5.	Distribution of e-mail/ brochure/information	766	−70%[9]	229.8	450
6.	Website	5696	–	5696	
7.	Other expenses	–	–	–	
8.	Offset of CO_2 emissions	0	offset 50 years +100%[10]	10,680	0
9.			offset 30 years +100%[10]	52,955	0
10.	TOTAL	149,151	offset 50 years	35,719	0
11.			offset 30 years	77,994	0

Description	Expenditure ordinary event [PLN]	The possibility of reduction / increase of costs [%]	Expenditure ecological event [PLN]	On line event
TOTAL EXPENDITURE	350,290	offset 50 years	247,228	91,300
		offset 30 years	289,503	
UNFORESEEN EXPENSES (5% of total costs)	17,515	offset 50 years	12,361	4565
		offset 30 years	14,475	
TOTAL	367,805	offset 50 years	259,589	95,865
		offset 30 years	303,978	
Surplus / deficit	–	–	–	-

Source: Report, Analiza ekonomiczna wybranych inicjatyw ekologicznych w branży MICE, Project *Zielona Energia Zmiany Społecznej*, Program Social Innovation funded by the National Centre for Research and Development in Poland.

Table 5: The assumptions for the calculations in Table 4.

Assumption
1   50% journey took place with a private car,   • cost of travel by private car at a distance of 100 km is 83.58 PLN (at the rate of 0.8358 PLN/km)   • the cost of the bus on the same route is 15 PLN, and the cost of train 22 PLN, the average for public transport (100 km) to 19.50 PLN   Source of prices: http://wartowiedziec.org/attachments/article/22417/ Plan_zrownowazonego_rozwoju_publicznego_transportu_zbiorowego_dla_wojew%C3%B3dztwa_do
2   it was assumed that the cost of organic food is 30% higher   Source: http://greendietbuffet.pl/produkty–ekologicznie–zdrowsze–czy–tylko–drozsze/
3   it was assumed that 90% participants use public transport
4   it was assumed that the average cost of a standard room in hotels of the with one to four stars, with green certificate is about 30% higher than in the objects of the same type without this certificate. Data was established on the basis of: Nicolai V. Kuminoff, Congwen Zhang, and Jeta Rudi 2010 Are Travelers Willing to Pay a Premium to Stay at a "Green" Hotel? Evidence from an Internal Meta–Analysis of Hedonic Price Premia. *Agricultural and Resource Economics Review*, 39(3): 468–484.

	resignation of preparing invitations and tickets printed for the benefit of electronic documents was assumed, the remaining 30% of the cost is the preparation of documents in electronic form, eg. the design, layout, graphic design etc.
6	resignation from the preparation of printed promotional materials was assumed, the remaining 50% is to the cost of advertisement in the media
7,8	resignation of preparing materials on CD, DVD and printed materials was assumed, in favor of the materials submitted electronically
9	resignation from the distribution of information material in paper form was assumed, the remaining 30% are costs of distributing information via e-mail

10	offset costs are included only in environmental events and depend on the amount of greenhouse gas emissions that a company wants to offset. To calculation of offset cost total emitted CO_2 was assumed, which was calculated using calculator of AerisFuturo Foundation (available at http://aerisfuturo.pl/kalkulator/kalkulator.html).
	 For the calculation of emissions assumed the following data:
	 • the duration of the event – three days
	 • number of participants (including organizers) – 315 people
	 • transport of organizers – 3 cars (the average distance of 500 km/car)
	 • amount of paper used – 10 reams
	 • bus travels of participants (100 people, average distance of 150 km/participant)
	 • train travels of participants (100 people, average distance of 500 km/participant)
	 • plane travels of participants (100 people, average distance of 1000 km/participant)
	 • number of nights – 700
	 • mixed meals – 600
	 • electricity consumption – 8713 kWh
	 • consumption of natural gas – 740 m³
	 • water consumption (social and living purpose) – 30 m³
	 • amount of waste generated – 0.5 kg/participant
	 • The costs of offset calculated for:
	   – planting of 360 trees and the calculated amount of CO_2 assimilation in 50 years
	   – planting of 1765 trees and the calculated amount of CO_2 assimilation in 30 years
	   – To estimate data of conference organization benefits also from the report: *EAUC Annual Conference 2013, Carbon Footprint Report,* available on the website: http://www.eauc.org.uk/file_uploads/eauc_annual_conference_footprint.pdf.

Source: Report, Analiza ekonomiczna wybranych inicjatyw ekologicznych w branży MICE, Project *Zielona Energia Zmiany Społecznej,* Program Social Innovation funded by the National Centre for Research and Development in Poland.

Conclusions

Trade and business meetings are an important part of business, ranging from antiquity to the present day. The global market and rapidly changing environment require changes in the functioning of modern enterprises, including reduction of costs and adaptation to changing customers' tastes and preferences. Businesses are trying to meet these expectations by seeking access to widely understood business information. Fairs, conferences and business meetings are places where this kind of information is available. Therefore, this study shows the benefits of online trade fairs and compared the costs to that of similar events organized in the traditional way.

According to the data presented above, organizing an event in ecologically friendly manner can bring environmental, social and economic benefits. It builds a good image of the company and shows the company's innovation. Organizing business meetings online is still cheaper and gives a number of additional environmental and social benefits. According to the data presented in Table 3, costs of participation in online trade fairs are small, depending on the package range from 600 PLN to 1800 PLN, which results from the fact that the cost of organizing such events represents one third of the cost of traditional meetings and are about 60% lower than face-to-face green events.

Taking into account that many companies are expanding their markets by looking for business partners not only in the country but in the whole world, building their branches abroad, the possibility of contacts online is particularly important. It allows for direct contact with customers, suppliers and cooperatives, saving cost, time and environmental impact.

Notes

[1] Instytut Gospodarki Surowcami Mineralnymi i Energią Polskiej Akademii Nauk.

References

Aeris Futuro Foundation. The Aeris Futuro Foundation's CO2 Calculator. Available at URL http://aerisfuturo.pl/kalkulator/kalkulator.html [Last accessed 01.10.2016].

Borodako, K, Berbeka, J, Niemczyk, A, and Seweryn R 2014 *Raport: Ekonomiczne znaczenie przemysłu spotkań dla gospodarki Krakowa*, Kraków, wrzesień.

Borodako, K 2013 *Turystyka biznesowa w Krakowie na tle wybranych miast polskich*, Prace Geograficzne, zeszyt 134, Instytut Geografii i Gospodarki Przestrzennej UJ.

Celuch, K 2013 *Raport „Przemysł spotkań i wydarzeń w Polsce – Poland Meetings and Events Industry Report 2013"*, PCB, Warszawa.

Gerega, A 2010 *Rachunek zysków i strat w prawie bilansowym i w regulacjach międzynarodowych,* Studenckie Naukowe Czasopismo Internetowe TH!NK, Nr 1 (2) s. 15–24, Akademia Górniczo-Hutnicza, Wydział Zarządzania.

Greenstonecarbon 2013 Report: EAUC Annual Conference 2013, Carbon Footprint Report, dostęny na stronie Available at http://www.eauc.org.uk/file_uploads/eauc_annual_conference_footprint.pdf [Last accessed 15.10.2016].

Kostecka, J, Pączka, G, and Piękoś, P 2013 *Prośrodowiskowe zasady organizacji konferencji,* Inżynieria i Ochrona Środowiska, t. 16, nr 4, s. 499–510.

Sustainable events guide 2012 United Nations Environment Programme.

Tomczyk, N 2013 *Zarządzanie turystyką biznesową na przykładzie wybranych convention bureaux w Polsce,* Praca magisterska, Instytut Geografii Miast i Turyzmu, Uniwersytet Łódzki.

Case 2: Market readiness for a residential ventilation system designed for providing better household living conditions and lower energy costs. The case of Lindab in Romania

Tudor EDU* and Iliuta Costel NEGRICEA*

*PhD; Associate Professor of Marketing, Romanian-American University, Bucharest, Romania

Introduction

In 2016, Lindab Romania wanted to include its product assortment a ventilation system for residential use. In this regard the company is faced with the question of whether such a system would be sought after in Romania. Narrowing down from this problem definition, the present study focuses on uncovering buying and non-buying reasons for such a system in Romania in order to match them with the benefits provided by the ventilation system, which can be effectively summarised in healthier indoor environment and lower electricity and gas bills.

The research methodology was centred on qualitative research in the form of in-depth interviews and group discussions for prompting possible reasons and restrictions for buying a mechanical ventilation system for household purposes.

How to cite this book chapter:
EDU, T. and NEGRICEA, I. C. 2019. Case 2: Market readiness for a residential ventilation system designed for providing better household living conditions and lower energy costs. The case of Lindab in Romania. In: Gąsior, A. (ed.) *Pro-ecological Restructuring of Companies: Case Studies*, Pp. 199–209. London: Ubiquity Press. DOI: https://doi.org/10.5334/bbk.q. License: CC-BY 4.0

The main conclusion of the study is that house owners are delighted to have healthier indoor environment and lower electricity and gas bills but very few have the financial means or are willing to invest in acquiring the residential ventilation system.

Research methodology

The goal of the study being that of uncovering buying and non-buying motives for a new product, qualitative research was considered the most appropriate method because of its effectiveness in understanding issues very seldom easily expressed by individuals, such as values, beliefs or attitudes (Marshall 1996). According to Corbin and Strauss (2014), through qualitative research, consumer experiences can be explored, while Sharan (2009) extends this idea, underlining that even insights attached by consumers to such experiences can be identified. In this case study two qualitative research techniques were selected due to their effectiveness in generating data on topics not previously covered, in-depth interviews and focus groups. The in-depth interview, as a data collection tool, stands out for the richness of the findings (Ritchie, Lewis & Elam 2003), helping a researcher in understanding why each respondent judges one topic in a particular way (King 2004). On the other hand, the focus group, as a tool for gathering data, represents a group discussion, which is considered to be very effective especially because of the interactions between the members often building up to situations similar to those ones in real life (Kreuger & Casey 2000). In qualitative research, special consideration should be given to the sampling methodology and sample size. Because the main purpose of using qualitative research is to provide a wealth of data and not to generalise the findings to the entire population, the sampling methodology is a non-random one, the researcher having a wide liberty of including in the sample the respondents deemed most suitable (Malhotra 2010; Coyne 1997). Closely connected with the sampling methodology is the sample size. Unlike quantitative research, the sample size in qualitative research is small. According to Marshall, Cardon, Poddar and Fontenot (2013), Morse (1994), Bernard (2000) and Creswell (1998) a sample of at least 30 individuals would deliver appropriate findings when using in-depth interviews, while according to Finch and Lewis (2003), six to eight individuals or, according to Malhotra (2010), eight to 12 individuals per each focus group should be considered in two to three group discussions for about 80% theme coverage or three to six group discussions for about 90% theme coverage (Guest, Namey & McKenna 2016).

The data collection in this study was performed based on a group discussion moderated by the researchers and semi-structured in-depth interviews also conducted by the researchers.

A judgemental sample of 44 individuals was considered comprising people from four groups:

1. individuals building a house or planning to build one: 8 people
2. individuals who bought Lindab products in the past 12 months: 9 people
3. Lindab's sales agents: 28 people
4. Lindab's partners: 5 people

The judgemental sampling procedure was chosen for several reasons:

- To collect data from all stakeholders
- To build a comprehensive understanding of the research goal
- To perform an exploratory research, meaning to uncover answers to "why questions" and not to "how many or how often"

Lindab – An International Leader in Construction Solutions

Lindab claims, "Simplifying is our passion, ultimate comfort is our vision".

Lindab is a leading international manufacturer of industrial and residential construction solutions based in Sweden but currently present in 32 countries. According to the Interim report (Lindab 2016a), Lindab recorded, in 2015, sales of approximately 812 million EUR, employing around 5100 people and making about 80% of its sales from the non-residential sector. Geographically, the biggest part of its sales (44%) came from the Nordic countries, followed by Western Europe (33%), Central and Eastern Europe and other Soviet states (19%) and other markets (4%). Lindab has a network of 140 branches and around 3000 partners (Lindab 2016a).

Lindab defines itself as an innovator, delivering top quality energy-efficient and environmentally friendly products focused on improving the standard of living (Lindab 2016b). By aiming at comfort and simplicity, Lindab strives to be recognised as a pillar of sustainable building, Corporate Social Responsibility actions being at the forefront of all business endeavours (Lindab 2016c). Lindab markets five groups of products and solutions: building products, covering floors, walls and roofs; building solutions for residential and industrial purposes; ventilation products; indoor climate solutions (air diffusers, waterborne climate systems and acoustics) and complete building systems for industrial purposes (Lindab 2016d).

The residential ventilation system was designed by Lindab to be implemented in dwellings focusing on three aspects: energy consumption, indoor climate and recurrent costs. The benefits rendered by the residential ventilation system can be summarised in healthier indoor climate (supressing pollen, moisture, mould and condensation), lower running costs (the system saving up to 7000kWh/apartment/year), easy maintenance and a nice design of the equipment, ducts and valves. From a technical perspective, the ventilation system is an integrated solution comprising a double-flow heat recovery system, filtering and warming or cooling the incoming air, an airtight system of ducts, and valves and grills.

All these components can be blended perfectly with various types of interior designs. Lindab offers the residential ventilation system as a turn-key solution including counselling, deploying and maintenance (Lindab 2016e).

Market Readiness for the Residential Ventilation System in Romania

The research goal, that of uncovering buying and non-buying motives for the residential ventilation system in Romania, was split into eight objectives, five common to all groups and three appropriate for either one or two groups, covering the following areas:

- identifying meanings pertaining to mechanical ventilation given by individuals currently building a house or planning to build one – *objective set for prospects*
- identifying if the mechanical ventilation system would be purchased based on the benefits rendered through its features:
  o healthier indoor environment
  o lower home heating and/or cooling bill
- identifying if prospects would pay a price ranging between 3500 and 4000 EUR (+VAT) for the mechanical ventilation system considering an investment recovery time frame of eight to 11 years
- identifying if a payment plan including maintenance would be an incentive for a prospect in buying the mechanical ventilation system
- identifying if a discount ranging between 10% and 20% would be an incentive for a prospect in buying the mechanical ventilation system
- identifying if a prospect would rather work with only one supplier or several suppliers considering the incurred costs
- identifying reasons for buying or rejecting the mechanical ventilation system by prospects if the cost would not be a constraint – *objective for prospects*
- identifying the construction stage at which Lindab's sales agents and partners should approach a prospect about the mechanical ventilation system – *objective for sales agents and partners*

Five instruments were designed for collecting data. For each group of respondents under investigation semi-structured in-depth interviews were used while for the sales agents a focus group was organised additionally to the in-depth interviews (see Table 1).

The data analysis was performed using content analysis for each sample group, considering that some research objectives were formulated for one or two groups.

Table 1: Groups and research instruments.

Group and sample size	Type of qualitative research instrument used
Individuals building a house or planning to build one: 8 people	In-depth interviews (8 interviews)
Individuals who bought Lindab products in the past 12 months: 9 people	In-depth interviews (9 interviews)
Lindab's sales agents: 28 people	In-depth interviews (22 interviews) and focus group (1 group discussion – 6 people)
Lindab's partners: 5 people	In-depth interviews (5 interviews)

Source: developed by the authors.

The research objectives were used to build the discussion topics for each group under investigation. The discussion topics and the appropriate conclusions for each group are presented below.

Group 1 – Individuals building a house or planning to build one

For this group, nine discussion topics were developed to provide answers necessary to cover the formulated objectives:

1. Meanings given to ventilation
2. Advantages of a mechanical ventilation system
3. Buying intention based on healthier indoor environment as a benefit provided by the mechanical ventilation system
4. Buying intention based on lower heating and/or cooling costs as benefits provided by the mechanical ventilation system
5. Opinions about the appropriateness of buying the mechanical ventilation system based on an investment recovery within a period of eight to 11 years
6. Opinions about paying a price ranging between 3500 and 4000 EUR (+VAT) for the mechanical ventilation system
7. Opinions related to a payment plan for the mechanical ventilation system
8. Opinions about working with a single company or several companies for installing the mechanical ventilation system considering the incurred costs
9. Opinions related to the appropriateness of buying the mechanical ventilation system if its cost would not be an issue

Main findings for this group:

The prospect is aware of the home ventilation need in order to maintain a healthy indoor climate and provide better well-being for the entire family. Although many prospects overlap mechanical ventilation and air conditioning, they comprehend the benefits of a mechanical ventilation system (MVS) in the form of maintaining health, keeping constant ambient temperature, heating/cooling cost efficiency and convenience. Cuts in the heating/cooling expenses are an argument that can justify buying an MVS. But the cost reduction is placed in the context of the total cost and product lifetime expectancy. Also, the health benefits are a strong incentive in buying the MVS, but one cannot discriminate which one is more important. The prospects consider that the 8–11-year return-on-investment interval is too long, this being correlated with their opinions on the acquisition price, the MVS being considered expensive. On the other hand, a payment plan is considered a good idea by the prospects, but a monthly instalment of 150 EUR is perceived as being too strenuous on the budget, alternatives with lower monthly fees and longer period of times being considered more suitable. Some prospects would consider installing the MVS with several companies due to cost reasons while other prospects are open towards deploying the MVS with a single company to control the process. In conclusion, the MVS is highly commended by the prospects, the only hindrance in acquiring it being its cost.

Group 2 – Individuals who bought Lindab products in the past 12 months

For this group, six discussion topics were developed to provide answers necessary to cover the formulated objectives:

1. Buying intention based on healthier indoor environment as a benefit provided by the mechanical ventilation system
2. Buying intention based on lower heating and/or cooling costs as benefits provided by the mechanical ventilation system
3. Opinions about the appropriateness of buying the mechanical ventilation system based on investment recovery within a period of eight to 11 years
4. Opinions about paying a price ranging between 3500 and 4000 EUR (+VAT) for the mechanical ventilation system
5. Opinions related to a payment plan for the mechanical ventilation system
6. Opinions about working with a single company or several companies for installing the mechanical ventilation system considering the incurred costs

Main findings for this group:

For Lindab's current customers (for other products than the mechanical ventilation system) the reasons for purchasing the mechanical ventilation system

(MVS) are mainly rational. The family health benefits seem to be less important than rational elements like the return on investment or MVS's installation or maintenance costs. It is also mentioned that the MVS is feasible for polluted and crowded areas, for office buildings and less adequate for residential ones. Lindab's current customers consider that lowering the actual costs of house heating/cooling costs is the main acquisition reason of the MVS. Because Lindab's current customers are technically and financially proficient in what it takes to build a house, it is advisable that rational explanations of the cost reduction through the usage of the MVS be properly communicated. These rational explanations can be the strongest argument in convincing this segment about the benefits of the MVS. The 8–11-year return-on-investment time frame is considered too long. The underlying reasons for this conclusion are the system's lifetime expectancy and the envisaged high maintenance costs. Lindab's current customers (for other products than the MVS) would prefer a shorter return-on-investment time interval. The acceptance of a 3500–4000 EUR (plus VAT) price is correlated with the effort incurred in the structural changes necessary to install the system and with the costs of the interior design changes. The price level is directly related to the health and financial benefits rendered by the MVS. Also, the competitive advantage and the lifetime expectancy are important in the MVS's price acceptance. A payment plan is not considered an incentive but it can be taken into consideration if the instalments are advantageous and the interest rate is low. However, a monthly rate of 150 EUR is considered high, many respondents believing that such an instalment is an important element in the procurement process of the MVS. Buying an MVS from one supplier is acceptable to Lindab's current clients. Quality, risk reduction activities and capabilities related with installation, operation and maintenance are the main reasons supporting a buying decision.

Group 3 – Lindab's sales agents

For this group, ten discussion topics were developed to provide answers necessary to cover the formulated objectives, the data being gathered in a focus group and through in-depth interviews:

1. Buying intention based on healthier indoor environment as a benefit provided by the mechanical ventilation system
2. Buying intention based on lower heating costs as benefits provided by the mechanical ventilation system
3. Buying intention based on cooler indoor temperature through fresh air in-take as a benefit provided by the mechanical ventilation system
4. Opinions about the appropriateness of buying the mechanical ventilation system based on investment recovery within a period of eight to 11 years

5. Opinions about paying a price ranging between 3500 and 4000 EUR (+VAT) for the mechanical ventilation system
6. Buying intention based on a 10% discount offered to the prospect
7. Opinions related to a payment plan for the mechanical ventilation system
8. Opinions about working with a single company or several companies for installing the mechanical ventilation system considering the incurred costs
9. Opinions about the most appropriate construction phase for approaching a prospect for the mechanical ventilation system
10. Opinions about the appropriateness of introducing the mechanical ventilation system in Lindab's product assortment

Main findings for this group:

Lindab's sales agents presume that the mechanical ventilation system (MVS) would be purchased for residential purposes by individuals with medium-to-high income for the health benefits rendered by the MVS. The sales agents believe that these benefits are more important than the money the prospects can save on heating/cooling bills. Also, linked with the customer profile (medium-to-high income and health benefits), the agents presume that the MVS will sell even better if integrated with new heating/cooling technologies. Also, they believe the difference between air conditioning systems and the MVS is not clear and prospects would not buy the MVS because it can cool or heat premises considering its price unless the MVS's features are thoroughly explained and documented. The 8–11-year return-on-investment time frame is considered too long by most sales agents. However, a few sales agents consider this time frame to be a benefit but this should be properly documented. The sales agents consider, as mentioned above, that the MVS would be acquired mainly by individuals with medium-to-high income that value highly the health benefits but they believe that a discount of at least 10% would speed up the selling process and lure in more prospects. A payment plan is considered a suitable alternative for attracting more prospects as a significant number of prospects discover the appropriateness of a ventilation system while they are in the building process and such a system is not initially budgeted. The sales agents have mixed feelings concerning the prospects' tendencies of working with a single business or several companies when installing a ventilation system. Those underlining one company emphasise trust and less effort from the prospects while those mentioning several companies focus on smaller costs. The sales agents believe the MVS can be proposed to the market in all construction stages. Most importantly, the sales agents strongly believe that the MVS can be a successful product and should be included in Lindab's portfolio primarily due to its features covering health and welfare as it will render more sales especially cross-sold with the roofing systems.

Group 4 – Lindab's partners

For this group, seven discussion topics were developed to provide answers necessary to cover the formulated objectives in in-depth interviews:

1. Buying intention based on healthier indoor environment as a benefit provided by the mechanical ventilation system
2. Buying intention based on lower cooling/heating costs as benefits provided by the mechanical ventilation system
3. Opinions about the appropriateness of buying the mechanical ventilation system based on investment recovery within a period of eight to 11 years
4. Opinions about paying a price ranging between 3500 and 4000 EUR (+VAT) for the mechanical ventilation system
5. Opinions related to a payment plan for the mechanical ventilation system
6. Opinions about working with a single company or several companies for installing the mechanical ventilation system considering the incurred costs
7. Opinions about the most appropriate construction phase for approaching a prospect for the mechanical ventilation system

Main findings for this group:

Lindab's partners believe that the Mechanical Ventilation System (MVS) would be purchased by individuals for the health benefits but by the affluent ones (medium to high income) as in many cases they value more the health benefits in comparison to the financial/cost ones. This is in sync with what the partners believe about the return-on-investment time frame (8–11 years) as being too long and not an adequate idea to use in the marketing communication. Also, considering the MVS's acquisition price, the partners believe that the price is high and Lindab should target prospects with medium to high income. The partners believe that a payment plan for the MVS would enlarge the opportunity pool by raising interest from more prospects but they underlined the fact that they would not want to be involved in financing the MVS. The partners believe that most prospects would want to work with a single company for installing a ventilation system being open to pay a higher price but not exceeding 20–30%. The partners also believe that the MVS can be proposed to prospects in all construction stages of a house.

Conclusions

This research sheds some light on motives for buying and not buying the mechanical ventilation system (MVS). The most important reasons for buying the MVS are the health benefits provided by the system, the reduction of monthly costs for heating and/or cooling the dwelling and keeping a constant ambient temperature. An important finding is that the prospects and the buyers of other Lindab products consider the heating/cooling cost reduction as the most important reason for acquiring such a system while Lindab's sales agents and partners believe that the health benefits surpass the financial ones. The most important obstacle in buying the MVS is its cost, the respective value rendering a long return-on-investment time frame. Closely connected with this reality, a payment plan is perceived by the demand side as a solution to mitigate the financial burden. Another important conclusion that can be drawn is that the only group considering the environmental benefits as being important in the buying decision of such a system is the one comprising Lindab's clients, an explanation for this situation being that probably the Romanian construction market is not yet very conscious about the importance of environmental issues.

Based on the findings, Lindab should try to sell its mechanical ventilation system focusing on the financial benefits rendered by the system augmented with the health reasons and constant ambient temperature and stressing the option of the payment plan to reduce the financial strain. Such a marketing approach is reinforced by Lindab's premium brand position on the Romanian market, the brand being often used by prospects and actual buyers as a standard in product comparisons. However, these considerations must be further exploited in qualitative and quantitative studies to comprehend if the uncovered buying motives and their bundling could be used for an enduring market positioning endeavour.

References

Bernard, H R 2000 *Social Research Methods*. Thousand Oaks, CA: Sage.

Corbin, J and Strauss, A 2014 *Basics of Qualitative Research – Techniques and Procedures for Developing Grounded Theory*, 4th ed., Thousand Oaks, CA: Sage.

Coyne, I T 1997 Sampling in qualitative research. Purposeful and theoretical sampling, merging or clear boundaries? *Journal of Advanced Nursing*, Vol. 26: 623–630.

Creswell, J 1998 *Qualitative Inquiry and Research Design. Choosing among Five Traditions*. Thousand Oaks, CA: Sage.

Finch, H and Lewis, J 2003 Focus Groups. In Ritchie, J & Lewis, J (eds.), *Qualitative Research Practice – A Guide for Social Science Students and Researchers* (pp. 171–198), London: Sage.

Guest, G, Namey, E and McKenna, K 2016 How many focus groups are enough? Building an evidence base for non-probability sample sizes. *Field Methods*, published online before print, DOI: http://doi.org/10.1177/1525822X16639015

King, N 2004 Using interviews in qualitative research. In Cassell, C & Symon, G (eds.), *Essential Guide to Qualitative Methods in Organizational Research*, London: Sage.

Kreuger, R A and Casey, M A 2000 *Focus Groups: A Practical Guide for Applied Research,* 3rd edition. Thousand Oaks, CA: Sage.

Lindab 2016a Interim report January-June 2016. Available at http://www. lindabgroup.com/english/ir/reports/Documents/Interimreport-16-q2.pdf [Last accessed 1 August 2016].

Lindab 2016b About Lindab/ business concept. Available at http://www.lindab. com/global/pro/about-lindab/businessconcept/pages/default.aspx   [Last accessed 2 August 2016].

Lindab 2016c About Lindab/ CSR. Available at http://www.lindab.com/global/ pro/about-lindab/csr/pages/default.aspx [Last accessed 2 August 2016].

Lindab 2016d About Lindab/ our products. Available at http://www.lindab. com/global/pro/about-lindab/our-products-solutions/pages/default.aspx [Last accessed 2 August 2016].

Lindab 2016e About Lindab/ Lindab-inside. Available at http://www.lindab. com/global/pro/lindab-inside/Pages/default.aspx [Last accessed 2 August 2016].

Malhotra, K N 2010 *Marketing Research, An Applied Orientation,* Global Edition, 6th ed., Upper Saddle River, NJ: Prentice Hall.

Marshall, M 1996 Sampling for qualitative research. *Family Practice,* 13(6): 522–525.

Marshall, B, Cardon, P, Poddar, A and Fontenot, R 2013 Does sample size matter in qualitative research? A review of qualitative interviews in IS research, *Journal of Computer Information Systems,* 54(1) Fall: 11–22.

Morse, J M 1994 Designing funded qualitative research. In Denzin, N K & Lincoln, Y S (eds.), *Handbook of Qualitative Research* (2nd ed.) (pp. 220–235), Thousand Oaks, CA: Sage.

Ritchie, J, Lewis, J and Elam, G 2003 Designing and Selecting Samples. In Ritchie, J & Lewis, J (eds.), *Qualitative Research Practice – A Guide for Social Science Students and Researchers* (pp. 77–108), London: Sage.

Sharan, M 2009 *Qualitative Research: A Guide to Design and Implementation,* San Francisco: Wiley & Sons.

Final Conclusions

To conclude, the aim of this book was to present turbulent environment, pro-ecological performance of the enterprises and eco-innovations based on the case studies carried out in Poland, Romania and Ukraine, which means in different countries from and outside the European Union. In this sense, the book was not a theoretical approach to develop existing concepts but the practical presentation of the companies' problems. Based on this, the series of case studies have analysed challenges the firms have to cope with. The presented practical solutions have enriched reader's perspective in the area of restructuring processes.

The first case study shows how legal and political factors influence the restructuring policy of a company under pressure of different interest groups in Romania. The case demonstrated that the studied companies have a reactive rather than proactive attitude towards pro-ecological actions.

The second case study presents how the Ukrainian company strengthens its competitive position on the international egg market by adapting to consumers' needs and by fulfilling requirements of a European egg market and by introducing ecological standards into its production processes. This case study demonstrates the importance of pro-ecological behaviour for building a competitive position on the market.

The third case shows the state of pro-ecological awareness in a Polish company. This paper discusses the problems faced by restructured enterprises in terms of ecological aspects and the pro-ecological measures they undertake for the improvement or prevention of any deterioration of the enterprise's nearest natural surrounding. For the future performance, the management board should take more actions to increase employees' awareness of pro-eco-logical aspects in the activity of their company.

The chapter on turbulent environments is followed by pro-ecological performance of the enterprises.

The first part of this section is an extended case study on pro-environmental activity of a large German company, ThyssenGas. It can be said that the activity of this company is not favorable to the environment. However, high technology that the company uses in its process and the restructuring of its operation has allowed this firm to become as green as possible.

The next case describes the situation in Ukraine on the example of the "LLC Leader" pig farm and its problems with the disposal of bio-waste such as fae-ces. The company found the solution to this problem: using faeces to produce biogas. This is shown by the example of the farm as an environmentally friendly way to recycle biological waste.

The third case characterized the Polish HS Company. This is an industrial processing company that manufactures components of machinery and equipment. The company decided to take a strategic reorientation related to financial and organisational problems, with the participation of its core stakeholders, namely employees. The adopted strategy resulted in new solutions not only in the organization of the processes but also as regards the staff conducting business in a manner friendly to the environment, health and safety at work.

The fourth subsection presents an example of a Ukrainian producer of alcoholic beverages, "Obolon". The purpose of the analysis of this entity is to indicate the influence of environmental factors on its activity as well as a broader discussion of actions taken by the company, especially with regard to CSR.

The next case study concerns a Romanian firm's situation. It offers an example of how by using simple methods any company may achieve the goal of the environmental stewardship by creating a working environment that fosters the pro-ecological behaviour of firms' employees.

The last case contains a description of pro-environmental investments in Poland. Two projects have been analysed: GreenEvo and ETV, as flagship examples of pro-environmental investments in new technologies. In effect, it should be stated that creating new environmentally friendly technologies is one of the main tasks of a contemporary business and there is a need for intensifying actions of capital investment. Market entities have to significantly increase the funding of its new environmental technologies.

In the third chapter on eco-innovations, an emphasis has been put on competitiveness, which is particularly important in companies in the era of globalization.

The first case shows the Polish company ABC Colorex Ltd, which is implementing environmentally friendly production. This plant pays attention to the legal conditions as well as efficiency of production. The actions intended to implement eco design by introducing non-chromate technology of conversion coating for aluminum elements. Based on the analysis, it was found that the company implements the principles of sustainable design in the powder coating industry. According to the policy of the European Union, which supports eco design as well as sustainable design, this chemical sector should strive for innovative solutions and improvements in production.

The second case presents aspects of the pro-ecological restructuring for jobs. This is a modern trend for sustainable development of an Ukrainian bank. Due to specialization of quaternary sector, the problems of ecological restructuring are not crucially important comparing both primary and secondary sectors. Restructuring appears in the professional training according to the implementation of the ecological restructuration. It brings many advantages to the companies implementing the process as well as to the whole economy.

The next section describes the current state and development opportunities of eco-innovations in Poland. Selected regulations and guidelines relating to eco-innovation were presented. The right direction of the future changes seems to be the evaluation of environmental impact that may contribute to the protection of the environment as well as the increase of economy's competitiveness. International legislation standards obligatory in all countries are one of the main factors contributing to the improvement of producers' and consumers' practices to make such an environmental change to introduce the life cycle thinking.

The last subsection contains two examples showing final benefits for users in two countries: Poland and Romania.

The main aim of the Polish case is to show the benefits for the final users, resulting from the use of an innovative platform for an online trade fair, which contributes to lowering costs of participation in trade fairs, conferences and business meetings and is an example of a good practice in environmental and social activities. It is a solution in the field of technological and organizational innovation. According to the data presented, it can be stated that organizing eco-events may bring environmental, social and economic benefits by building a good image of the company and showing the company's innovation. Nonetheless, organizing business meetings online is still cheaper and gives a number of additional environmental and social benefits.

The Romanian case shows a dilemma about company Lindab which, in 2016, wanted to introduce in its product assortment a ventilation system for residential use. An important finding is that the prospects and the buyers of other Lindab products consider the heating/cooling cost reduction as the most important reason for acquiring such a system, while Lindab's sales agents and partners believe that the health benefits surpass the financial ones. One of the important conclusions stemming from this case is that the only group considering the environmental benefits to be important in the purchasing decision of such a system is the one of Lindab's clients – an explanation for this situation probably being that the Romanian construction market is not yet very conscious of the importance of environmental issues.

www.ingramcontent.com/pod-product-compliance
Lightning Source LLC
Chambersburg PA
CBHW071545200326
41519CB00021BB/6614